THE COURT-MARTIAL OF LT. CALLEY

By Richard Hammer
BETWEEN LIFE AND DEATH
ONE MORNING IN THE WAR
THE COURT-MARTIAL OF LT. CALLEY

RICHARD HAMMER

The Court-Martial of Lt. Calley

WITH DRAWINGS BY HOWARD J. BRODIE

COWARD, McCANN
& GEOGHEGAN, INC.
New York

For
ARLENE

CONTENTS

His Majesty, King Piyadesi, in the ninth year of his reign conquered the Kalingas.

One Hundred and fifty thousand persons were thence carried away captive, one hundred thousand were slain, and many times that number perished.

Ever since the annexation of the Kalingas, His Majesty has jealously protected the Law of Piety, has been devoted to that law, and has proclaimed its precepts.

His Majesty feels remorse on account of the conquest of the Kalingas, because during the subjugation of a previously unconquered country, slaughter, death, and taking away captive of the people necessarily occur, whereat His Majesty feels profound sorrow and regret.

—Rock Edict XIII (256 B.C.)

Part One:
Of Heroes, War and Murder

1
A Hero for Our Time

We dreamed of heroes when we were young. They were men who did noble and brave deeds without thought of themselves or of rewards; they were more courageous and selfless than anyone we knew; they were bigger than life; they ennobled us through our dreams of them and through our reenactments (in our minds and at play) of their deeds. Somehow, by their existence and what they had done, and how they had done those deeds, they made life better and more livable, made the future a time of limitless potential, a time to anticipate with expectations of what we might do.

When we were young, it was a time of heroes, a more innocent time, perhaps, when we believed in heroes, believed we needed them and believed they symbolized the best of their times and, because above all they were men, the possibilities that heroism was open to all of us. We could look back through history as we learned it (with all the romantic distortions of our schoolbooks), through the books we read and the movies we saw, and find the times filled with heroes of our past. Their names came without effort into our minds, or, if we didn't know their names because they were nameless, at least we knew what they had done. The list of our heroes—those blends of romantic fact, fiction, and dreams—was almost endless and could be recalled in no particular order, just as we happened to find them in our minds: Ivanhoe and Scott's other knights of chivalry and valor; Galahad and Lancelot and King Arthur; Richard the Lionhearted; Columbus and Sir Francis Drake and

1

those who sailed uncharted seas filled with strange beasts and demons toward some unknown end; John Alden and Roger Williams; the heroes of the Revolution, Sam Adams and Washington at Valley Forge and Jefferson at Philadelphia, Ethan Allen and the Green Mountain Boys, Lafayette, Nathan Hale, whose last words we could all repeat as though we too were about to be hanged as a spy, the best of all deaths in defense of our country, we felt then (and, if we had been able to look beyond the narrow jingoism of our own history, we might have seen the same thing in Major John André); Natty Bumpo, the deerstalker, breaking through the wilderness in Fenimore Cooper's imagination; Tom Sawyer and Huck Finn, who made us jealous and restless in our own restricted lives; Commodore Perry, and Andy Jackson at the Battle of New Orleans and, at his right hand, the pirate Laffite; Davy Crockett and the men of the Alamo; Buffalo Bill and Wild Bill Hickok and the other scouts and trappers who cleared the plains and opened the West for a more peaceful people (when we were young, who among us gave a thought to those who had owned the land and were being dispossessed—though, if we looked within ourselves, most of us had at least a glimmering admiration for, and even enacted in our play, Sitting Bull and Crazy Horse and Geronimo and, in my native New England, even King Philip); the men in gray and blue at Gettysburg and Bull Run; Teddy Roosevelt charging up San Juan Hill; Sergeant Alvin York, in the only guise we knew him, as Gary Cooper, pretending he was shooting turkeys and not Germans on some battlefield whose name we never knew in the France of World War I; the men of the Lafayette Escadrille with leather helmets and goggles flying off into the morning sun; Jimmy Cagney as some unremembered Irish kid redeemed as a member of the Fighting Sixty-Ninth when he fell on a grenade in the trenches and saved all his buddies; and, more recent still, Colin Kelly diving his crippled bomber into a Japanese warship right after Pearl Harbor (was it all a myth? did he really not sink anything?), or Jimmy Doolittle bombing Tokyo, or the men of the Flying Tigers and the RAF, none of whose names we ever knew, if we ever heard any.

They were the heroes of our youth, they and so many more. They were special—selfless, loyal, modest, unaware of their heroism or bravery. To think of them, to enact their roles in a dream or a game, was to enter a realm of greatness and grandeur.

Even the antiheroes of our youth (though certainly we did not think of them in terms of antiheroism, or even, really, in terms of villainy) were a special breed, sharing a kind of vastness of spirit and expansiveness with our heroes. Their deeds were always of more enormity, or at least we thought so, than those of an ordinary desperado; they killed more, but with a kind of joy or in self-defense (and we could never see their victims as real people, as victims who would not get up and walk away later); they robbed on a grander scale and then showed generosity with the loot. They were all Robin Hoods though their names might be Dillinger or Baby Face Nelson or Machine Gun Kelly or Billy the Kid or Jesse James or Blackbeard or Henry Morgan. They were, so often, the counterparts of our heroes, and because our heroes needed someone of nearly equal stature in opposition for their heroism to attain its necessary magnitude, they, too, assumed those huge dimensions.

So we grew up in this country in this century, dreaming of heroes and antiheroes, in a time filled with heroes and antiheroes. They were always with us and they helped form our ideas of the possibilities of men as we grew. They revealed to us what a hero, and even an antihero, ought to be and was. They became for us more than that, they became symbols of their times and of their wars (for, aside from our sports heroes, the DiMaggios and Williamses and Harmons and Baughs and the rest, who inhabited another, special plane of their own, our heroes had grown out of battle, out of what we used to see as the ultimate test of a man).

I thought of heroes, and my feelings about them in my own youth, the day at the end of March, 1971, when they marched Rusty Calley down the steps of the one-story brick courthouse at Fort Benning, Georgia, when they marched him, surrounded by military police but unshackled, down the sidewalk, past the waiting, beseeching television cameras and microphones and reporters shouting questions at him and the crowds cheering him from across the street, to a waiting car and then to the post stockade. And I thought often about what I had once—and perhaps still—thought heroes were in the days and weeks following that afternoon when First Lieutenant William Laws Calley, Jr., had been proclaimed by a jury of his military peers a murderer. And I wondered if I were alone with my memories, if they had all been worthless delusions. For among many at Fort Benning itself and, it seemed, for millions out beyond the gates of that military reservation in the nation itself, Calley was being proclaimed not a murderer of the innocent but a hero—a hero for our time.

For a year and a half I had been living with this case, talking with the soldiers who had once served under him in his platoon and with others who had been at that hamlet in Quang Ngai Province in South Viet-Nam that the United States Army called My Lai (4) on March 16, 1968, and had participated in or been witness to the slaughter of an unknown and uncounted number of Vietnamese civilians—old men, women, children, babies—perhaps more than five hundred. I had wandered through the ruins of that hamlet (actually a subhamlet that the Vietnamese called not My Lai (4) but Xom Lang or Thuan Yen in the village of Son My) and seen the wasteland left by those American troops. I had talked for days with many of those who had survived that awful morning. For four and a half months I had sat in that small Fort Benning courtroom listening to testimony, watching Calley, and coming to know him as well as an observer and not a friend could.

Was he a hero, a hero for this age, for this time of America? Was this small (five-foot three-inch), pudgy (more than 160 pounds, soft and flabby from lack of physical activity), often red-faced, increasingly bald, with a prominent forelock curling down the middle of his forehead, by his own admission and by all the records not very bright or perceptive twenty-seven-year-old lieutenant the hero so many seemed to be proclaiming him?

Was he the hero to rank, now, with those who had dwelt in the pantheons of our youth, in the Valhallas of our days of innocence? Was Rusty Calley really the hero, the symbol of that nightmare called the Viet-Nam War? Were the things he had done, then, to be called the heroic deeds of the modern hero, to rank with the deeds of all those other dead heroes of our past? Or was he even to be the antihero of our time and his deeds to measure with the deeds of all those dead antiheroes?

Calley might be a lot of things—the fall guy for all those above him and below him who had been at My Lai or had known about My Lai, the fall guy for those who had perpetrated all the other My Lais, the fall guy for the whole, bloody Viet-Nam War, the fall guy for American policy in Viet-Nam and for those who had developed it and ordered its execution. But it was hard to think of him, impossible to think of him as a hero or to consider his acts of heroic stature.

He had been convicted of murder, of slaughtering an unknown number, but no fewer than twenty-two unarmed, unresisting Vietnamese civilians at My Lai (4) in a few hours on the morning of March 16, 1968. He had been convicted of murder not in the heat of combat but during the course of what was almost an unhampered stroll in the warm Vietnamese sun.

There had been nothing quick or summary about his conviction. It had taken two weeks more than three years from that March morning in Viet-Nam to bring it about. It had taken the longest court-martial in military history—forty-five days of court testimony spread over more than four months. It had taken the weight of an Everest of evidence, both circumstantial and direct—one hundred four witnesses and more than seven hundred exhibits and depositions. It had taken a long, slow, and excruciating jury deliberation before the verdict of guilt for premeditated murder had been reached—eighty-nine hours and fifty-eight minutes of argument and discussion in the deliberation room and no one knows how much inner dialogue and anguish over thirteen days. And the jury that convicted Calley was not a panel of desk-bound armchair officers with no combat experience basing its decision on hypothetical—and, some said, unworkable—principles with no relation to real life or to combat. That jury was composed of six officers, all combat veterans, five veterans of the war in Viet-Nam. None of them wanted to believe that Calley or any officer, or any soldier, in the United States Army could be guilty of the crimes the government had said he committed.

Most of us who sat in that small, fifty-nine-seat courtroom at Fort Benning with its patriotic motif so blatant—its carpets and seat cushions red, its walls white, its draperies blue, the judge's bench flanked by an American flag and a Fort Benning Student Brigade Flag with its blue background and the motto "Follow Me" etched over a numeral "1"—and listened to all the evidence during the months of trial were convinced that the jurors, if they followed the evidence and were not swayed by outside considerations—particularly the complicity of others not on trial at Fort Benning who might, or might not, face future courts-martial themselves, or the sense of need to protect the Army by protecting one of their own—could have arrived at no other decision than the one they did.

But as Calley was marched out the courthouse door, it was, across the nation, as though there had been no trial and little evidence, as though he had been summarily convicted. It was as though this young lieutenant, like some ugly duckling metamorphosed into a swan, had been transformed before our eyes from the murderer of unresisting, unarmed, innocent old men, women, children, and babies into the symbol of the American soldier in the Viet-Nam War, into the symbol of the American soldier in the world. Into a hero. It seemed that perhaps the nation had come so far down a twisted road in the last few years that it was willing to throw into the ashcan of useless impediments one of the foundations of western religion and philosophy, one of the foundations of the nation itself: that a man is ultimately responsible for his own mistakes, errors, sins, and crimes and must himself pay for them and make his own atonement.

In that violent reaction that followed the verdict against Calley—a reaction which found even President Richard M.

Nixon embroiled, not to uphold the law but to contravene it—it seemed that most Americans forgot, if they ever knew or cared to know, what it was that the young lieutenant had done at My Lai on that "dark and bloody" March morning in 1968. And in forgetting or ignoring it, they could not know what had happened there, what it showed about Calley, about the war in Viet-Nam, and about America—and what their own reaction showed about themselves and this country.

2
Laws Even in War

To put a man in a uniform, to arm him with a rifle or machine gun or some other weapon and send him thousands of miles from home to fight in a war—even, as in Viet-Nam, a war he did not believe in or understand in a place he did not want to be against an unseen and unknown enemy who was sometimes an innocent-appearing farmer or even a child or a woman and almost simultaneously an armed enemy—does not give that man, become a soldier, a license to kill everything in his path, does not put him on some plane above and beyond the jurisdiction of the rules of law that guide human behavior, not only in war but in all human endeavor. More than a hundred years ago, in 1863, Francis Lieber, in setting down the regulations for the conduct of Union soldiers in the Civil War, wrote: "Men who take up arms against one another in public war do not cease on this account to be moral human beings, responsible to one another and to God."

As the court-martial of Lieutenant Calley wound its slow way through the late fall, winter, and early spring of 1970-1971, with its revelations not just about My Lai but about the general conduct of the war in Viet-Nam by the American Army, about the policies developed by the United States government and military to wage that war, and about the attitudes and practices of American soldiers toward Vietnamese they theoretically had been sent to defend and protect, it became ever more apparent that Lieber's dictum had been forgotten, or ignored, or never learned. And it became manifest that Americans in

Viet-Nam were ignoring as well—if they were even aware of—the long-established fact that war is not anarchic, not conducted outside the realm of law, but is restricted by detailed codes of law and conduct.

If war is the most uncivilized and barbaric of human actions, the last and most brutal resort of men and nations when all other resorts to reason, debate, argument, and persuasion have failed, societies nevertheless have long recognized that the very survival of civilization, the survival as moral human beings of both those waging the war and those caught in its path, demands that war be fought within a framework of law and that its effects be limited as far as possible. As long as there must be wars—and the human condition gives no indication that the day of universal peace is near—their impact must be circumscribed. Someday, after all, peace will return to even the most war-ravaged land, and the aim of the belligerents is supposed to be to ensure that something and someone is left to pick up the pieces when that day arrives, that the destruction has not been so vast that all that remains is an uninhabited desert or a wasteland peopled with mental, physical, and moral cripples, though there is grave evidence that such has been the fate of Viet-Nam.

War, no less than any other human activity—even an immoral, needless, and obscene war—is supposed to be conducted within a framework of well-codified international and military law. There are rules to protect the innocent, to guarantee the safety of prisoners (in order, among other things, to guarantee the safety of one's own soldiers when captured), to maintain discipline in troops that would otherwise vanish if pillage and license were permitted free rein, to curb the tendency toward blood lust that fills some in the heat of battle or in the presence of the weak and helpless, and to limit war's destruction and havoc.

If it all sounds like trying to civilize uncivilized behavior, like trying to make rules for a game when the object should be not to make rules but to end the game, like a passionless intellectual discussion of the most passionate and unintellectual brutalities, think for a moment what would happen without such rules.

In all law—military and civilian, domestic and international—there is a basic element that some call the theory of the "reasonable" or "prudent" man. There are some acts, no matter the circumstances or the provocation, that a reasonable man knows he should not commit and that if he commits them it is a crime. A reasonable man, for instance, ought to know that murdering children who are only standing around is a crime even if no one has taken the trouble to explain that fact to him. A reasonable man ought to know—even if he has never received instructions on it and in fact has been told by someone above him to do it, that it is all right—that robbery and looting and pillage are illegal acts and that if he's caught he's very likely to be punished. And a soldier in war, no less than a civilian in peace at home, is bound by this doctrine and is considered to be a reasonable man.

But there are also written laws that spell out permissible and impermissible acts in wartime. It is against the background of this very large body of international and military law—and the circumvention and outright violation of those laws by the American government and the military in the war in Viet-Nam and the ignorance of the language of those laws by the average American soldier who has, at most, only been told that they exist but has received little or no indoctrination or instruction in them—that the war in Viet-Nam has been fought and out of which the slaughter at My Lai and the trial of Lieutenant Calley must be viewed.

Without some understanding of what those laws specify as legal and illegal during a war, it is impossible to really grasp the crimes the United States has committed in Viet-Nam, the magnitude of what happened at My Lai, or Calley's own personal responsibility for his actions that morning in March. Otherwise, it is too easy, and too many Americans have taken that route, to say that what happened at My Lai, what has happened throughout Viet-Nam, is just war, something that happens in every war and so nobody should be held culpable.

Calley's court-martial did not occur in a vacuum or in

isolation. That the crimes he was charged with may have grown, perhaps—as his attorneys and he himself constantly maintained—from an overzealous implementation of orders and of generally recognized American military policy in Viet-Nam was a fact always present at his trial and a fact that gave that trial implications and impact far beyond just the considerations of the guilt or innocence of one young lieutenant. His crimes, though—and the crimes of the American policy-makers in the war—are violations not just of the "reasonable" and "prudent" man doctrine but of specific strictures in the Army's Uniform Code of Military Justice and Law of Land Warfare and of international law relating to the conduct of war and the behavior of soldiers, law that the United States has subscribed to and, in some cases, even has taken the lead in promulgating.

To understand the court-martial in all its ramifications, to understand the responsibility and the culpability of the nation and its leaders for the crimes of My Lai and of all Viet-Nam, it is necessary to understand what is expected of a nation, its leaders, and its soldiers in war. And those expectations, in the form of law, have been set down succinctly and with few ambiguities not once but many times.

THE HAGUE CONVENTION ON LAND WARFARE, 1907

Article 3: The armed forces of the belligerent parties may consist of combatants and non-combatants. In the case of capture by the enemy, both have a right to be treated as prisoners of war.

Article 4: Prisoners of war are in the power of the hostile Government, but not of the individuals or corps who capture them.

They must be humanely treated.

All their personal belongings, except arms, horses, and military papers, remain their property. . . .

Article 22: The right of belligerents to adopt means of injuring the enemy is not unlimited.

Article 23: In addition to the prohibitions provided by special

Conventions, it is specifically forbidden—. . .

(b) To kill or wound treacherously individuals belonging to the hostile nation or army;

(c) To kill or wound an enemy who, having laid down his arms, or having no longer means of defense, has surrendered at discretion;

(d) To declare that no quarter will be given;

(e) To employ arms, projectiles or materials calculated to cause unnecessary suffering; . . .

(g) To destroy or seize the enemy's property, unless such destruction or seizure be imperatively demanded by the necessities of war;

(h) To declare abolished, suspended, or inadmissible in a court of law the rights and actions of the nationals of the hostile party. . . .

Article 25: The attack or bombardment, by whatever means, of towns, villages, dwellings, or buildings which are undefended is prohibited. . . .

Article 28: The pillage of a town or place, even when taken by assault, is prohibited. . . .

THE NUREMBERG PRINCIPLES, 1946

Principle I: Any person who commits an act which constitutes a crime under international law is responsible therefor and liable to punishment. . . .

Principle III: The fact that a person who committed an act which constitutes a crime under international law acted as Head of State or responsible government official does not relieve him from responsibility under international law.

Principle IV: That fact that a person acted pursuant to order of his Government or of a superior does not relieve him from responsibility under international law, provided a moral choice was in fact possible to him.

THE GENEVA CONVENTIONS ON THE LAWS OF WAR, 1949

Article 3: In the case of armed conflict not of an international character occurring in the territory of one of the High Contracting Parties, each Party to the conflict shall be bound to apply, as a minimum, the following provisions:

(1) Persons taking no active part in the hostilities, including members of armed forces who have laid down their arms and those placed *hors de combat* by sickness, wounds, detention, or any other cause, shall in all circumstances be treated humanely, without any adverse distinction founded on race, color, religion, or faith, sex, birth, or wealth, or any other similar criteria.

To this end, the following acts are and ˏshall remain prohibited at any time and in any place whatsoever with respect to the above-mentioned persons:

(a) violence to life and person, in particular murder of all kinds, mutilation, cruel treatment, and torture;

(b) taking of hostages;

(c) outrages upon personal dignity, in particular humiliating and degrading treatment;

(d) the passing of sentences and the carrying out of executions without previous judgment pronounced by a regularly constituted court, affording all the judicial guarantees which are recognized as indispensable by civilized peoples.

(2) The wounded and sick shall be collected and cared for. . . .

THE UNITED STATES ARMY FIELD MANUAL
The Law of Land Warfare, 1956

2. *Purposes of the Law of War*

The conduct of armed hostilities on land is regulated by the law of land warfare which is both written and unwritten. It is inspired by the desire to diminish the evils of war by:

a. Protecting both combatants and non-combatants from unnecessary suffering;

b. Safeguarding certain fundamental human rights of persons who fall into the hands of the enemy, particularly prisoners of war, the wounded and sick, and civilians; and

c. Facilitating the restoration of peace. . . .

3. *Basic Principles*

a. *Prohibitory Effect.* The law of war places limits on the exercise of a belligerent's power in the interests mentioned in paragraph 2 and requires that belligerents refrain from employing any kind or degree of violence which is not actually necessary for military purposes and that they conduct hostilities with regard for the principles of humanity and chivalry.

The prohibitory effect of the law of war is not minimized by "military necessity" which has been defined as that principle which justifies those measures not forbidden by international law which are indispensable for securing the complete submission of the enemy as soon as possible. Military necessity has been generally rejected as a defense for acts forbidden by the customary and conventional laws of war inasmuch as the latter have been developed and framed with consideration for the concept of military necessity.

b. *Binding on States and Individuals.* The law of war is binding not only upon States as such but also upon individuals and, in particular, the members of their armed forces. . . .

498. *Crimes Under International Law*

Any person, whether a member of the armed forces or a civilian, who commits an act which constitutes a crime under international law is responsible thereof and liable to punishment. . . .

499. *War Crimes*

The term "war crime" is a technical expression for a violation of the law of war by any person or persons, military or civilian. Every violation of the law of war is a war crime. . . .

501. *Responsibility for Acts of Subordinates*

In some cases, military commanders may be responsible for war crimes committed by subordinate members of the armed forces, or other persons subject to their control. Thus, for instance, when troops commit massacres and atrocities against the civilian population of occupied territory or against prisoners of war, the responsibility may rest not only with the actual perpetrators but also with the commander. Such a responsibility arises directly when the acts in questions have been committed in pursuance of an order of the commander concerned. The commander is also responsible if he has actual knowledge, or should have knowledge, through reports received by him or through other means, that troops or other persons subject to his control are about to commit or have committed a war crime and he fails to take the necessary and reasonable steps to insure compliance with the law of war or to punish violators thereof. . . .

505. *Universality of Jurisdiction*

. . . b. *Persons Charged with War Crimes.* The United States normally punishes war crimes as such only if they are committed by enemy nationals or by persons serving the interests of the enemy State. Violations of the law of war committed by persons subject to military law of the United States will usually constitute violations of the Uniform Code of Military Justice and, if so, will be prosecuted under that Code. . . . Commanding officers of United States troops must insure that war crimes committed by members of their forces against enemy personnel are promptly and adequately punished.

508. *Penal Sanctions*

The punishment imposed for a violation of the law of war must be proportionate to the gravity of the offense. The death penalty may be imposed for grave breaches of the law. . . .

509. *Defense of Superior Orders*

a. The fact that the law of war has been violated pursuant to an order of a superior authority, whether military or civil, does not deprive the act in question of its character as a war crime, nor does it constitute a defense in the trial of an accused individual, unless he did not know and could not reasonably have been expected to know that the act was unlawful. In all cases where the order is held not to constitute a defense to an allegation of war crime, the fact that the individual was acting pursuant to orders may be considered in mitigation of punishment.

b. In considering the question of whether a superior order

constitutes a valid defense, the court shall take into consideration the fact that obedience to lawful military orders is the duty of every member of the armed forces; that the latter cannot be expected, in conditions of war discipline, to weigh scrupulously the legal merits of the order received; that certain rules of warfare may be controversial; or that an act otherwise amounting to a war crime may be done in obedience to orders conceived as a measure of reprisal. At the same time it must be borne in mind that members of the armed forces are bound to obey only lawful orders.

510. *Government Officials*

The fact that a person who committed an act which constitutes a war crime acted as the head of a State or as a responsible government official does not relieve him from responsibility for his act.

So there is a vast body of law—international and internal—governing the conduct of nations and men fighting wars. Most of the elements of that law are relatively simple, so that even if they were not codified, any reasonable man of normal intelligence, which is supposed to cover just about every soldier, should know that such acts are on their face illegal under any circumstances.

It was against the background of these laws that Calley was tried at Fort Benning—though, because he came under jurisdiction of the Army, he was, as the Law of Land Warfare specifies, charged with violation of Article 118, Murder, of the Uniform Code of Military Justice. And it was in light of these laws that, despite all efforts to evade it, the Army itself and much of the nation found themselves in the dock with the lieutenant.

3

A Famous Victory

Though no one realized it at the time, the chain that would lead inevitably to the court-martial of Lieutenant Calley and the national torment that tore the nation began with a letter written from Phoenix, Arizona, on March 29, 1969. It was just a year and thirteen days after Company C, 1st Battalion, 20th Infantry, had gone for the first time to meet the enemy in pitched battle in Viet-Nam. Charlie Company—along with two other infantry companies, Company B, 4th Battalion, 3rd Infantry, and Company A, 3rd Battalion, 1st Infantry, an artillery battery, and some miscellaneous units—had been assigned to the 11th Light Infantry Brigade's special Task Force Barker in northern Quang Ngai Province in central Viet-Nam, the area of operations of its overall parent, the Americal (23rd) Division.

On March 16, 1968, it left its fire base, called LZ-Dotti, under orders to search and destroy an area east of Quang Ngai city, actually the village of Son My, thought to be the base camp of the experienced, tough, and long-lived 48th Viet Cong Local Force Battalion. With a strength of 105 men, supplemented by artillery and helicopter gunships, the men of Charlie Company were told that in this, their first battle, they would be meeting a force of perhaps 250 Viet Cong and could expect heavy casualties.

The troops landed, advanced with heavy fire into a hamlet called My Lai (4) on the Army maps, one platoon under Lieutenant Calley sweeping through the southern half of the hamlet, a second platoon under Lieutenant Stephen Brooks sweeping through the northern half and a third platoon under Lieutenant Jeffrey LaCross following in the wake along with the headquarters section of company commander Captain Ernest L. Medina. But there were no enemy soldiers there, only old men, women, children, and infants, and not a shot was fired from them at the advancing Americans, they offered no resistance. This did not inhibit the troops, and when they left My Lai (4), not a house was standing, not a well was unpolluted, not an animal was still alive, and almost all the people— perhaps as many as 500 of them—who were in the hamlet were dead.

It had been a massacre, but no one said anything and nothing happened. In the year that followed, many of the men in Charlie Company finished their tours in Viet-Nam, came home, and were discharged. Calley himself signed up for a second tour in Viet-Nam and for a time even served as a liaison officer with the Vietnamese population in his area. Neither he nor anyone else suspected what the future would bring.

How could they? The attack on My Lai had been hailed as a famous victory by none other than the then-commander of all United States forces in Viet-Nam, General William C. Westmoreland. Within days after the assault, he sent the troops a message, hailing the fact that they had "dealt enemy heavy blow. Congratulations to officers and men of C-1-20 for outstanding action."

And the after-action report filed on March 28, 1968, by Lieutenant Colonel Frank A. Barker, commander of Task Force Barker, read like the tale of a smashing victory over a major enemy:

"*Intelligence:* Enemy forces in the area of operation were estimated to be one local force battalion located in the vicinity of My Lai. This information was based upon previous combat operations in this area, visual reconnaissance, and PW and agent reports. During the operation it was estimated that only two local force companies supported by two to three local guerrilla platoons opposed the friendly forces. The area of operation consisted of six hamlets to varying degree of ruin, each separated by rice paddies which were bounded by a series of hedgerows and tree lines. The area was also honeycombed with tunnels and bunkers. The many hedgerows offered the enemy considerable cover and concealment from the attacking friendly forces. However the clear weather permitted maximum utilization of reconnaissance aircraft and helicopter gunships to seek out and destroy enemy defensive positions.

"Mission: To destroy enemy forces and fortification in a VC base camp and to capture enemy personnel, weapons, and supplies.

"Concept of Operation: Task Force Barker conducts a helicopter assault on 160730 March 68 on a VC base camp . . . with Company C, 1st Battalion, 20th Infantry landing to the west and Company B, 4th Battalion, 3rd Infantry landing to the southwest of the VC base camp. Company A, 3rd Battalion, 1st Infantry moves by foot to blocking positions north of the base camp prior to the helicopter assault. USN Swift Boats screen the coastal area to the east of the base camp and Company B (Aero Scout) 123rd Avn Bn screens to the south to block or destroy enemy forces attempting to withdraw. An artillery preparation and gunship suppressive fires are planned for both landing zones. Artillery blocking fires are planned on all paths of escape which the enemy might use. Upon landing, the two rifle companies assault enemy positions making a detailed search of all buildings, bunkers, and tunnels as they move.

"Execution: The order was issued on 14 March 1968. Coordination with supporting arms reconnaissance and positioning of forces was conducted on 15 March 1968. On 160726 March 68 a three-minute artillery preparation began on the first landing zone and at 0730 hours the first lift of Co C touched down while helicopter gunships provided suppressive fires. At 0747 hours the last lift of Co C was completed. The initial preparation resulted in 68 VC KIA's in the enemy's combat

outpost positions. Co C then immediately attacked to the east receiving enemy small arms fire as they pressed forward. At 0809 H a three-minute artillery preparation on the second landing zone began and the first lift for Co B touched down at 0815 hours. At 0827 the last lift of Co B was completed and Co B moved to the north and east receiving only light enemy resistance initially. As Co B approached the area of the VC base camp, enemy defensive fire increased. One platoon from Co B flanked the enemy positions and engaged one enemy platoon resulting in 30 enemy KIA. Throughout the day both Co B and Co C received sporadic sniper fire and encountered numerous enemy booby traps. Co A in blocking positions to the north had only light contact against small enemy elements attempting to withdraw to the north. Attempts of the enemy to escape along the beach or to the south were successfully countered by the Swift Boats and the Aero Scout Company. By 1630 hours the surviving enemy elements had broken all contact with friendly forces by infiltrating with civilians leaving the area. At 1715 hours Co C linked-up with Co B and both units went into a perimeter defense for the night in preparation for conducting search and destroy operations the next day. With the establishment of the night defensive position at 161800 March 1968 the operation was terminated.

"Results:
   a. Enemy losses:
      (1) Personnel:
         128 KIA
         11 VCS CIA [sympathizers captured in action]
      (2) Equipment captured:
          1 M-1 rifle
          2 M-1 carbines
        10 Chicom hand grenades
         8 US M-26 hand grenades
      410 rounds small arms ammo
         4 US steel helmets with liners
         5 US canteens with covers
         7 US pistol belts

> 9 sets US web equipment
> 2 short wave transistor radios
> 3 boxes of medical supplies
> (3) Equipment and facilities destroyed:
> 16 booby traps
> 1 large tunnel complex
> 14 small tunnel complexes
> 8 bunkers
> numerous sets of web equipment
> b. Friendly losses:
> 2 US KIA
> 11 US WIA [wounded in action]

"Commander Analysis: This operation was well planned, well executed, and successful. Friendly casualties were light and the enemy suffered heavily. On this operation the civilian population supporting the VC in the area numbered approximately 200. This created a problem in population control and medical care of those civilians caught in the fire of the opposing forces. However, the infantry unit on the ground and helicopters were able to assist civilians in leaving the area and in caring for and or evacuating the wounded.

"Recommendations: Operations conducted in an area where large numbers of refugees might be generated should provide for civil affairs, psyops [psychological warfare operations], medical, intelligence, and police teams to be brought to the area as early as practicable after the arrival of combat troops. This would facilitate population control and medical care, and would permit the sorting out of VC which have mingled among the population for cover. The presence of these teams would free infantry personnel for combat operations."

It was a fairy tale dreamed up in the headquarters of Task Force Barker to cover an operation which, as described, had taken place only in the reveries of an Army public information officer.

Did anyone question it, though? It seemed not, at least not

then. Barker's report was accepted as true, though it would have been thought that someone would find a little fanciful the discrepancy between the number of Viet Cong killed and the number of weapons captured—only three rifles, and all of them American of ancient make.

But perhaps someone was a little distressed at Chu Lai, at the headquarters of the Americal Division. Distressed, at least, over the use of some terms. For less than a month later, on April 13, 1968, a directive went out from Colonel Nels A. Parson, division chief of staff: "Effective immediately the term 'search and destroy' will not be used in correspondence originating within this command.

"Unfortunately, this term has been taken out of context and the emphasis placed on the word 'destroy.' It is then used to describe hamlets and villages in an area in which heavy fighting has occurred. Further, 'search and destroy' has occasionally been used to foster the impression that military operations wantonly create, without regard to human suffering, large numbers of refugees.

"To preclude unintentional misuse or incorrect description of combat operations other terms will be used. Phrases which are fully descriptive are sweep operations, search and clear, search and hold, cordon and search, and reconnaissance in force. Other applicable but less commonly used descriptive phrases for consideration are meeting engagement and movement to contact.

"These instructions do not preclude the use of words and phrases indicating offensive or defensive actions providing they give the reader no basis for assuming a lack of compassion on the part of members of this command."

Perhaps there it all might have died had it not been for a young man who was not even at My Lai. Ronald Ridenhour had only heard stories of what had happened that morning in March from friends who had been there, and the more he heard the more distressed he became. But he waited until he returned home, until he had been discharged, before doing anything about the turbulent emotions that were stirring within him. On March 29, 1969, he finally sat down at his desk in his home in Phoenix and wrote a letter to the Department of the Army, sending copies to the Defense Department, other government officials, and several Congressmen and Senators.

Everything that happened from that point on sprang from this letter, with its misspellings, its uncertainties about facts, but with its general ring of truth:

"It was late in April, 1968, that I first heard of 'Pinkville' and what allegedly happened there. I received the first report with some skepticism, but in the following months I was to hear similar stories from such a wide variety of people that it became impossible for me to disbelieve that something rather dark and bloody did indeed occur sometime in March, 1968, in a village called 'Pinkville' in the Republic of Viet-Nam.

"The circumstances that led to my having access to the reports I'm about to relate need explanation. I was inducted in March, 1967, into the U.S. Army. After receiving various training I was assigned to the 70th Infantry Detachment (LRP), 11th Light Infantry Brigade at Schofield Barracks, Hawaii, in early October, 1967. That unit, the 70th Infantry Detachment (LRP), was disbanded a week before the 11th Brigade shipped out for Viet-Nam on the 5th of December, 1967. All of the men from whom I later heard reports of the 'Pinkville' incident were reassigned to 'C' Company, 1st Battalion, 20th Infantry, 11th Light Infantry Brigade. I was reassigned to the aviation section of Headquarters Headquarters Company, 11th LIB. After we had been in Viet-Nam for 3 or 4 months many of the men from the 70th Inf. Det. (LRP) began to transfer into the same unit, 'E' Company, 51st Infantry (LRP).

"In late April, 1968, I was awaiting orders for a transfer from HHC, 11th Brigade to Company 'E,' 51st Inf. (LRP), when I happened to run into Pfc. 'Butch' Gruver, whom I had known in Hawaii. Gruver told me he had been assigned to 'C' Company 1st of the 10th until April 1st when he transferred to the unit I was headed for. During the course of our conversation he told me the first of many reports I was to hear of 'Pinkville.'

"'Charlie' Company, 1/20 had been assigned to Task Force Barker in late February, 1968, to help conduct 'search and destroy' operations on the Batangan Peninsula, Barker's area of operations. The task force was operating out of LZ-Dotti, located five or six miles north of Quang Ngai city on Vietnamese National Highway 1. Gruver said that Charlie Company had sustained casualties, primarily from mines and booby traps, almost every day from the first day they arrived on the peninsula. One village area was particularly troublesome and seemed to be infested with booby traps and enemy soldiers. It was located about six miles northeast of Quang Ngai city at approximate coordinates B.S. 728795. It was a notorious area and the men of Task Force Barker had a special name for it; they called it 'Pinkville.' [Actually, the name Pinkville came not from the troublesome nature of that particular place but rather from its color on Army maps; many population centers in villages are so colored; in this case, the Pinkville was the major hamlet, or subhamlet in Son My village, called by the Vietnamese My Khe and by the American Army My Lai (1).] Its mission: destroy the trouble spot and all its inhabitants.

"When 'Butch' told me this I didn't quite believe that what he was telling me was true, but he assured me that it was and went on to describe what had happened. The other two companies that made up the task force cordoned off the village so that 'Charlie' Company could move through to destroy the structures and kill the inhabitants. Any villagers who ran from Charlie Company were stopped by the encircling companies. I asked 'Butch' several times if all the people were killed. He said he thought they were, men, women, and children. He recalled seeing a small boy, about three or four years old, standing by the trail with a gunshot wound in one arm. The boy was clutching his wounded arm with his other hand, while blood trickled between his fingers. He was staring around himself in shock and disbelief at what he saw. 'He just stood there with big eyes staring around like he didn't understand, he didn't believe what was happening. Then the captain's RTO put a burst of 16 fire into him.' It was so bad, Gruver said, that one of the men in his squad shot himself in the foot in order to be medivac-ed out of the area so that he would not have to participate in the slaughter. Although he had not seen it, Gruver had been told by people he considered trustworthy that one of the company's officers, 2nd Lieutenant Kally (this spelling may be incorrect) had rounded up several groups of villagers (each group consisting of a minimum of 20 persons of both sexes and all ages). According to the story, Kally then machine-gunned each group. Gruver estimated that the population of the village had been 300 to 400 people and that very few, if any, escaped.

"After hearing this account I couldn't quite accept it. Somehow I just couldn't believe that not only had so many young American men participated in such an act of barbarism, but that their officers had ordered it. There were other men in the unit I was soon to be assigned to, 'E' Company, 51st Infantry (LRP), who had been in Charlie Company at the time that Gruver alleged the incident at 'Pinkville' had occurred. I became determined to ask them about 'Pinkville' so that I might compare their accounts with Pfc Gruver's.

"When I arrived at 'Echo' Company, 51st Infantry (LRP) the men I looked for were Pfc's Michael Terry and William Doherty. Both were veterans of Charlie Company, 1/20 and 'Pinkville.' Instead of contradicting 'Butch' Gruver's story they corroborated it, adding some tasty tidbits of information of their own. Terry and Doherty had been in the same squad and their platoon was the third platoon of 'C' Company to pass through the village. Most of the people they came to were already dead. Those that weren't were sought out and shot. The platoon left nothing alive, neither livestock nor people. Around noon the two soldiers' squad stopped to eat. 'Billy and I started to get out our chow,' Terry said, 'but close to us was a bunch of Vietnamese in a heap, and some of them were moaning. Kally (2nd Lt. Kally) had been through before us and all of them had been shot, but many weren't dead. It was obvious that they weren't going to get any medical attention so Billy and I got up and went over to where they were. I guess we

sort of finished them off.' Terry went on to say that he and
Doherty then returned to where their packs were and ate
lunch. He estimated the size of the village to be 200 to 300
people. Doherty thought that the population of 'Pinkville' had
been 400 people.

"If Terry, Doherty and Gruver could be believed, then not
only had 'Charlie' Company received orders to slaughter all the
inhabitants of the village, but those orders had come from the
commanding officer of Task Force Barker, or possibly even
higher in the chain of command. Pfc Terry stated that when
Captain Medina (Charlie Company's commanding officer
Captain Ernest Medina) issued the order for the destruction of
'Pinkville' he had been hesitant, as if it were something he
didn't want to do but had to. Others I spoke to concurred with
Terry on this.

"It was June before I spoke to anyone who had something of
significance to add to what I had already been told of the
'Pinkville' incident. It was the end of June, 1968, when I ran
into Sergeant Larry LaCroix at the USO in Chu Lai. LaCroix
had been in 2nd Lt. Kally's platoon on the day Task Force
Barker swept through 'Pinkville.' What he told me verified the
stories of the others, but he also had something new to add. He
had been a witness to Kally's gunning down of at least three
separate groups of villagers. 'It was terrible. They were
slaughtering the villagers like so many sheep. Kally's men were
dragging people out of bunkers and hootches and putting them
together in a group. The people in the group were men,
women, and children of all ages. As soon as he felt that the
group was big enough, Kally ordered an M-60 (machine gun)
set up and the people killed. LaCroix said that he bore witness
to this procedure at least three times. The three groups were of
different sizes, one of about twenty people, one of about thirty
people, and one of about forty people. When the first group
was put together Kalley ordered Pfc Torres to man the
machine gun and open fire on the villagers that had been
grouped together. This Torres did, but before everyone in the
group was down he ceased fire and refused to fire again. After

ordering Torres to recommence firing several times, Lieutenant Kally took over the M-60 and finished shooting the remaining villagers in that first group himself. Sergeant LaCroix told me that Kally didn't bother to order anyone to take the machine gun when the other two groups of villagers were formed. He simply manned it himself and shot down all villagers in both groups.'

"This account of Sergeant LaCroix's confirmed the rumors that Gruver, Terry and Doherty had previously told me about Lieutenant Kally. It also convinced me that there was a very substantial amount of truth to the stories that all of these men had told. If I needed more convincing, I was to receive it.

"It was in the middle of November, 1968, just a few weeks before I was to return to the United States for separation from the army that I talked to Pfc Michael Bernhardt. Bernhardt had served his entire year in Viet-Nam in 'Charlie' Company 1/20 and he too was about to go home. 'Bernie' substantiated the tales told by the other men I had talked to in vivid and bloody detail and added this. 'Bernie' had absolutely refused to take part in the massacre of the villagers of 'Pinkville' that morning and he thought it was rather strange that the officers of the company had not made an issue of it. But that evening 'Medina (Captain Ernest Medina) came up to me ("Bernie") and told me not to do anything stupid like write my congressman' about what had happened that day. Bernhardt assured Captain Medina that he had no such thing in mind. He had nine months left in Viet-Nam and felt that it was dangerous enough just fighting the acknowledged enemy.

"Exactly what did, in fact, occur in the village of 'Pinkville' in March, 1968, I do not know for *certain*, but I am convinced that it was something very black indeed. I remain irrevocably persuaded that if you and I do truly believe in the principles of justice and the equality of every man, however humble, before the law, that form the very backbone that this country is founded on, then we must press forward a widespread and public investigation of this matter with all our combined efforts. I think that it was Winston Churchill who once said 'A country without a conscience is a country without a soul, and a country without a soul is a country that cannot survive.' I feel that I must take some positive action on this matter. I hope that you will launch an investigation immediately and keep me informed of your progress. If you cannot, then I don't know what other course of action to take.

"I have considered sending this to newspapers, magazines, and broadcasting companies, but I somehow feel that investigation and action by the Congress of the United States is the appropriate procedure, and as a conscientious citizen I have no desire to further besmirch the image of the American serviceman in the eyes of the world. I feel that this action, while probably it would promote attention, would not bring about the constructive actions that the direct actions of the Congress of the United States would."

And so with this letter began the investigation into what happened at My Lai, an investigation that for more than six months was conducted by the Army itself and unknown to the public. *

Spurred by persistent requests for action from Ridenhour's Congressman, Morris K. Udall of Arizona, the Department of the Army began to dig into the facts in the letter. Around the country and to Viet-Nam flew Army investigators, interviewing those mentioned by Ridenhour and new names cited by other members of the company. And slowly the evidence accumulated that was to lead to the charges against Calley, Medina and, eventually, twenty-three other members of the Americal Division, including that division's commanding

*For a full discussion of the revelations to the public and the world of the massacre and the events surrounding and following those revelations, and for a full treatment of the people and the village in Viet-Nam where the massacre took place, see Richard Hammer, *One Morning in the War: The Tragedy at Son My* (Coward-McCann, 1970); also, Seymour M. Hersh, *My Lai 4: The Massacre and Its Aftermath* (Random House, 1970); the heavily expurgated and censured *Report of the Department of the Army Review of the Preliminary Investigations into the My Lai Incident* (the report of the Peers Inquiry), 1970; and the Report of the Armed Services Investigating Subcommittee of the House of Representatives, *Investigation of the My Lai Incident,* 1970.

officer at the time of the massacre. It became all too apparent in the Pentagon that though much of what Ridenhour had related could not be substantiated, the basic facts were all too true. The question rose: What to do?

Calley himself, the prime target from beginning to end, first learned of the investigation and of the possibility that he would stand court-martial for murder at My Lai at the beginning of June, 1969, nearly fifteen months after the slaughter. He had extended his tour in Viet-Nam and was then serving with Company G of the 75th Rangers. "It was back in about, I believe about the twentieth—it was the last third of May," he remembered, "and I was called down to division, and one of the clerks there had a TWX from DA [a message from the Department of the Army] that reassigned me to Fort McLellan, Alabama, to the chemical school there. And the date was— reporting day was thirty-one May. And everybody took it for granted that DA had not posted my thirty-day leave on that, because I shouldn't have left until thirty-one June. So we all agreed that it was a mistake. And that was the first time I heard about it."

Because of his belief that the Army had made a mistake in not giving him thirty days to report, Calley was in no rush to respond to his reassignment. He considered it only an ordinary directive. But "on six June, I was to be back down to division and they said they had another wire from DA and DA was upset because the orders were in fact for me to be in—be at DA for three days TDY on no later than thirty-one May. So within two hours I was leaving Chu Lai and I was back in the United States on the sixth."

No explanation other than reassignment was given to Calley for his return home, and no explanation at all was given him as to why the rush. On June 10 he found out. He was ordered to report to the Inspector General's office in Washington, where "I was advised of my rights and I might possibly stand charges for murder. They said I would possibly be charged for murder for action at My Lai Four."

A month later, Calley was assigned to the Student Brigade at Fort Benning, his future unclear, uncertain as to whether those charges would actually be lodged against him. It seemed, then, almost a race against the clock, with the clock winning, for the Army did not seem to be rushing anything. On his return, Calley had put in for discharge and he was scheduled to be out of the Army on September 6; if charges were not filed before that day, he would be a civilian and beyond the reach of military justice.

But one evening in the first days of September, four young lawyers, captains all, in the Judge Advocate General's (JAG) Corps at Fort Benning sat around talking and growing angrier and angrier. About six weeks earlier, almost coinciding with Calley's arrival at the base, they had been briefed on the Army's investigation into the My Lai incident and had been told that the case, if there was indeed to be one, would be assigned to their office.

There was much these young legal captains did not know at that moment about the slaughter of Vietnamese; but they knew enough to be fairly certain that violations of international law regarding war crimes and violations of the Army's own law of war and of Article 118 of the UCMJ relating to murder had taken place at My Lai.

What seemed to be increasingly clear that hot early September night in Georgia, eight thousand miles and a year and a half from the scene of the massacre in Viet-Nam, was that the Army and the United States government seemed to be extremely hesitant about following through—with Calley, who was their responsibility, and with anyone else who might fall into the net. The case was just too volatile and the political repercussions of revelations about a slaughter of unarmed Vietnamese civilians by American soldiers might be so intense and so vast and the public repugnance over the war might be so great as a result of such disclosures as to lead to renewed and greater protests in the streets and on the campuses than had already taken place in recent years. The resulting outcry might well put in jeopardy President Nixon's professed aim of "winding down the war" in a slow and what he claimed was a steady fashion; Nixon's plans might be washed away in a torrent of cries to "end the war now."

What gave that meeting its special urgency, though, was the imminent separation of Calley from the Army—only a matter of days away. If the case against him were not pressed immediately, it would be too late. He would be beyond the reach of all justice, for as far as anyone knew there was and is no way to bring a man to trial for crimes committed while in the service once he has been discharged. Once a civilian, he would be liable for action only in civilian courts, but civilian courts have no jurisdiction over crimes committed by men in the service and particularly crimes committed outside the United States.

Something had to be done and done fast if Calley were not to escape into the sanctuary of civilian life. Yet, one of the officers at that meeting said later, orders had come from the Pentagon to "do nothing until you hear from us."

Almost in desperation, the four captains—none a career soldier, all serving the standard four-year draftee's hitch in JAG—decided to take matters upon themselves. They would press a charge of murder and thereby forestall Calley's discharge. But they were well aware that if they took such an action, and that action went counter to the desires of their superiors at Fort Benning and at the Pentagon, retribution would surely descend. The wiser course, they finally agreed, was to let one of their number take the necessary steps and suffer the consequences while at least one of the remaining three would be able to carry the case forward.

That night they flipped coins. The winner—or the loser— was a twenty-six-year-old Georgia lawyer named Captain William Ralph Hill. "All of us," Hill said, "were frustrated that the case was becoming politically oriented. We knew it was sensitive, but we were determined we would go right by the book."

Hill went to Colonel Lon D. Marlow, then commander of the

Student Brigade at Fort Benning, and so Calley's commanding officer. He urged Marlow to issue a murder charge against the lieutenant before it was too late. According to Hill, Marlow refused. Such an action, the colonel told the captain, might offend President Nixon. "If I don't do what the President wants me to," Hill said Marlow told him, "I'm a fool or a jackass, and I'm inclined to the latter."

If Marlow would not take action, then there was only one other course. Hill decided to take it upon himself to sign the murder charge. But almost simultaneously with his decision, on September 4, the Pentagon—perhaps with knowledge of the rebellion of the legal captains and what repercussions that might have—told the JAG office at Fort Benning to go ahead on its own and press charges if it felt the evidence was sufficient. Hill was given the honor of signing those charges.

That afternoon a release was sent to the press; in two short paragraphs it said that the Army had that day charged First Lieutenant William L. Calley, Jr., with violation of Article 118 of the UCMJ. If a full investigation under Article 32 of the UCMJ (similar to a grand jury investigation) showed the charges had merit, Calley would stand court-martial for the murder of an unknown number of Vietnamese civilians.

The news was all but ignored by the nation's press; in *The New York Times*, for example, it rated a brief paragraph on a back page under a minuscule headline, and was not followed up. It was not for another two months that the nation began to hear the story and began to grasp its magnitude, not until an enterprising young journalist named Seymour M. Hersh was tipped to the story by a friend at the Pentagon and, with almost incredible perseverance, tracked down every lead he could develop in the United States (for this work, Hersh would later win the Pulitzer Prize and almost every other journalistic award for reporting).

So, in November, 1969, the story of the massacre at My Lai (4) was on the front pages around the world. And as the details piled on each other, the scope of the investigation widened far beyond just the lonely figure of Calley. (Hill was out of the case by then. Soon after the charges against Calley were filed at Fort Benning, he was transferred to the 11th Armored Cavalry Regiment at Bien Hoa, South Viet-Nam.)

If the furor was initially over Calley, and he would always remain the central figure and the one name that immediately came to mind when My Lai was mentioned, the net was scooping up others in rapid order. But Calley remained in the middle. He was in a unique position. He had both taken orders from those above that led to the massacre, and given orders to perpetrate it; and he had not only given orders to kill but had participated in the killing itself. Below him in the chain were the soldiers and noncommissioned officers who had followed his directives and killed; above him were the higher officers with whom the policy and the directives had originated but who themselves had not taken part in the actual slaughter. Calley was thus the sole initiator and participant still alive. (The leader of the second platoon of Charlie Company, Lieutenant Stephen Brooks, whose men did no less than Calley's and who, if his troops are to be believed, was no laggard in joining them, was later killed in Viet-Nam and so no charges could be brought against him.)

The web of unsupported rumor and of supported fact and evidence that had ensnared Calley was, in the weeks and months after he was charged, to ensnare those both higher and lower in the chain of responsibility. Before the initial surge was over in March, 1970, more than two dozen others still in the military, and so still subject to military justice, were to find themselves facing possible courts-martial for their roles in the events surrounding My Lai.

As a result of the investigations of the Army's Criminal Investigations Division both in the United States and in Viet-Nam, eleven other soldiers, including two officers, were accused of actual participation in the slaughter of the innocent at My Lai that March morning, and a third officer was charged with murder in a nearby hamlet in Son My village—a hamlet the American Army called My Khe (4) and which the Vietnamese knew as My Hoi.

Captain Ernest L. Medina, thirty-three at the time he was charged, was cited for failure to report the massacre and on capital charges of murder—both of individuals at My Lai and of the overall responsibility for at least 175 civilian murders committed by his troops (that number, never certain anyway, as no numbers at My Lai were ever certain, was later reduced to at least 100).

Captain Eugene M. Kotouc, thirty-six, an intelligence officer assigned to Task Force Barker, was charged with "assault, maiming, and murder" of a prisoner picked up during the sweep whom he had interrogated at the evening bivouac later.

Staff Sergeant David Mitchell, a squad leader in Calley's platoon, was accused of assault with intent to murder at least thirty Vietnamese.

Sergeant Charles E. Hutto, a member not of Calley's first platoon but of Brooks's second, was charged with murder, rape, and assault with intent to commit murder of six civilians at My Lai.

Sergeant Esequiel Torres was charged with "premeditated murder of an unknown number of unidentified Vietnamese persons, not less than three, by means of shooting them with a machine gun," and with intent to murder at least three others with his machine gun. Torres also faced an additional charge: that sometime prior to the attack on My Lai, in February, he murdered another Vietnamese civilian "by means of hanging him by the neck with a rope."

Corporal (later Sergeant) Kenneth Schiel, a highly decorated soldier, was charged with premeditated murder.

Specialist 4 William F. Doherty was charged with murder.

Specialist 4 Robert W. T'Souvas was charged with the murder of two Vietnamese by machine-gunning them to death.

Private Max D. Hutson was charged with machine-gunning to death at least fifteen civilians, and with rape.

Private Gerald A. Smith was charged with the murder of one man, one woman, and five unidentified civilians. He was also charged with "an indecent assault upon an unidentified female Vietnamese civilian by tearing and opening her blouse, by touching her on or about the chest and by fondling her breasts with intent to gratify his lust."

Staff Sergeant Kenneth L. Hodges was charged with assault with intent to commit murder and with rape.

And just days before he was to be discharged from the Army, Captain Thomas K. Willingham, who on March 16, 1968, had been a lieutenant in command of a platoon not of Charlie Company but of Bravo Company which attacked the hamlets along the beach a couple of miles from My Lai (4), was charged with an unspecified number of murders during his platoon's sweep.

And the net reached out and enveloped those on a higher level. A special investigating panel of the Army under Lieutenant General William R. Peers began looking into just what had happened at My Lai and whether there had been, as all the evidence seemed to show, a deliberate attempt by higher officers to cover up the atrocity. Appointed in late November, the Peers committee finished its work three and a half months later, concluding in March, 1970, that there had indeed been "serious deficiencies in the actions taken by officials in the Americal Division, the 11th Brigade and Task Force Barker, after the incident at Son My. . . . Certain officials in these units did not, after information came to their attention, take appropriate action to investigate or report."

The Peers report was turned over to the Army, and a couple of weeks later charges were brought against many of those named by the Peers panel.

Major General Samuel W. Koster, in 1968 commander of the Americal Division, was charged with failure to obey lawful regulations and dereliction of duty in covering up the massacre. The charges against Koster were a serious blow to the Army. He was considered one of the brightest of the young generals (he was not yet fifty), was a protegé of General Westmoreland, was then commandant of the United States Military Academy at West Point, and was slated, according to rumors around the Pentagon, for higher posts; it was said that he would soon take over command of American forces in

Germany and, if he continued to brighten his stars as he had in the past, he might one day become Army chief-of-staff.

Brigadier General George H. Young, Jr., Koster's assistant division commander of the Americal, was charged with failure to obey lawful orders and dereliction of duty by helping to cover up the massacre.

These same charges were lodged down the line against a number of other officers: Colonel Robert B. Luper, commander of the 11th Artillery's 6th Battery; Colonel Nels A. Parson, the Americal Division chief-of-staff; Colonel Oran K. Henderson, commander of the 11th Brigade; Lieutenant Colonel David G. Gavin, senior American adviser in the Son Tinh District of Quang Ngai Province, the district which encompassed Son My village and My Lai; Lieutenant Colonel William D. Guinn, Jr., deputy American adviser in Quang Ngai Province; Major Charles C. Calhoun, executive officer and operations officer of Task Force Barker; Major Frederic W. Watke, commander of Company B, 123rd Aviation Battalion; Captain Kenneth W. Boatman, a forward artillery observer attached to Bravo Company on March 16, 1968; Captain Dennis H. Johnson, attached to the 52nd Military Intelligence Department in Quang Ngai Province.

In addition, Colonel Henderson was charged with making false statements and swearing falsely under oath during investigations into My Lai; similar charges were lodged against Major Robert W. McKnight, operations officer of the 11th Brigade, and against Captain Willingham. And a charge of possible misconduct was leveled against Captain Boatman.

If he had lived, Lieutenant Colonel Frank A. Barker, the commander of the task force named for him, the task force which assaulted My Lai, would almost certainly have faced these same charges and might also have been cited for graver crimes resulting from the attack. But Barker was killed in a helicopter accident in June, 1968, three months after My Lai, and though his name was ever-present in the tales of the day, death had rescued him from the disgrace of formal charges.

Faced with this imposing array of officers and enlisted men, ranging from a major general down to privates, all charged with crimes growing out of the attack on Son My village that on conviction could mean anything from a simple reprimand to the death sentence, the Army was in a quandary as to how to deal with all of them and all the implications, and how to deal with them legally.

There seemed at least two choices. It could try the men singly, one at a time. Or it could hold a mass trial at which all twenty-five charged (and any others who might subsequently be charged, for the Army was then, and is still, looking into the conduct of other officers and enlisted men that day) would be placed in a dock together. Such a mass trial would have the benefit, some thought when the idea was first broached, of disposing of the entire Son My incident and all its implications at one time; it would be something of a board of inquiry in addition to a trial and during it all the facts surrounding the massacre might be made public—how and why it was planned and initiated, exactly what happened everywhere in the village during the action, and why and how it had been concealed afterward. It would also be a means of disposing of Son My in one large, bitter drink over a relatively brief time, certainly no more than a few months, rather than feeding bits and pieces of the story to the world through individual trials which would keep the name My Lai, and Son My, with all its implications in the headlines and on the nation's conscience for a protracted period, perhaps for years.

But for many high officers in the Army, a mass trial had an aura of horror. The Army and the President were maintaining that My Lai was an aberration, not common practice, and the sight of all those soldiers in the dock, including generals, would seem to give the lie to that contention. And the thought of such a spectacle, with two dozen or more American soldiers, including generals, lined up in the dock like a little Nuremberg, a real-life war crimes trial involving this time not Germans or Japanese but Americans, was just more than they could stomach. The disgrace that such a spectacle would bring to the American Army, and to the United States, in the eyes of the nation and the world was more than they were willing to bear.

During the spring of 1970, a number of discussions were held between the Pentagon and the Department of Justice during which the merits and demerits of the mass trial concept were debated. According to some sources, the Justice Department leaned toward a mass tribunal as a way to get it all over with fast; but the Army refused to move. It was insistent throughout that no mass trial be held, that neither the nation nor the Army could afford that.

So the second option won out. Each man charged would face the possibility of court-martial on his own; the officers and men would be tried, if they were tried, alone and one at a time; it would be up to the individual prosecutors and judges to decide whether to limit the evidence presented so that it dealt only narrowly with the individual acts charged, and thereby prevent a full disclosure of the ramifications of My Lai, or to broaden the trial to cover the entire scope of the operation.

And, as though to blunt even further the possibilities that any of the trials would take on the aura of a major war crimes tribunal, the accused soldiers were not centered at one base but were scattered to a number of bases where each would face his own trial, that is, if the convening officer—the commanding general of each base—decided the evidence was sufficient to present such a presumption of guilt that a court-martial was indicated (and, indeed, such a presumption is practically necessary before a court-martial is held). In the Army's legal lexicon, the charging of a soldier is only the first step toward court-martial, similar to arrest in civilian life. It is followed by pretrial hearings under Article 32 of the UCMJ to sift the seriousness of the crimes and what evidence there is that the accused may be guilty. If, after investigation and hearings, enough evidence has been bared to convince the commanding general of a substantial presumption that the crime was committed and the accused was the perpetrator, then a court-martial is scheduled. (This procedure has long been a subject of major criticism of the system of military justice, for it should be apparent what effect a court-martial must have on officers selected to sit as the jury when they know that the commanding officer of their base has convened that court-martial, meaning he is just about convinced of guilt.)

Thus Calley was at Fort Benning, where it would be up to General Orwin C. Talbott, commanding general, to decide whether he would actually be tried.

Mitchell was at Fort Hood, Texas, and the commanding general there would make the decision. The commanding general at Fort McPherson, Georgia, would have the ultimate say in the cases of Medina, Kotouc, and most of the other enlisted men. Lieutenant General Jonathan O. Seaman, commander of the First Army at Fort Meade, Maryland, would make the ultimate decision about all the higher officers charged with covering up the incident (and General Seaman's own actions as a commander in Viet-Nam have lately been called into question by *ad hoc* citizens and veterans groups investigating war crimes committed by American soldiers in Viet-Nam).

Through the spring and summer of 1970, Americans then waited to learn what, if anything, the Army would do. Would the Army press forward and actually bring anyone to trial, or would the charges be dropped after the heat of the initial disclosures had begun to cool? There was the feeling among many who watched closely or were involved in some aspect of the My Lai affair that it would all, eventually, come full circle, and at the end if anyone at all remained it would be only Rusty Calley.

And, indeed, charges against some of the officers and enlisted men were quietly dropped during those months, especially against those officers stationed under General Seaman's jurisdiction at Fort Meade. Almost the first to be told that the Army would do nothing to him, because the evidence of crimes was sketchy and less than conclusive from the Army's standpoint, was Captain Willingham. He promptly left the service. And when he vanished from the ranks of the accused, the light that had flickered for only a moment over the second wave of killings on March 16, 1968, at My Hoi, or My Khe (4), was extinguished, never to be lit again. What happened at that subhamlet in Son My would remain, it seemed, forever arcane and obscure.

At Fort Hood, however, the decision was made to proceed with the court-martial of David Mitchell, the second man (after Calley) against whom charges had been brought. In many ways, it was only fitting that the first My Lai court-martial would be that of a black soldier, given the disproportionate role that blacks had played in Viet-Nam combat.

If anyone had hoped to learn anything about My Lai from the Mitchell court-martial, though, those hopes were doomed as soon as the trial began. Mitchell, a Louisiana black who had volunteered for the Army in 1960 and had hoped to make it his career (a hope he still holds), came to court on October 6, 1970. The military judge announced almost immediately that he would not permit any testimony by soldiers who had appeared before the House subcommittee investigating My Lai because that subcommittee had refused to make available a transcript of those hearings. Captain Michael Swann, the Army prosecutor, called only three witnesses, only one of whom said he had actually seen Mitchell shoot civilians at My Lai; the other two said they had seen the sergeant fire his M-16 into a ditch where civilians had been herded but had not actually seen the results of that fire. After these three witnesses, Swann rested his case. "I feel," he said, "I've proved my case. The government never undertook in this case to prosecute a My Lai massacre. All the government undertook to do was to show that Staff Sergeant David Mitchell stood at the edge of a ditch and shot women and children with his M-16 rifle."

But it was obvious that Swann had not even proved that. Ossie Brown, Mitchell's volunteer civilian lawyer, called more than twenty former soldiers as his witnesses; some testified that the government witnesses were known as liars; others said they were not sure where Mitchell was that morning, and most, if they had seen any killing at all, put the blame on Calley. Mitchell himself testified with tears in his eyes that, "I'm still not sure what happened and who was in my squad that day. But

I'm positive that I did not shoot anyone. I know what I did and what I did not do."

In his summation, Ossie Brown struck the note that would be heard again and again—and had already been sounded by supporters of the incriminated soldiers. He defended Mitchell and everyone who had been at My Lai as soldiers doing their duty. "I don't like to see the prosecution of any young man sent to fight for his country," Brown declared. "Some elements are trying to undermine and destroy the military of this country. They'd love to gut the military because when you gut the military, you destroy a country. . . . We need soldiers such as Sergeant Mitchell. Let's not betray him."

The jury was out less than seven hours—some of the jurors admitted later they reached a verdict soon after retiring and only stayed out so long to make things look good. Sergeant Mitchell, they said, was not guilty.

With that verdict, Mitchell said on the courthouse steps, he was determined to stay in the Army and continue his career. But though he had been acquitted, a continued military future for him did not seem bright. About two months later, his service file was "flagged"—he could not be promoted or assigned new duties, he would remain static—while a further investigation was made by the Pentagon of all those involved in the My Lai incident. It was apparent that the Army wanted to wash its hands of Mitchell and everyone else and that all would have to find a life outside the service.

Next the Army turned to another enlisted man, at Fort McPherson. In February, 1971, Sergeant Charles Hutto went to trial. Just as at Fort Hood, though, the Army prosecutor, this time Captain Franklin Wurtzel, called only three witnesses, and none could recall seeing Hutto fire a single shot at My Lai. All Wurtzel had going for him was a signed statement by Hutto saying that the night before the attack, he and other troops had received orders from Captain Medina "to kill all the animals and to destroy all the food." The next day, as the assault was in progress, Hutto's statement to the CID said, "orders came down to kill all the people, destroy the food and kill all the animals. I don't remember who gave the order, but I guess it came from headquarters." Hutto, his statement concluded, followed those orders exactly.

Hutto's defense was a simple one, and his civilian lawyer, Edward Magill of Miami, stressed it over and over again during his closing argument: Hutto had never thought to question whether an order to kill people was an illegal order that ought not to be obeyed "because he had never heard of an illegal order. The only thing the Army ever said to Charlie Hutto is that he was to obey orders without question."

It took the six officers on the Hutto jury less than two hours to acquit the sergeant. And a couple of days later—as soon as he could—Hutto was out of the Army and on his way back home to Louisiana, beyond any further action the military might want to take against him.

With the acquittal of both Mitchell and Hutto, it seemed clear that there was no chance of getting a conviction in the case of an enlisted man. There seemed a penchant of officers on military juries to accept the plea that obedience to orders was a total defense for an enlisted man, despite what international law and the Army's own rules said, and if that plea were made, as it had been implicitly in the Mitchell case and explicitly in the Hutto case and as it would certainly be made in other enlisted men's cases, then the officers would acquit, no matter the evidence and no matter the law. And so the decision was made to drop the charges against all enlisted men cited for actual crimes during the My Lai attack. To prosecute them, it was agreed in the Army, would be just a waste of time.

And at Fort Meade, General Seaman was reaching the same conclusion about the feasibility of prosecuting those higher officers charged with crimes growing out of the cover-up. One by one, and then in groups, the charges against them were dismissed. One of the last to be freed was General Koster. Late in January, General Seaman announced that all charges against him had been dropped "in the interest of justice." This was so,

General Seaman said, even though there was "some evidence" that Koster knew that civilians had been killed at My Lai and had failed to investigate.

The dismissal of charges against Koster and other high officers left a taste of ashes in the mouths of many who were concerned that the Army was being something less than diligent in its attempts to bring to justice those high officers involved at My Lai, that it was prepared to sacrifice a lieutenant and perhaps a captain, but no one any higher. Robert MacCrate, a Wall Street lawyer who had served as special counsel to the Peers inquiry, called Seaman's action "a serious disservice to the Army. I am shocked by the action of the commanding general in dismissing at this time the charges against General Koster, because charges are still pending against men who were within his command."

The reaction of MacCrate and some in Congress caused the Pentagon to take at least minimal action. The general was officially censured and General Westmoreland, the Army chief-of-staff, recommended that Koster be broken from major general to brigadier general and that his second in command, General Young, be broken to colonel. Secretary of the Army Stanley Resor, in one of his final acts before resigning in May, did reduce General Koster one grade, though he did not break General Young; however, he stripped both men of their Distinguished Service Medals. Their careers in the Army, once considered so shining and full of potential, were effectively at an end. But that was the extent of their punishment. In June, 1971, General Young retired with full pension.

With these dismissals, the responsibility for the My Lai massacre seemed to have come that full circle. Of the twenty-five originally charged with some measure of blame, only four were left.

Two sergeants—Mitchell and Hutto—had been court-martialed and acquitted. Charges against all the other enlisted men had been dropped. Of the dozen high officers charged, eleven had gone free. These were the men who remained:

Calley and Medina and Kotouc, charged with actual crimes, and Henderson, the brigade commander, with covering up those crimes. One of them would later go free in a trial that was in its own way a duplicate of the Mitchell-Hutto affairs.

In April, 1971, after the Calley court-martial was already over, Kotouc went to trial at Fort McPherson. Some charges already dropped, he was now cited only with maiming a prisoner by cutting off his finger during the interrogation. The court-martial lasted just three days. There was direct evidence that Kotouc had done exactly what he was charged with doing.

Kotouc was an unlikely military man. A burly, red-faced, sloppily dressed Nebraskan who took delight in joking with reporters, in erupting into enormous horse laughs, and who found nothing strange in walking out of court with a cigarette dangling from one side of his mouth and a toothpick from the other, he had been sent to Viet-Nam, he said, even though a year earlier he had been declared physically unfit for combat because he was hard of hearing. And when he got to the American Division headquarters at Chu Lai, he had wandered around looking for something to do and wondering why he had been sent to Viet-Nam in the first place. Everywhere he went he was sent to some other officer, but nobody had anything for him to do. "They asked me what I'd like to do," Kotouc said, "and I told them I'd like to go home." Instead, they sent him to the officers' club until someone could dream up an assignment for him. What they came up with was to make him an intelligence officer assigned to the 11th Brigade, the man who would ultimately develop the intelligence that led to the assault on My Lai.

What happened that late afternoon of March 16 at the night bivouac, fittingly enough in a cemetery a mile or more east of My Lai, was all an accident, Kotouc contended. He had been trying to interrogate this Viet Cong suspect, see, and when the man refused to answer his questions, Kotouc had taken out a seven-inch knive, had the man's fingers spread on a board, and begun to thrust the knife between them to intimidate him. It didn't work. "The guy just looked at me," Kotouc said, "and so

I gave him another little crack. This time I missed the board and hit the terrorist's hand. The little end of the finger popped off."

Was any first aid given? No, but then none was needed, for soon afterward the Vietnamese National Police who were on the scene took the suspect away and shot him.

It took the jury less than an hour to acquit Kotouc, who was properly elated and declared that he, too, was going to remain in the Army.

So it was down to three. At Fort Meade, in early April, desultory hearings began for Colonel Henderson on the cover-up charges. But it seemed from the manner they were being conducted that the Army was being cowed by Henderson's civilian lawyer, Henry Rothblatt of New York, who in the past had successfully defended Green Berets charged with murder and who indicated that if the Army persisted in "persecuting" Henderson he was prepared to call as witnesses everyone from General Westmoreland to the service secretaries, and perhaps those even higher. The hearings wended an inconclusive way through the spring and into the summer of 1971, with no end in sight.

At Fort McPherson, there was Ernest Medina. His trial, too, was constantly pushed farther and farther into the future; each time a date was announced, it would be canceled and rescheduled for later. It seemed that the Army had little taste for combat with Medina's chief civilian counsel, the flamboyant F. Lee Bailey, who had often predicted that Medina would never come to trial. And the Army, too, seemed to have little desire to meet in court even Medina's two military lawyers, both serving four-year hitches in JAG before returning to civilian life—Mark Kadish, a bright, ambitious young New York lawyer, and John Truman of Missouri, a nephew of the former President.

And so we were back where it had all begun. Back to the man in the middle. Back to Rusty Calley.

4
Sartoris vs. Snopes

By the time the name My Lai had begun to permeate and roil the American conscience, most of the leading actors who would perform on the courthouse stage had already begun to assemble at Fort Benning.

If there had been doubt at first over whether Calley would ever stand trial, it seemed to be quickly washed away. General Talbott, commanding general of the base, was swiftly convinced that the evidence necessitated a court-martial, and on November 24, 1969, he ordered such a trial, at some undetermined date in the future. That afternoon, Calley was formally charged with violating Article 118 of the UCMJ on four major specifications and two additional specifications:

"Specification 1: In that First Lieutenant William L. Calley, Jr., US Army, 40th Company, The Student Brigade, US Army Infantry School, Fort Benning, Georgia (then a member of Company C, 1st Battalion, 20th Infantry) did, at My Lai 4, Quang Ngai Province, Republic of South Viet-Nam, on or about 16 March 1968, with premeditation, murder four Oriental human beings, occupants of the village of My Lai 4, whose names and sexes are unknown, by means of shooting them with a rifle.

"Specification 2: . . . with premeditation, murder an unknown number, not less than 30 Oriental human beings, males and females of various ages, whose names are unknown, occupants of the village of My Lai 4, by means of shooting them with a rifle.

"Specification 3: . . . with premeditation, murder three Oriental human beings whose names and sexes are unknown, occupants of the village of My Lai 4, by means of shooting them with a rifle.

"Specification 4: . . . with premeditation, murder an unknown number of Oriental human beings, not less than seventy, males and females of various ages, whose names are unknown, occupants of the village of My Lai 4, by means of shooting them with a rifle.

"Additional charge:

"Specification 1: . . . with premeditation, murder one Oriental male human being, an occupant of the village of My Lai 4, whose name and age is unknown, by shooting him with a rifle.

"Specification 2: . . . with premeditation, murder one Oriental human being, an occupant of the village of My Lai 4, approximately two years old, whose name and sex is unknown, by shooting him with a rifle."

Before the case came to trial, specifications one and three of the initial charge would be dropped, and Calley would stand accused of two major specifications—the premeditated murder of "not less than thirty Oriental human beings" and of "not less than seventy Oriental human beings"—and two additional specifications—the premeditated murder of "one Oriental male human being" and of "one Oriental human being . . . approximately two years old."

In all, Calley was charged with the premeditated murder at My Lai (4) of at least 102 "Oriental human beings," a quaint and condescending archaism whose implied meaning the Army did not grasp for many months. When finally the military began to see what that language implied about the American military view of other, foreign people, the term "Oriental" was finally dropped from the specifications and Calley was charged with killing 102 just plain "human beings." And he was charged with killing them in a time sequence that corresponded to the order of the specifications, and at specific locations which the government would have to cite.

Captain Aubrey M. Daniel, III
From the left Colonel Clifford H. Ford, Major
Charles C. McIntosh, Major Carl R. Bierbaum,
Major Walter D. Kinnard, Major Harvey G. Brown,
Captain Ronald J. Salem.

If those charges were all true, then Calley would stand as author of one of the largest mass murders ever committed, certainly ever committed by an American.

The man who would try to prove that this was so was Captain Aubrey Marshall Daniel III, a twenty-eight-year-old draftee who was in the middle of a four-year Army service and was then senior trial counsel at JAG at Fort Benning.

In the fall of 1969, the five-foot ten-inch, slim, blond (his hair almost always neatly trimmed but longer than the military style and in sharp contrast to the standard Fort Benning "skinhead"), and ruggedly handsome Daniel was only another obscure military lawyer in the JAG hierarchy, one with little experience in the law outside his limited military service. It seemed unfair at the time to put the burden of such a major, crucial, and symbolic prosecution on such a raw lawyer. And there were many who were concerned that with his lack of experience he would be overmatched and torn to pieces by the experienced trial counsel who would surely handle the defense.

If any clues could be drawn from his background, there were indeed dangers that such a grim future was in store for Daniel once the court-martial began. Born in 1941 at Monks Corner, a tiny South Carolina hamlet, Daniel spent the first nine years of his life shuttling around West Virginia and Kentucky, wherever his father's construction and strip-mining ventures took the family. When he was nine, the family returned to his father's home town of Orange, Virginia, near Richmond, and it was there, in the atmosphere of the Old South, with its stern moral code and an undeviating vision of right and wrong, with its romantic recollections of chivalry, that Daniel grew up. His schooling was that of a young Southern aristocrat—the genteel Woodberry Forest prep school, and the University of Virginia, from which he was graduated in 1963. "By the time I'd reached the second year of college," Daniel says with the inflection of the upper South in his speech, "I knew I wouldn't be content with a regular degree. Although I had no family in the law field, my dad had always urged me toward entering some profession.

So I entered law. I have always had the love of the trial. The dramatics of it. The degree of uncertainty as to how the trial will come out."

But in those college days, the intensity and dedication and drive that would mark the older, more mature Daniel were not yet so apparent. His marks were not good enough for a prestigious law school like the University of Virginia, so he took his law degree from the T. C. Williams School of Law of the University of Richmond (and, at the same time, took himself a wife, Shirley, whom he calls "Bunky," a religion major whom he met at Virginia). On graduation, with a new law degree, he went to work as a very junior lawyer in the prestigious Richmond law firm of Minor, Thompson, Savage, and Smithers. Nine months later, that career came to a sudden halt. He received his draft notice and immediately applied for a direct commission in the Army's legal corps, JAG.

As a military lawyer, Daniel both prosecuted and defended the usual AWOL, theft, assault, homicide, and other cases that flow across a young military lawyer's desk. He was considered by those who worked with him, or opposed him in court, a good, solid lawyer who prepared well, was articulate and knowledgeable on his feet, had a natural gift for trial work. But few would have guessed just how good Aubrey Daniel could be or the mark he would make. He was, as far as could be seen, just another JAG lawyer serving out his four years at Fort Benning before going back to a civilian life, a man who liked to eat well, knew something about wines, spent his free hours on the golf course, trying to break eighty, or playing with his young daughter who was, in the fall of 1969, only a year-and-a-half old. And he and his wife would spend an occasional evening playing a few rubbers of bridge with Colonel Reid W. Kennedy, the military judge at Fort Benning, and his wife Dorothy.

When the Calley file first crossed his desk, Daniel's views about the war in Viet-Nam were still uncertain; his interest was the law, his family, and finishing out his Army service. If he had thought much at all about the war, it was in terms of the patriotism he had learned growing up in the upper South, in the Virginia Tidewater. There must be a need to do a dirty job over there if the government had made that decision. It did not really occur to him then to seriously question the basic policies being made by his government.

But as his involvement in the Calley case intensified, Daniel's attitudes began to change. He was one of those four angry young captains who flipped coins that early September night at Fort Benning, one of those young military lawyers prepared to stage a minor revolt against the military brass if Calley was not charged. And the more he learned, the more he heard from witnesses, the more he began to ask in his own mind questions about the morality, legitimacy, and rightness of the American adventure in Southeast Asia.

Daniel's gifts as a lawyer, which had been at least partially obscured by the lack of real demand in the military law cases he had been handling, burst forth with his assignment as Calley's prosecutor. To that job, he brought tenacity, diligence, dedication. He and his assistant trial counsel (the military term for prosecutor), Captain John Patrick Partin, personally interviewed every witness who could shed any light on the events at My Lai, both those who might testify for the government and those who might appear for the defense (with the sole exception of Calley himself; the first time Daniel had a crack at Calley was when he cross-examined him on the witness stand during the court-martial). They went over every document they could find, read almost everything that had been written on the case, worked so long and so hard that both, by the end of the trial, had that look of fatigue deep in the bones, of sallow skin that had not seen sunlight. Both before and during the court-martial, Daniel would often return to his office in the court-house at Fort Benning after supper and work far past midnight; his wife was more than a little ambivalent about the whole thing, recognizing Daniel's commitment and at the same time wanting on occasion to see her husband, especially later when she again became pregnant.

(Partin, Daniel's assistant, a twenty-five-year-old native of

Tullahoma, Tennessee, and graduate of the University of Virginia School of Law, found himself in the case almost as soon as he entered the Army; he arrived at Fort Benning on September 1, 1969, and from then until April, 1971, Calley was his sole concern.)

Though a naturally gregarious man, from the moment he was assigned the case until it finally went to the jury more than eighteen months later, Daniel turned more and more to his own resources, shunning anything and anyone that would cause a deviation from what he had come to see not just as a legal but also as a moral duty. He stopped playing bridge with the Kennedys once Kennedy was assigned as the judge for the case; the socializing, he felt, might look bad. Unlike many lawyers, he refused to have anything to do with opposing counsel above and beyond the ordinary courtesies, and even then he was strained. Though his wife and the wife of one of Calley's military lawyers, Major Kenneth A. Raby, often attended court together, Daniel rarely had more than a brief nod for Raby. And he rebuffed all attempts at cordiality from Calley's civilian counsel, George W. Latimer, much to Latimer's surprise and discomfort (though one of the reasons may well have been his growing disgust with some of Latimer's trial tactics and his increasing lack of respect for what he thought was Latimer's failures of preparation and ineptitude in the courtroom).

Throughout the trial, unlike other lawyers, Daniel avoided almost all contact with the dozens of reporters who flocked to Fort Benning and who eagerly sought him out—and who were in a position to publicize him extensively. A question to Daniel almost always drew the response, "No comment," no matter what the question—even if it was only who his next witness might be. That reached the point where reporters began calling him "N.C." Daniel. Even when the case was finally before the jury and there was nothing more he could do but wait, Daniel, though beginning to relax a little, still found it difficult to shed the manner of the previous eighteen months. There was a night while the jury was in deliberation when Daniel and I were at a small party. During the trial we had sometimes had short conversations and I had given him on a couple of occasions some information I thought he might be able to use—some of which he did use (as I had also given Calley and his lawyers information that came my way that I felt might serve them), and toward the last he had begun to relax just a trifle and trade a few bantering remarks. At that party, after a few drinks and some talk, a photographer asked us to pose together. Daniel's old reticence came to the surface almost immediately, as he shyed away, then it faded. And the picture, with both of us holding glasses and smiling warily at each other, was taken. The habits of the trial were hard to break.

With the selection of Daniel as prosecutor, the scene at Fort Benning was set for a reenactment of an old morality play that had been staged often in the United States and particularly in the South. For as the court-martial progressed, it became increasingly apparent that the two central characters in opposition to each other were Daniel and Calley (not Calley's attorney).

Daniel was a scion of the Old South with a stern and unbending moral code. "My God," Reid Kennedy said about him at the end, "he really is a puritan, isn't he? He really does see everything in terms of right and wrong; he doesn't see the gradations." Daniel came to see the issues in this court-martial as moral issues as much as they were legal, as issues in which there *was* right and wrong, good and evil, and he came to see himself upholding the right, the good, the moral, the old and ancient traditions of the moral man and his responsibilities to his fellowman—views which so often seem to dominate the lives and are articulated so often by aristocrats, particularly those of the upper South, of Virginia.

Calley was almost patently Daniel's opposite. He was the child of the new South, déclassé, amoral, ill-educated, uncertain, anxious, even overanxious to please, his eyes on ends without consideration for the means by which those ends were attained, unable to understand, it seemed, that some things could be inherently evil and wrong and others inherently good and right.

Thus what was played out in the courtroom at Fort Benning became, just below the surface, a renewal of that struggle portrayed by Faulkner, the struggle between the Sartorises and the Snopses, the struggle between those trying to uphold an old, chivalrous morality and those in the grip of a new morality, or amorality, grown from modern technological, rootless, and traditionless society.

As Daniel was the product of a heavily tradition-filled upper South, so Calley was the product of the rootless newer times, with tradition shunted to an abandoned cellar, in the Miami of the new South. He grew up on the south Florida coast, the second of four children (the others all girls) in a relatively prosperous middle-class home. His father was a successful businessman, running his own company that sold heavy construction equipment. Money was not a major problem in those early years. But the family was not particularly close, and Calley always felt himself something of a loner; the only member of his family he ever felt he could talk to was his older sister (when the charges were brought against him, his father complained that he hadn't heard from Rusty in months and the only things he knew were what he read in the newspapers).

In school Calley was a below-average student from the beginning. His grades, he said, "were generally poor." To compensate, perhaps, for this, for his loneliness at home, for his small size, to seek attention, he would sit beside the teacher in music class and turn the pages, volunteer to stay after school to clean the blackboards and erasers, anything at all that would bring him recognition.

But the recognition he got came more from his failings. There was little to distinguish him except for his small size and his failures. The pattern of failure that was to dominate his life reached a kind of initial peak when he was in the seventh grade. "I failed the year for cheating, basically," Calley said. According to his story, "I wrote the—well, it was a final exam, and I wrote some answers down on my paper and passed them to somebody else." (When Calley told this story, one observer in court was moved to remark, "Can you image the guy who had to get his answers from Calley?") Caught, Calley was forced to repeat that seventh grade, though he transferred to another school in Miami for that year.

Two years later, in ninth grade, after something of a battle with a teacher, he left public school in the middle of the term, going off to Florida Military Academy at Fort Lauderdale. "My parents wanted me to go, but I think I joined in and conceded to go when I had an argument with the teacher."

A year later he changed schools again, this time going to Georgia Military Academy. There, according to Calley, he did "very well; well, I did well." But he remained there only for a year, and returned to Miami Edison Senior High School in the eleventh grade. Back in public school, "my grades were poor. I went to military school and they came up. I went back to public school, they declined—mainly because I didn't study, and my social life." He graduated in 1962, "in the bottom quarter of my class"—666th out of a class of 731.

Despite his lack of ability or interest in things academic, he went after more education, enrolling that fall at Palm Beach Junior College. There he had to earn his own money to support himself, and "I went out and got myself a job as a busboy. After that, for a couple of weeks in the same restaurant, I took a job as a dishwasher. Then I had a job on Palm Beach as a bellman that lasted through the main, heavy season. And after that, I worked as a short-order cook, not that I know how to cook, but I worked as a short-order cook. I worked drying cars in a Minute Car Wash. And just an assortment of small jobs. I had no other income from any other source, other than what I earned."

And at school, he was again a failure. His marks were "definitely poor. I dropped out of most of my classes and I took failing marks in them." Of the seven courses he enrolled in during his one year in junior college, he failed four, got one D and two C's.

Then he drifted for a while, as he had really been drifting throughout his life. Though he had had, he said, "an active social life," he had "never really had—ran around with—a group that was closely knit. I just had a lot of associates, but no real 'life-or-death' companions." The kind of life he lived "came to bore me."

Out of college, a failure, drifting, he found nothing to give his life meaning or direction, and there was nothing within him to provide those qualities, to help him wash away a feeling of ennui. He tried in 1964 to enlist in the Army, but "I was rejected. I was tone deaf."

The Florida East Coast Railway was then on strike and in order to keep operating was hiring nonunion strike-breakers at higher wages than it had paid its regular employees. Calley was hired on as a switchman; a couple of months later he was promoted to conductor on a freight train, the youngest conductor in the system, earning more than $300 some weeks. One day, while on that job, he was arrested in Fort Lauderdale for permitting his forty-seven-car train to block traffic during the rush hour; he was acquitted when he explained that the brakes had malfunctioned. Three months later, Calley once again stalled his train, this time for an hour rather than a half-hour as before. And though he felt he was doing a good job and enjoying the work, the railroad was not all that satisfied. He was late to work often, failed to complete paperwork correctly, and even once got fifteen demerits for permitting several cars on his train to break free of his idling engine.

The job finally came to an end in December, 1965, when the workers began coming back to work, even though the strike was not officially settled. Calley was sharply downgraded on the seniority ladder to the point "where I couldn't bid in the regular jobs. I might get out one or two days a week."

So he quit and headed for North Carolina. His father's business in Florida had gone bankrupt, and the family had moved to North Carolina, where it had a summer house. There Calley's mother developed cancer. "I found the situation was much worse than I thought it was," Calley said of his visit there around Christmas. "My mother was termed terminal. And there wasn't that much money coming in, so I stayed up there and supported the family."

When Calley had "depleted all my money that I had saved

up, and there wasn't any real work up there in the wintertime," he got into the Buick Wildcat he had bought with some of his trainman's earnings and took off for New Orleans. There he went to work for a commercial investigating firm that did work for insurance companies. "We didn't evaluate incidents themselves," he explained. "We would get requests from underwriters to check out policies, such as if somebody had a hundred-thousand-dollar policy on a house. You would go out and take a picture and see that the house wasn't submerged under water, or it was worth a hundred thousand dollars, that the policy was actually properly represented. And also we would do that with automobile insurance; if a man had three or four children, he had to report them to the insurance company. Things like that."

When the firm tried to move Calley to Baton Rouge, "I went off on my own working directly for underwriters." As a private eye, Calley again found himself inadequate to the job. "Well, I ended up down in Mexico looking for certain individuals and I just realized very rapidly that I just didn't have any mental capacity to try to figure out where a person would be hiding. And I just found out that I just wasn't cut out for that type of business. So I left that. It's a frustrating-type thing to have somebody—I was going up and asking somebody who they were, and if they wouldn't tell me, I had no recourse to find out. So it was just—I really wasn't adequate at the job." In the middle of his Mexican investigation, he quit without completing the assignment.

It was back to the road. Calley headed for San Francisco, hoping to find something, uncertain what. But he had little time to even look. His mail was forwarded to him, and in it "was a couple of draft notices. Well, actually they weren't draft notices as such, they were letters from my draft board. Some of them stated for me to report to the induction center for reevaluation, and some of them said I was delinquent, and some of them said I had violated my draft." Calley, with his tone-deafness, had been classified 1-Y; the Army, needing fodder for Viet-Nam, was reclassifying 1-Y's. Calley started back to Miami to report. "I got stuck in Albuquerque, New Mexico. And when I left San Francisco, my finances were not that high. I did have some car failure which almost depleted all my finances. I went in and talked to a recruiter and asked him what somebody does in a situation like that. And he quickly told me, 'You enlist.' I called my draft board, and they said, yes, if I went on and enlisted, they would not draft me, basically."

Calley was in the Army, sent to Fort Bliss, Texas, for basic training, and then to Fort Lewis, Washington, where he became a clerk-typist. That job, it seemed, was meant for him. He graduated in the top half of the clerk's school at Fort Lewis and fell readily into the work. But someone, examining his records, with his school background and his military school experience, decided he was officer material, especially with the Army's need for officers, second lieutenants, for Viet-Nam. On March 16, 1967—a year to the day before the attack on My Lai—Calley reported to Officer Candidate School at Fort Benning, where, four years later, his military career would end in a shambles.

OCS was a bitter struggle for Calley. He was considered again a below-average candidate, was constantly criticized for lack of "command presence and command voice." Again he graduated in "the bottom one-quarter of my class"—120th out of 156.

His first assignment as a new second lieutenant: to ship out for Hawaii and join the 11th Light Infantry Brigade, to join as a platoon leader Captain Ernest Medina's Charlie Company. A few months later he would be off to Viet-Nam and his destiny.

This was the man who was now about to face court-martial for, he consistently declared, obeying his orders. If he were to be convicted in the courtroom on the same base where he had won his bars, his prosecutor, Aubrey Daniel, would have to work against what seemed enormous odds. There was, first, the natural tendency of the military—and it would hold true of a military jury—to look on acts committed in war, no matter their gravity or atrociousness, as acts of war and thus excusable. Daniel would have to persuade a military jury that the acts committed by Calley at My Lai were not in any way legitimate acts of war or excusable but were, in fact, crimes deserving of the severest punishment.

And then there was Daniel's opposition—the lawyers at the defense table, older, more experienced, theoretically at least more knowledgeable in the area of military law and, one of them, George Latimer, at least, considered a master of trial tactics and forensics in the field of the court-martial. It seemed that Daniel would be greatly overmatched.

When Calley was first charged, and the seriousness of those charges—and the government's, or at least Daniel's, intention to press hard for conviction—became apparent, the immediate quest was to find a lawyer who could give the young lieutenant the strongest kind of defense. The late Jim Lukas, the Scripps-Howard war correspondent, rallied to Calley's defense. He called an old friend, Charles Black of the *Columbus* (Georgia) *Enquirer*, and told him that Edward Bennett Williams was interested and, if Calley wanted, would handle the case. Williams, of course, is one of the nation's leading defense lawyers, having handled in the past such unpopular clients as the late Senator Joseph R. McCarthy, Jimmy Hoffa, and Bobby Baker.

But when Black passed the word to Calley, the response was negative. Calley's instinct and desire, he said, was to stay away from a lawyer who would make the case a *cause célèbre* or who would play it for the headlines. What he wanted, he maintained, was someone who would play it "low-keyed" and would understand him and not so overwhelm everything that he would be lost in the courtroom histrionics.

Then, too, he already had someone in mind. Soon after the charges were filed, Calley had received a letter expressing sympathy and support from George W. Latimer, then sixty-nine, of Salt Lake City, who had represented in the past one of the Green Berets accused of murdering a Vietnamese double, or triple, agent. Latimer's name was already known to Calley;

in discussion with friends at Fort Benning it had come up, and he had been told Latimer was a brilliant courtroom lawyer and an expert in military law. If anyone would be ideal, it would be Latimer. And so it was to Salt Lake City that Calley turned. He called Latimer to thank him for his letter, and before he hung up had asked Latimer to represent him.

In that conversation, as in many that followed, Latimer asked little of Calley's side; in fact, then and almost through the entire trial, he refused to listen whenever Calley tried to narrate his version of the morning in My Lai. He insisted only that he believed in Calley's innocence and did not want to hear details. He requested the answer only to a basic question: "Do you believe your own self that what you did was right?" When Calley replied, "Yes," Latimer took the case.

On the basis of his background, Latimer did, indeed, seem the ideal choice. Though he was nearly seventy—a particular sore point with him; Latimer consistently refused to answer questions about his age and when some reporters printed it, he became outwardly incensed and berated them—Latimer did not, at least before the court-martial began, give outward signs that age had dimmed his histrionic or legal abilities. The only disability he showed was deafness in one ear, and he wore a small, barely visible hearing aid. In other ways, he projected a trim, sprightly, dapper appearance. Latimer, his sparse gray hair always neatly brushed back, was easily the best-dressed man in the courtroom, his clothes slightly mod, in bright hues with brilliantly colored shirts and coordinated ties (all selected, he maintained, by his wife Rhoda—"shirts, ties, suits, she buys everything").

In military law, Latimer was considered almost without peer. His connections with the Army dated back more than fifty years, to 1917, when at the age of seventeen he joined the Utah National Guard during World War I. After the war, he worked his way through the University of Utah and became a practicing attorney in his home state in 1924, and over the next seventeen years won a reputation as one of Utah's premier trial counsels. When the United States entered World War II,

Latimer immediately put on a uniform again, rising to full colonel and the position of chief-of-staff with the 40th Infantry Division in the South Pacific. He took part in four invasion assaults, earning four battle stars and a Legion of Merit, and developing a number of war stories of his own which, he said, "I tend to exaggerate more and more as the years go by." In the war, Latimer insisted, "I was always a combat soldier. I never saw a court-martial until I tried my first one, as a civilian."

When the war ended, Latimer returned to Utah and made a successful run in 1947 on the Republic ticket for the Utah Supreme Court. There he sat for five years until, in 1951, President Harry S. Truman appointed him to the Court of Military Appeals, the highest military court and supposedly the service equivalent to the United States Supreme Court.

In his decade on that bench, Latimer won a reputation as the great dissenter and the determined guardian of the rights of the individual soldier. At one point during the Calley court-martial, Judge Kennedy was to tell Latimer how much he had always admired his work on the Court of Military Appeals and how much he had always depended on Latimer's dissents for his own views of military laws. And Kennedy was to tell some reporters later how one of the things he most looked forward to when he was assigned the Calley case was to watching Latimer at work in his courtroom—and how disappointed he had been at what he saw.

In 1961 Latimer returned to civilian life in Salt Lake City and to a partnership in Parsons, Behle and Latimer, with such clients as United States Steel, Texas Gulf Sulphur, Kennecott Copper, and a number of insurance companies. But even though then a civilian and no longer a judge, Latimer did not abandon his interest in military justice and was constantly involved in defending soldiers facing courts-martial and on appeal. "None of my boys is in Leavenworth," he boasts, though several were convicted but freed on appeal.

It was this background that Latimer brought to the Calley defense and which led many to believe he would devour Daniel. He was a military legal legend.

* * *

But Latimer was not alone at Calley's side. There were another civilian counsel and two military lawyers.

What recommended Richard B. Kay of Cleveland, Ohio, as assistant civilian defense counsel to Calley was that he was a volunteer, serving without pay. A fifty-two-year-old bachelor, the tall, slim, often neatly but unobtrusively dressed Kay, with his dark, slightly graying hair slicked back from a high forehead, volunteered for the defense team in August, 1970, and was promptly accepted. (That seemed one of the marks of the Calley defense: almost all its experts, both advisers and witnesses, were unpaid volunteers, which led one observer to note that the defense "got exactly what it paid for; it got its money's worth.")

Kay seemed to add little to the defense either in legal knowledge or ability. In Cleveland, Kay's specialty was accident, negligence, and some real estate law. And he himself had had troubles with the law in the past; some years before he had been convicted of bribery; handling his own appeals, it took him nearly five years to have that conviction reversed.

During the trial, Kay told several reporters that this was the first criminal case he had handled in years. "They're just too hard," he said. And if his performance in court at Fort Benning was any indication, he was telling the truth as it concerned him. All during the court-martial, Judge Kennedy gave him lessons and lectures in military law, in courtroom procedures and conduct and revealed, as did almost everyone else, a great weariness and impatience with Kay's tactics and manner. With every witness he questioned, and before asking his questions—even if he had only a single one—he undeviatingly would stride from the defense table across the courtroom to the jury box. Whenever Daniel posed an objection to a Kay question, Judge Kennedy almost invariably sustained it (though his tendency was to overrule almost all of Daniel's other objections) and put Kay down, at which point Kay would look at the judge and then around the courtroom with a hurt, pained expression.

But then Kay, beyond his professed concern for Calley, had

entered the trial hoping to use it as a springboard to bigger things. Once a liberal Republican in Ohio, he had become by 1968 an ardent supporter of George C. Wallace and in 1970 had run for Senator from Ohio on a Wallace ticket. It was Kay's hope, and he was not shy in proclaiming it, that he would gain enough fame from his participation in the Calley case to propel him into the vice-presidential spot on the Wallace ticket in 1972. When Stephan Lesher of *Newsweek* pressed Kay on the point one afternoon, Kay said, "Well, you drop an item like that and it could really take off."

What Kay provided for many reporters was a pipeline into the defense strategy—what little there was of it. He seemed either to shun the company of other defense lawyers and associates or not to be welcomed by them. (Latimer, as it happened, spent almost the entire trial in a small apartment on the base with his wife, rarely appearing in public, though he was to say when it was over that he would have welcomed invitations to dinner and a little wine.) As the court-martial progressed, Kay took to wandering almost every evening into the Heritage Inn in Columbus, where many reporters were staying, strolling into the dining room to look for a reporter to join him for dinner. Such dinners were invariably filled with talk of Kay and his ambitions and the latest gossip from the defense chambers. It was Kay, for instance, who told reporters before Calley took the stand that nobody on the defense side had yet heard his story of My Lai. When some incredulity was expressed, Kay said, "A couple of times Calley tried to tell us, but every time he did, Judge Latimer would stop him. The judge would hold up his hand and say, 'I know you're innocent and that's all I need to know. I don't want to hear the story.'"

Throughout the trial, reporters constantly speculated on the groping and often ill-defined tactics of the defense both in its cross-examination and in the presentation of its own case; Kay's tales often helped clear up mysteries.

By the end of the trial, Kay seemed increasingly isolated from his defense colleagues, and just before the case went to the jury he approached a reporter at dinner and told him to try to create a stir in the press to demand that Latimer hand the final arguments over to Kay. Otherwise, he said, Calley was doomed.

Initially the most derided man at the defense table was Calley's chief military counsel, Major Kenneth Albert Raby, a thirty-five-year-old South Dakotan who was making military law in JAG a career. Considered by military legal experts a brilliant scholar—all during the court-martial, Raby seemed to know every legal citation and precedent by rote and could quote them to the court, often to Judge Kennedy's exasperation—Al Raby had graduated near the top of his class from the Law School of the State University of South Dakota in 1960, where he had been editor in chief of the law review. Almost immediately, he had gone into military service, had risen to chief of military justice at Fort Dix, New Jersey, deputy staff judge advocate of the Americal Division in Viet-Nam from July, 1968, to July, 1969, and was, when he became chief military defense counsel for Calley, the legal team chief at Fort Benning.

Raby's forte, unfortunately, was in scholarship and not trial law. In court, he was stilted and pedantic and, whenever he won a point, would turn in triumph to the audience with a stiff smile that seemed almost supercilious. His manner and appearance made him the butt of snide and slanderous humor—his ramrod-straight posture, his perpetually iron-creased uniforms led some to say that he spent his nights in a clothes press; his always skin-close crew cuts led some to wonder whether he got a haircut every morning with a straight razor.

But as the months passed, Raby gradually won both the respect and the admiration of many in the press, and some came to see the warmth and dedication of the man behind the stiff, distant front. By the end of the trial, the barriers had fallen enough so that a measure of friendship was apparent between Raby and some reporters, and he began to joke about his experiences in military law. And when the trial was over, almost everyone who had watched from beginning to end was convinced that Al Raby was the best man on the defense side. It was he who tried to steer the defense into a challenge to the legality of the Viet-Nam War and the policies developed to fight that war; to challenge the kind of training given American troops; to point out the weapons used by Americans that were in violation of international agreements. He was, however, constantly diverted from these lines by Latimer, who feared such tactics might upset the military jury.

On one of the last days at Fort Benning while the jury was still out, Raby rather plaintively asked me whether, now that it was almost over, I were going away to write about how terrible he had been.

He needn't have worried.

If Raby had been the most derided man at the defense table, the most ignored was twenty-seven-year-old Captain Brooks S. Doyle, Jr. A native of Pennsylvania and a graduate of Wake Forest University Law School, Doyle had been given the job of researching the witnesses for the defense. But his work was profitless. While Latimer and Raby were preparing their case through much of 1970, Doyle was sent around the country to interview all potential witnesses, prosecution and defense, and tape their stories. On one of these trips, his tape recorder was stolen. A call back to Fort Benning revealed that he would have to wait for some time to get a new one, so Doyle bought one himself and some tapes as well. But short of funds, he would interview and makes notes from the tapes each night, then erase those tapes to use again. It really didn't matter. All his work ended up in several file cabinets in the defense office. Those cabinets were locked and no one ever looked at what was in them.

The man who would stand between the adversaries—Daniel and Partin on one side, Calley, Latimer, Raby, Kay, and Doyle on the other—and whose rulings would guide the court-martial either into a narrow channel or a broad ocean of inquiry into the events at My Lai was a fifty-year-old career military judge, Colonel Reid W. Kennedy (promoted as the trial began from lieutenant colonel to colonel, perhaps so that no one in the court would outrank him).

Kennedy was perhaps the most human figure in the drama. A tall, straight man with iron-gray hair in a ragged crew cut, a craggy face and horn-rimmed glasses, who almost never wore a uniform beneath his black judicial robes (and when he did, it invariably led to sardonic questions), Kennedy brought humor and a sense of balance to his courtroom.

A graduate of Drake University Law School, his military career began in 1943 as an enlisted man in World War II, where he saw service in Europe. After the war, he was in private practice in Iowa, though continuing his attachment to the military, winning a commission in the Iowa National Guard. When the Korean War began, and after he had been defeated for reelection as county attorney in Spencer, Iowa, Kennedy decided to make the military his career. Between 1954 and 1958, he was staff judge advocate—the top legal officer in a military unit—with the 101st Airborne Division, and from there went to the 1st Cavalry Division in Korea. At the end of that tour, Kennedy went to the Command and General Staff College at Fort Leavenworth and later to the Armed Forces Staff College. After a tour as staff judge advocate in Viet-Nam, he arrived at Fort Benning in July, 1967, as military judge of the Army's Fifth Judicial District.

If not a great legal scholar, Kennedy nevertheless was essentially a fair man who did not let his own biases or personal opinions dictate his conduct of the Calley court-martial. His aim, it seemed, was to make certain that Calley had a fair trial, and if he leaned in any direction in his rulings it was toward the defense in an effort to ensure that fairness. As the trial went on he clearly saw that Aubrey Daniel was perfectly capable of handling himself without any assistance from the bench, while the defense was proving itself increasingly inept. On a dozen different occasions, he overruled Daniel's objections even though agreeing with the prosecutor that legally those objections were correct and ought to be upheld. He felt that if he were going to make errors, they would be errors that helped the defense. For the verdict could not be overturned on appeal because them; reversible errors are those made in favor of the prosecution.

And Kennedy brought one thing more to his handling of the case—a gift for the low-keyed aside which could suddenly lift the oppressive atmosphere which so frequently filled the court. And his humor was as often directed at his own foibles and failings as at those of the lawyers appearing before him.

Kennedy was essentially a highly conservative man. When he was first assigned as judge for the Calley case, he had a great suspicion of the press, and would utter stern injunctions about what could and could not be done by reporters covering a trial in his courtroom. But through the months, that suspicion gradually relaxed, and there came a day in December when in open court he was given to explain how his own attitudes had changed and how he had begun to admire those in the press he had watched and come to know.

The reaction was a mutual one. Reporters grew to know and admire Reid Kennedy, to spend hours after court talking with him, playing bridge and even, as the months passed, dropping by at his home to raise a glass now and again. Toward the end of the trial, he gave a large barbecue for reporters at his home, donning an apron and cooking the steaks himself.

And as he got to know the reporters, most of whom he considered ultra-liberals, Kennedy was not above pointing to his own conservatism and using it to get a reaction. There was a rumor around Fort Benning that Kennedy wanted to contribute to the Wallace campaign in 1968 and had been dissuaded by his colleagues and his wife, Dorothy, a native New Yorker and former department store model who did as much as anyone to ease the mutual suspicion that had earlier existed between Kennedy and the outsiders.

At one party for the judge and his wife, Kennedy, with a drink in his hand, looked around at the circle of reporters in their off-hours and asked, "Say, has anyone here seen the movie, *Joe?*" Several people said they had. Kennedy paused and looked around, then said, "You know, I identify with Joe."

Dorothy Kennedy was to say later, "Reid loves to bait liberals."

Part Two:
Calley on Trial -
The Prosecution

5
"It Was So Repulsive"

That moment had come at last toward which everything since that "dark and bloody" morning at My Lai had been inevitably directed. It was Tuesday morning, November 17, 1970, and the court-martial of First Lieutenant William L. Calley, Jr., was about to begin.

Though it was not known, as the trial began, what the fate of those others selected for possible courts-martial would be, it was even then evident that this would be the critical case. If Calley were acquitted, that would probably be the end of the Army's attempts to try anyone for the crimes committed at My Lai. If this one man, this young lieutenant—the man in the middle who had taken orders and given them, who had killed and ordered killing—were freed, then the Army would go no higher or lower, for more evidence seemed to exist against Calley than anyone else, and My Lai would be written off as just an unfortunate incident. The dead would lie in their nameless and unmarked graves outside My Lai, victims of no one, of nothing more than war.

If, though, Calley were convicted, then at least a measure of blame would have been assessed and through his conviction there would be an acknowledgment, however small, that My Lai—and perhaps other, smaller My Lais, perhaps even the war itself—was indeed an unspeakable act. And if Calley were convicted, then perhaps the Army might go after others, those above him who had sent him to My Lai, who had indoctrinated him and his troops so that they could commit an atrocity without thought. But even, as seemed more likely, if the prosecutions growing out of My Lai ended with only Calley tried and convicted, still the Army and the nation would have acknowledged that there was indeed something "dark and bloody" at My Lai and in Viet-Nam.

For Aubrey Daniel, there was no question of what he had to do, of the tack he would have to take in this case. His job was to prosecute Calley, to present all the evidence he could find to convict Calley of the murder of those Vietnamese who had been caught at My Lai that morning the American troops arrived. As he saw it, it was not his job, no matter his personal beliefs, to prosecute the war or others involved in the massacre. If he tried to do that, it might be fatal to his case. If he were to attempt to try those above Calley who might have given him orders and who, thus, might bear greater moral and as much legal responsibility for what happened, and those below Calley who had been carrying out the lieutenant's commands, then he would have little chance of persuading those six soldiers on the jury to bring in a verdict of guilty. If he tried to move along that road, he would be asking them to convict themselves for crimes in Viet-Nam, to convict the nation for crimes there. It was almost certain that was hopeless. Daniel's job was to convict Calley and no one else; to try to go beyond that would be to lose his case and, probably, to end all hopes of assessing any guilt on anyone for My Lai or for Viet-Nam.

If the war itself, if the government and the Army and its commanders were to be placed in the dock with Calley at Fort Benning, that would be the job of the defense, not of the prosecution. (And it was what Al Raby wanted to do and what George Latimer stopped him from doing fully.) In the American system of justice and law, it was Calley who was on trial at Fort Benning and no one else.

And so at last we had come to that moment, the moment to try Calley. All the legal debris was out of the way, all the preliminary hearings over and decided, all the motions made and disposed of. Now there was Calley on one side and the weight of the government, in the person of Aubrey Daniel, on the other. We had come to that moment, two years, eight months, and a day after Calley and his men entered the hamlet the American Army had misnamed My Lai (4).

It was a strange, hushed scene as court opened that morning in the one-story brick Building Five at Fort Benning. All fifty-nine seats in the courtroom were filled. We were a long way, more than eight thousand miles, from the rice paddies of Quang Ngai Province in Viet-Nam, a long way from My Lai. And there was something unreal about that scene. Every face in the court, military and civilian, was white. There was not a Vietnamese anywhere, and there would never be a Vietnamese face all through the trial. (During one of the recesses later, I asked a Vietnamese friend why he didn't go down to Fort Benning either as an observer or a reporter; he shook his head and said, "It's a show of the American Army; I would be out of place, an embarrassment.") And, in fact, throughout the trial there was rarely anything but white faces in that courtroom. An occasional black officer might appear for a day or two, but that was rare. The only blacks in regular attendance were the black soldiers and former soldiers who showed up as witnesses. Until the last week, when the death watch for the jury was in progress, there was only a single day when a nonwhite appeared in the press section; on December 7, in the morning, a Japanese reporter came to court; the inappropriateness of that particular day was remarked upon; the reporter left later in the day, not to return.

It was, then, a show for the world conducted by Americans, with Americans, white Americans, as the principal spectators, actors, and participants.

On one side of the courtroom, the six jurors sat stiffly in the jury box, their uniforms pressed and cleaned, the rows of battle ribbons ranked on their breasts, their faces expressionless—as they would remain with rare exceptions in the months ahead. They were sealed off from the court by a low wooden partition.

Looking down over them and over the court, like

some guiding benevolent eagle, flanked by the witness box, American flag, and the Student Brigade flag, was the military judge, Colonel Reid Kennedy in his black robes.

Directly across from the jury, and off to Kennedy's left, was the long wooden defense table, at one end of which rested a reading stand and a microphone. Calley sat like a child in the large cushioned chair at the other end, his back to the spectators, facing the judge. His feet seemed barely to reach the floor. His uniform, with no decorations at all save the Combat Infantryman's Badge and shoulder patches of the Americal Division (with five stars of the Southern Cross on a blue background) and the Student Brigade, seemed tight on him.

At the long side of the table sat Latimer, always neatly groomed and in the height of fashion, and Raby, his crew cut sheered almost to the skull, his uniform sharply pressed. Behind them sat Kay, his blue or gray suit hanging from his shoulders. Next to him was the silent, inconspicuous, and ignored Brooks Doyle. Down from Doyle toward the bench were the judge's two clerks, Captain Edward Hieronymous and Captain John LaFond, both busily taking notes and running errands.

Just beneath the judge at the base of the bench was the court stenographer. There were two of them, trading off at alternate sessions; one tapped quietly at a stenographic machine, the other repeated the spoken words softly into a voice recorder.

Near the center of the court, facing the bench, was the prosecution table and there, usually perched like a waiting tiger at the edge of his seat, was Daniel and next to him, leaning back or forward with rarely anything to do but study texts and legal papers, was John Partin.

Behind a railing dividng the court were the fifty-nine spectators, half of them reporters and the rest citizens of Columbus or its twin city, Phenix City, Alabama, or miliary personnel at the fort with time to spare, all of whom had waited since seven in the morning to draw for the public seats.

Calley rose from his seat at the end of the defense table. Judge Kennedy read the charge, "Lieutenant Calley, you are charged with violations of Article 118 of the Uniform Code of Military Justice. How do you plead?"

In a clear voice, Calley said, "I plead not guilty, sir." Then he sat down.

The court hushed. Aubrey Daniel rose, stepped away from the prosecution table, faced the jurors, and for twenty-two minutes outlined the government's case against Calley, his voice with its accents of the upper South low and calm, sometimes rising with emotion, anger, disdain, or disgust.

"Please the court," he began, using words which would become almost a trademark each time he rose. "The accused is charged with four specifications of premeditated murder. All involve the accused directly. All allege acts of murder. All took place at My Lai (4) on March 16, 1968, two years, eight months and a day ago. Gentlemen, this is an unusual case. The victims are unnamed, and the government cannot give their names. The victims' ages are not given, and the government does not know their ages. The victims' sexes are not delineated, and the government cannot delineate their sexes."

The jurors listened intently, as Daniel listed the charges: Calley had murdered a group of at least thirty civilians at a trail intersection just south of My Lai; he had murdered a group of at least seventy civilians at an irrigation ditch east of My Lai; he had murdered a man dressed in white, perhaps a monk, at that ditch; he murdered a child of two at that ditch. These were Calley's victims and this was the order in which he had killed them and the places where they had died. "He murdered them," Daniel said, "with premeditation and with intent to kill."

But it was not enough just to say that Calley had done these deeds. "I want you to know My Lai Four," Daniel said. "I want to put you there. We will try to put you there." The hamlet, he described, was a large hamlet in the village of Son My. To the south was a hill, named on the Army maps Hill 85; between it and My Lai ran a road called Highway 521. In the hamlet there were numerous houses, hootches, and other buildings; the area was thickly vegetated. A trail bisected the hamlet running north and south; another trail ran around the outside of the hamlet and intersected that north-south trail in the south. My Lai (4) was surrounded by rice paddies. This was the target of American troops on March 16, 1968.

Those who aimed at that target were the members of Charlie Company, part of Task Force Barker. The company was stationed at a fire base named LZ-Dotti northeast of My Lai (4); north of My Lai several miles was an artillery battery at another fire base named LZ-Uptight. It too was part of Task Force Barker, as were two other infantry companies, Alpha and Bravo.

Charlie Company was a standard rifle company with three platoons, a headquarters element, and a weapons platoon, all under command of Captain Ernest L. Medina. The lieutenant who commanded the first platoon was Calley.

On the morning of March 16, 1968, a short artillery barrage was directed against a landing zone just to the west of My Lai (4) to prepare it for the troops. When the artillery lifted, helicopter gunships directed a steady stream of fire around the hamlet.

At seven-thirty in the morning, the first lift of helicopters set down west of My Lai (4). That lift of nine choppers carried the first platoon, elements of the second platoon, and the headquarters elements. No resistance and no hostile fire came from the hamlet when the troops landed. At seven-forty the second and last helicopter lift brought in the rest of the second platoon and the third platoon. A total of 105 men landed outside My Lai.

At seven-forty-seven, the first and second platoons set up in an on-line formation at the western edge of My Lai (4) and prepared to sweep through it, firing steadily into the hamlet. The headquarters element set up a command post to the rear, and farther to the rear were the mortar platoon, equipped with a single mortar prepared for action, and the third platoon, held in reserve in case of necessity.

Firing steadily, both automatic and semi-automatic, the two platoons swept into My Lai (4), the first platoon to the south, the second platoon to the north. "Members of the accused's platoon," Daniel told the hushed courtroom, "entered the village [though actually a subhamlet of Son My village, it was invariably referred to as a village throughout the trial] and found old men, women, and children, none of them armed, in hootches. Some were eating breakfast. The men in Calley's platoon started gathering them up, some as a result of their training, and others at Calley's orders."

These people, unarmed and unresisting, were herded, Daniel said, to an intersection of the north-south and east-west trails just on the southern edge of the village. There they were placed under the guard of Private First Class Paul David Meadlo and Private Dennis I. Conti. Calley, who was with his radio operator, Charles Sledge, "called to Meadlo and Conti to take care of these people, these women, children, babies, and a few old men. They didn't know what he meant by take care of these people at that time. They didn't know that he had formed his intent to kill them."

As Daniel spoke these words, he turned and looked directly at Calley for the first time. Calley was making notes, doodling on a legal-size yellow pad in front of him. He did not raise his eyes to meet Daniel's.

Daniel turned back to the jury and picked up his narrative. Calley left the area accompanied by Sledge, he said. The civilians remained under guard, squatting by the side of the trail. Meadlo stood over them with his rifle. Conti walked away and returned with several more people who were added to the group.

Observing the scene were several soldiers. Members of the third platoon were moving through the paddies to the southeast. Ronald Haeberle, an Army photographer who was assigned to the company for a day's combat, looked to the east and saw the people under guard.

Murder was about to take place. "Lieutenant Calley returned and he said to Meadlo and Conti, 'Why haven't you taken care of these people?'

"'We have,' Meadlo told him. 'We're guarding them.'

"'I mean kill them . . . waste 'em.'"

Conti, who was carrying an M-79 grenade launcher, stepped

back. "Calley and Meadlo stood side-by-side. The people sat there on the ground, unarmed, offering no resistance at all. With a full burst of automatic fire. . .there were four bursts of automatic fire. . .Calley and Meadlo killed these people."

Again Daniel turned to look at Calley, who again did not look up. "Calley and Meadlo," Daniel continued, "shot these people, these unarmed and unresisting old men, women, and children. Some people tried to run. They were shot down in cold blood on that trail. Meadlo was crying. It was so repulsive. . .at what he had to do at the direction of Lieutenant Calley."

For some unexplicable reason, at that moment, Calley looked up. From where I was sitting that morning, I was the only spectator in the courtroom to have a clear view of his face. He looked at Daniel and smiled broadly, a grin which he held for several moments, and then he looked back down at his yellow pad.

Daniel turned away and continued his opening outline. "Private First Class James Dursi was guarding another group. He heard and saw what happened. He heard the firing as he moved his group to the irrigation ditch that circles south of the village eighty meters out. Dursi takes his group to the ditch where he is joined by Calley, by Staff Sergeant David Mitchell and by Meadlo who is still crying. Calley orders them to shove the people into the ditch. He orders them executed.

"Dursi refuses.

"Meadlo cries and fires.

"Dennis Conti, who wandered away from the intersection of the trails in a state of shock, returns from the rear and sees what is happening and leaves.

"Thomas Turner, to the north, looks and sees these people being executed by the accused and at his direction."

And there were others who saw the bloody scene at the ditch, Daniel declared. Chief Warrant Officer Hugh Thompson, piloting a helicopter, and his gunner, Larry Coburn, flew over and saw the bodies in the ditch "and couldn't believe what they had seen." Out in the paddies, Gregory Olsen, Lenny Lagunoy, and Charles Hall looked back and saw what was happening. Thompson landed his helicopter. Calley went over and Thompson told him to take care of the people, to take them to a medic. Then he took off.

"Calley returns to the ditch and orders Mitchell to finish anybody still living, and he proceeds to do so with single shots." With disgust and horror in his voice, speaking slowly and deliberately, Daniel added, "Over seventy people were executed at that ditch by the accused and at his direction."

But that was not the end. There was more still. Some of the men dispersed, Daniel said, while Calley, Sledge, and Mitchell moved up the ditch. "They came upon an old man sitting against a tree. The old man began to plead for his life. Lieutenant Calley butt-stroked him in the face and knocked him back into the canal.

"At the same time, somebody is shouting, 'A child is getting away! A child is getting away!' A child had managed to crawl miraculously from the ditch. Calley picked up the child and threw it into the ditch and shot him, killed it."

"There was," Daniel concluded, "no hostile fire. There was no combat. Calley executed unarmed men, women, and children. Gentlemen, at the conclusion of the evidence, I am going to ask you in the name of the United States government and justice to convict the accused of all charges and specifications."

For a long moment there was absolute silence as Daniel turned abruptly away and returned to his seat.

As the session ended and we began to leave, someone near me said, "God, he doesn't look like he could do all those things, does he? He looks like a little kid."

Somebody else replied, "Yeah, he hasn't killed any women and children in the courtroom yet."

And later, in the press room, one reporter was moved by Daniel's opening, and by what he had read and knew, to say, "All my life I've almost automatically sided with the defense whenever I've covered a court case; it's just kind of natural. Not this time. This is the first time I can remember when I'm all for the prosecution."

6
Bodies on a Trail

It had been a strong, often moving opening. But that was all it had been, an opening statement in a classic manner, well prepared, organized, calculated to stir the emotions of the jurors and the court. It was not proof, only a statement of what Daniel hoped to prove. It would take his witnesses and his exhibits to do that, if that could be done.

Like a master craftsman, almost as though following the formulas set out in the legal textbooks, Daniel proceeded to develop that case against Calley, to pile up the evidence slowly, fact on fact, until only one conclusion could be reached, until it screamed aloud.

Since the defense was willing to stipulate as fact very little—only that on March 16, 1968, an attack had been directed by Task Force Barker at My Lai (4), that the troops had been lifted from LZ-Dotti to a landing zone outside My Lai in two lifts, and the time of those lifts—Daniel would have to prove everything else that happened that morning. He would have to prove that there had been no combat, that there were dead bodies where he said they were, that they had been killed in the order he specified, and that Calley had killed them and ordered his men to kill them.

Daniel's aim, in both the preparation and presentation of this case, was neatness and order. He wanted to present a picture of the operation at My Lai with geometric precision, working from the outside in, from those on the fringes to those in the center who could directly involve Calley; and he wanted to present his case in such a way that the jurors could see it unfolding before them much as though they were sitting in helicopters overhead and watching, or as if a motion picture screen had been dropped before them and they were an audience watching the cameras recreate that morning, starting with a wide pan and moving into closer and closer range until every detail and every face was visible with all the blemishes. If Daniel had his way, the jurors would see him make order out of what had been, at best, chaos.

Just how he would go about this had been carefully planned and thought out, and by the time the court-martial began, he knew exactly how he intended to move. It was his aim to present the facts of the slaughter of the innocent at My Lai in such a way that the six jurors—all of whom had declared, and gave every indication of believing in, a presumption of innocence—would be forced to believe that a slaughter had taken place and that it was an inexcusable act. He wanted to convince them of that so completely, without once mentioning Calley's name after the opening statement, without once pointing out who had engaged in the slaughter by name, who had directed it, that the moment would come when they would be on the point of rising in the jury box and demanding a name. And so when he gave them that name, there would be no question of the acts committed; there would almost be a relief that at last the name had been spoken.

In the jury box, selected during the previous week from nearly seventy-five potential jurors, were six career officers who would finally judge the lieutenant's guilt or innocence. All six were combat veterans, five of combat in Viet-Nam. Most had said in *voir dire* examination that they believed orders must be obeyed; most had also said they believed that the Vietnamese placed a different, though not necessarily lower, value on human life than Americans did. And all had said they had only sketchy knowledge of My Lai, despite the vast amounts written and broadcast about it. There were no readers on this jury, no deep-questioning thinkers; they were men who believed in the Army and were devoting their lives to it. What stood out was a conviction on the part of all of them that such a thing must be exaggerated, that it could not have happened, not the way it had been reported. There was, as there must be in a jury, a clear presumption that Calley was innocent.

These were the jurors, the men who would weigh Calley on the evidence and on whatever other factors they personally brought to the deliberations:

Colonel Clifford Haun Ford, fifty-four, of Knoxville, Tennessee. A red-faced, gray-haired, well-groomed man who looked as though he should have been more portly than he was—who resembled a younger and less dissolute W.C. Fields—he was president of the jury, its senior officer and its foreman. He had entered the Army during World War II, had reenlisted in 1951 during the Korean War, had seen combat in Europe and in Korea, had won the Bronze Star with two oak leaf clusters, an Army Commendation Medal with two oak leaf clusters, and a Combat Infantryman's Badge. When selected to head the Calley jury, he was deputy director of operations and training at Fort Benning.

Major Charles Carl McIntosh, thirty-eight, of Brownsville, Pennsylvania. He had been in the Army since 1951, had been an enlisted man for eleven years before winning a commission in 1962. McIntosh was a burly, hard-faced man with a crew cut who looked as though he could have been a lineman on a professional football team or even a sumo wrestler. He had seen combat in both Korea, where he was wounded three times, and Viet-Nam. During his year in Viet-Nam, he had been an operations officer with the 1st Cavalry Division. During the trial, McIntosh's expression almost never varied from a pained grimace (the one time he did smile, he tried to hold it back until that was impossible, then looked quickly around to see if anyone had noticed). Among all the jurors, he sent the most questions to Kennedy to be asked of witnesses—such a steady torrent, in fact, that when he picked up a pad an audible groan would rise from the spectators. McIntosh displayed several rows of ribbons, including a Bronze Star with oak leaf cluster, a

Combat Infantryman's Badge with second award, and a Purple Heart with three oak leaf clusters.

Major Carl Ray Bierbaum was, many thought, the most human-looking of the jurors. Under a close crew cut, his face was mobile. He reacted to testimony, sometimes with smiles and sometimes with shock, and when it dragged and became repetitious, he. even looked bored. At thirty-seven, from Litchfield, Illinois, Bierbaum had been in the Army since graduation from high school in 1951. He won his commission in 1958 and had served two tours in Viet-Nam as a helicopter pilot. When the trial opened, Bierbaum's leg was in a cast. Some thought it was a result of a war wound, but he had broken it playing sports. Bierbaum, too, was heavily bemedaled, wearing on his chest the ribbons of an Air Medal with twenty-six oak leaf clusters, a Bronze Star with oak leaf cluster, a Distinguished Flying Cross, and a Combat Infantryman's Badge. He probably asked fewer questions of witnesses than any other juror.

Major Walter D. Kinnard had been born practically next door to Fort Benning, in Columbus, Georgia, thirty-three years before. A tall, husky, stone-faced man with a crew cut like the two majors to his right, Kinnard always wore paratrooper's boots to court and sat with his legs stretched in front of him, his hands folded over his stomach, looking straight ahead with an unreadable expression. He had entered the Army in 1954, gone to paratroop school, served as an enlisted man, and had won his commission through OCS in 1962. Like Bierbaum, he served two tours in Viet-Nam—as an assistant battalion commander in the United States Military Assistance Command in 1964-1965, and then in 1968-1969 as a company commander with the 173rd Airborne Brigade. Kinnard held the Silver Star and the Bronze Star with three oak leaf clusters.

Major Harvey Gene Brown was a captain when the court-martial began; over the Christmas recess, he received his majority and returned to court with the gleaming gold leaves on his shoulders and a broad, proud smile. A thirty-three-year-old Texan from Matador, Brown wore his hair a little longer than the other majors and sported a trim mustache which, with his glasses, made him look not unlike the actor Billy de Wolfe. He had been in Viet-Nam as part of the Military Assistance Command in 1965 and had won the Combat Infantryman's Badge and a Bronze Star with "V" device. Obviously entranced by tactics and logistics, he would often rise from his seat and peer at the blown-up aerial photograph of My Lai that stood on an easel at the front of the courtroom when a witness made reference to some movement through the hamlet.

Captain Ronald J. Salem was the junior member of the court. A tall, almost cadaverously thin man, Salem initially appeared at the trial chewing vigorously at a thick wad of gum (perhaps to help him forget the cigarettes he smoked constantly outside court). After a few days, Judge Kennedy spoke to him about the gum; it disappeared and from then until almost the end of the trial, Salem sat absolutely expressionless and unmoving, leading some in court to wonder whether he was still alive. At thirty-five, a native of Dearborn, Michigan, Salem had been in the Army between 1954 and 1957, then had reenlisted in 1963 and won his commission at Fort Benning's OCS in 1968. Immediately, he had shipped out to Viet-Nam, where he served as a platoon leader and then executive officer and commanding officer of a company in the 25th Division. In Viet-Nam he had won the Bronze Star and the Combat Infantryman's Badge. If anyone on the jury would be in a position to understand the pressures that had been on Calley as platoon leader, it would be Salem.

These were the men who would judge Calley.

Once the decision had been made, all those months before when the revelations about My Lai were first emerging, that those who had been there that March morning and those who were responsible for what happened there and for covering up the facts later would be tried singly, the importance of this one case, and of this one jury, loomed increasingly large.

So slowly, with deliberateness and caution and a consuming passion for detail, Daniel laid his foundation over the first week and more, piece by piece, eliciting from each witness only as much as he needed to fill out a particular corner of his picture, completing that corner before going on to the next. (Early on, when Daniel called a witness back for a second time to question him about another aspect of the picture he was creating, Judge Kennedy told him he would not be permitted to do that again. "I realize," the judge said, "that you're trying to present your case in an orderly fashion, neatly, so that it will all be understandable. Unfortunately, Captain Daniel, a court of law doesn't always work that way. I'm not going to permit you to recall witnesses after they've been dismissed. You're going to have to get everything you want out of a witness when he's on the stand for the first time.")

Question: What does a Vietnamese do when he's lying in the middle of the road?
Answer: Nothing.
Question: Why?
Answer: Because he's dead.

From the opening statement through the Thanksgiving recess to the first of December, that became a litany inside the courtroom and out—a refrain with which reporters, who heard it greeted each other.

With those words, or with words similar enough to make very little difference, Daniel and his witnesses—many of them personally friendly to Calley—infused the courtroom with images of piles of Vietnamese bodies, old men, women, children, babies, lying alongside the trail intersection just south of My Lai, and in the irrigation ditch a little way to the east.

Daniel took each of these early witnesses from the point where he boarded the helicopter at LZ-Dotti several miles to the north to the combat landing zone at the western edge of My Lai (4). And from there, with each witness tracing his path on a transparent plastic overlay set on a large aerial photograph of My Lai (4) taken some months prior to the assault, he took those witnesses to the spot on the southern edge of the hamlet, at the intersection of two trails—a spot all could easily locate because it was from only a few yards away that the company's only casualty of the day, Private Herbert Carter, was medivac-ed to Chu Lai with a wound in the foot that some said was self-inflicted. There they had suddenly come upon a nightmare of blood and death, a scene of mangled, riddled bodies; no one was certain how many, with the estimates ranging from a half-dozen to thirty or more. (But a picture taken of those bodies by Ronald Haeberle which once graced the cover of *Life* magazine and which became Prosecution Exhibits 12 and 12A during the trial, reveals at least twenty-five bodies piled one on another; most of the adults are women; nine of the dead are children, three infants.) From that intersection, some of the witnesses, though not all, traced a continuing meander to an irrigation ditch east of My Lai and told how there they had seen a mass of riddled corpses—old men, women, children, infants—strewn like discarded dolls. No one was certain how many there had been, the estimates ranging from dozens to more than a hundred.

From these first twenty witnesses—soldiers on the ground and pilots and crews in the air, and not one a member of Calley's platoon—Daniel got exactly what he wanted. By the time court adjourned for the Thanksgiving recess, having heard the last of these twenty, it had a clear picture of that morning at My Lai, up to but not including Calley's part, from those who had been there. It was a portrait of a sudden assault on an undefended hamlet from which, according to every witness but one, not a shot was fired, and whose people offered no resistance. It was a portrait of burning, of the killing of livestock, of the destruction of crops and homes, and of the indiscriminate slaughter of people. And it was a chilling picture of the discovery of at least two large piles of bodies—at locations and in the approximate numbers specified in the charges against Calley—giving witness to mass executions.

It was a numbing recital, an accumulation of detail upon detail, the recitation of the same story over and over again, each time with perhaps an additional element, until even the most skeptical—even the most convinced that American soldiers just didn't do such things—were unable to deny any longer the truth of My Lai, the truth of a massacre. When that point was reached, when the jury and the spectators had been steeped in the preludes, then and only then did Daniel permit Calley's name to enter, only then did he place him on the scene. But until that moment, Calley was the forgotten man in the trial; only one of these early witnesses even had a vague recollection that he might have seen the lieutenant at My Lai. All the others said they had never seen Calley there that day.

Roger Aloux, a tall, blond, bearded young man with horn-rimmed glasses, was a former artillery lieutenant who had been assigned as a forward observer to Charlie Company that morning. There had been no hostile fire, he said, no need to call in new artillery strikes. He had gone to the trail intersection with Captain Medina for the evacuation of Herb Carter, he said, and suddenly had come upon "eight to twelve, more or less," dead Vietnamese along the trail. He was the first to tell of that group, of seeing the dead that morning. He was the springboard from which everything would follow.

But it was with Aloux that Latimer tried the first of his many lines of defense: that the dead had all been killed by artillery and helicopters. And indeed, Latimer persuaded Aloux to say that the deaths could have been caused that way. But perhaps some of Aloux's effect might have been dissipated when he left the stand, for he leaned over and wished Calley good luck, and then Latimer revealed that he would be recalled later as a defense witness.

If that line, that the soldiers had killed nobody, was indeed a line Latimer intended to take anywhere, he was shaken in his resolve by almost every other witness. Ronald Haeberle, grown plump since his Army days, his sulky, petulant face framed by a Prince Valiant haircut, had taken the pictures whose visual portrayal of death at My Lai had shaken the nation, had been a record of death that none could deny and which would stun the jurors when they were finally shown them.

Haeberle told how he accompanied a squad of the third platoon toward Highway 521 south of My Lai as it checked out reports of dead Viet Cong in the area. As they were moving through the paddies, he looked back and saw a group of Vietnamese he thought numbered between fifty and seventy-five. "They were," he said, "sitting in their kind of squat. First there were five soldiers standing in front of the group. The people were all sitting there facing north. Then three of the GI's walked off into the distance. Then I heard automatic fire. I looked back. The automatic fire was coming from one of the two soldiers. He was firing toward the people. Some of the people were trying to get up and run. They couldn't and fell down. This one woman, I remember, she stood up and tried to make it—tried to run—with a small child in her arms. But she didn't make it."

"Were any of the people standing when it was over?" Daniel asked.

"No," Haeberle replied, "I didn't see anyone."

Later, Haeberle found himself at the intersection of the two trails just south of the hamlet where Herb Carter was being treated for his foot wound and waiting for the medivac chopper. Haeberle took several pictures of the scene and the soldiers around it (almost all of whom would appear to testify). Nearby, he came upon a group of bodies "lying on the trail all shot up." He was unsure of how many or if it was the group he had seen being shot some time before. This group of dead, he said, consisted "mainly of women, children, small babies." Out came one of the three cameras he had strung around his neck that day (two his own property and filled with color film; the third an Army-issue camera with black-and-white film) and onto color film—and later into the conscience of the nation—was seared one of the war's most famous, and gruesome, pictures.

It was with Latimer's cross-examination of Haeberle that many of us sitting in the press section to the rear of the court first began to suspect that he was not all he was supposed to be, that we began to ask some questions about the defense, about its preparation, direction, and tactics, to have some serious doubts about its ability, and to wonder whether Calley was really being as well defended as he should have been. We began to ask, in fact, whether the Latimer-directed defense team had any clear ideas of where it was going or even of what it was doing.

It was apparent to just about everyone in the court—and it should have been even more apparent to the defense, which had supposedly talked at length with almost all the prosecution witnesses—that Daniel was calling these early witnesses for a very limited and very specific purpose. These early witnesses would all repeat essentially the same story to the point of redundancy; even if the credibility of one could be destroyed, Daniel could follow with a dozen more to tell the same story, and the credibility of those dozen would be unshakable.

Haeberle's testimony, at least that part of it relating to the pictures he had taken, was just about incontrovertible. Those pictures had identifiable soldiers in them, and those soldiers when they testified would corroborate the authenticity of the pictures. And they, and others, would also testify to the existence of that stack of bodies on the trail where Haeberle said he had photographed them. To attack Haeberle's credibility and to attempt to destroy his character might be good courtroom histrionics, but it seemed of little value, for it would not destroy the existence or the truth of his photographs or the supporting testimony of the witnesses to follow. Haeberle's damage to the defense had been to photograph that March morning a scene of carnage at a place where the government said Calley had committed carnage. It was a visual record that would haunt the jurors and that nothing could erase.

Haeberle's testimony, then, was supportive of one government premise—that a large group of civilians had been killed at a specific location. But as a direct witness to Calley's participation in the killings, Haeberle was valueless. He could in no way implicate the lieutenant, and that was clear in his response to a series of questions by Latimer.

Latimer: Did you not testify that you never saw a lieutenant?
Haeberle: Yes, sir.
Latimer: When did you first see a lieutenant?

Haeberle: I did not see a lieutenant all that day.

Latimer: Then you did not see Lieutenant Calley? [It was one of Latimer's vocal quirks that he could not pronounce Calley's name correctly; it always came out sounding like Collie.]

Haeberle: I did not see Lieutenant Calley.

But Latimer was not content to let Haeberle off easily. Unlike his gentle approach to Aloux, who would later be one of his witnesses, Latimer's tactics with Haeberle were savage and sarcastic, from the moment Daniel turned the witness over to him. His first question set the tone for the several hours of cross-examination to follow: "Is it not a fact that you finagled out of most of your military training on the ground that you were going to be a photographer?" Haeberle, of course, denied that, at least as far as basic training went. He had, he admitted, "finagled" out of training in Hawaii, though, while training for photography.

Latimer never let up. He ridiculed Haeberle for not being able to read a map, for having to ask the various investigating committees before which he appeared to point out locations to him before he could orient himself. He demanded Haeberle's account books and income tax returns—which showed Haeberle had earned $35,499 from the sale of his color My Lai pictures, and launched a bitter attack on him as a biased witness seeking to make financial gain out of My Lai.

Latimer: Do you not have a definite interest in the outcome of this suit?

Haeberle: Yes, sir, I do have an interest in it.

Latimer: And isn't that interest in selling books and magazine articles?

Haeberle: No, sir.

Latimer: Then what is your interest?

Haeberle: In seeing a fair trial. . .

Latimer: Did you have an interview with Captain Doyle in May?

Haeberle: Yes.

Latimer: Did you not make the following statement to him: that you wished you'd waited until after the court-martial to sell the pictures because you would have made more money?

Haeberle: No, sir, I did not.

Latimer even came close to accusing Haeberle of theft of government property by not turning in to the Army the color pictures he had taken at My Lai with his own cameras at the same time he turned in the role of black-and-white photographs he had shot. None of the black and whites showed any carnage but centered instead on individual soldiers posing beside hootches—the kind of thing, Haeberle said, the Army public information division sends to hometown papers.

And then, his voice dripping with derision, Latimer excoriated Haeberle for failing to do his duty and thus for committing a crime himself.

Latimer: From the time you took those pictures until after you got back to the United States, no one had been told of the color film, is that right? Did you ever tell any officer about what you'd seen?

Haeberle: I can't specifically recall. Jay [Jay Roberts, an Army correspondent who accompanied Haeberle to My Lai] and I talked about it. But I can't specifically recall.

Latimer: You never told anyone in the chain of command about the atrocity and massacre?

Haeberle: No, sir.

Latimer: Weren't you shocked by what you'd seen? Weren't you upset by what you'd seen? Why didn't you report it?

Haeberle: I felt it was unusual but I wasn't the one to bring it up. We decided to keep quiet until someone came to us and not to start the ball rolling. . . .

Latimer: Have you never heard of a MAC-V order of 1967 that says it is the responsibility of all military personnel to report to their commanding officer any war crime they know of, that they should make every effort to discover war crimes, report them and preserve the physical evidence?

Haeberle: I never heard of that regulation before.

Latimer: Do you know that it is a serious offense not to comply with a regulation, known or unknown?

Haeberle: No.

Latimer: Did you ever consider the impact of your failure to disclose that you had these pictures or information to your commander or senior commanders?

Haeberle: No, sir, I did not.

Latimer: You had no feeling that failure to disclose that information was a dereliction of duty?

Haeberle: I've heard that.

Latimer: Is that the best excuse you can give us, that you didn't want to start the ball rolling?

Haeberle: That's what Jay Roberts and I talked about.

When Haeberle left the stand, his reputation had clearly been tarnished by the viciousness of Latimer's assault. He had shown that Haeberle was not the best of soldiers—but then Haeberle had never claimed he was a good soldier. He had shown that Haeberle had failed in his duty to report an atrocity—but then nobody else there that morning had reported it either, including Latimer's client, who had more knowledge of it, perhaps, than anyone. But Latimer had done nothing to discredit the pictures Haeberle had taken, and they were the only reason he had been called as a witness. Those pictures were still there, eloquent, unshakable.

It had been interesting theatrics, but where had Latimer been trying to go with Haeberle and for what purpose?

If any jurors still questioned whether there had been resistance at My Lai on March 16, the next witness was to do more than anyone to persuade them that there had been none, that there had been no combat. A baby-faced blond who looked much younger than his twenty-three years, Frank Beardslee had been aide and driver to Colonel Barker. During his year in Viet-Nam, he had seen no combat; whenever there had been an engagement with Barker's troops taking part, Beardslee had been with the colonel in his helicopter.

"Were you a rifleman?" Latimer asked on cross-examination.

"On paper or for real?" Beardslee shot back.

"For real?"

"No."

Just before the attack on My Lai, Barker had told Beardslee that he was being recommended for a Combat Infantryman's Badge. That decoration, Beardslee said he felt, "was not just another piece of junk you stuck on your chest. It meant something. It meant that you had seen combat." When Beardslee said that, one could feel the jury nod its agreement and from then on it listened with care to his every word. Beardslee said he told Barker that he would not accept a CIB unless he actually went on a combat mission. My Lai was coming up and Barker sent him to join Charlie Company for the attack.

Beardslee was all prepared to win his CIB. But when he landed outside My Lai, "there was no fire." And gradually the feeling of "fear, worry and concern" he felt at the moment the helicopter landed faded. When an order came to check out possible Viet Cong bodies to the south, near Highway 521, he joined with a squad of the third platoon, hoping for combat at last, and moved south. As they moved, he noticed, looking northeast toward My Lai (4), "fifteen or twenty Vietnamese standing and sitting. They were women and children." There were two or three GI's guarding them (by implication, this must have been the same group Haeberle saw and thought numbered fifty to seventy-five). Later Beardslee returned to the area where the group had been, alive when he last saw the people. "What I saw were all dead. They were in the exact same location as the group I saw before. All women and children." He identified Haeberle's photograph, Prosecution Exhibit 12A, as that group. The location he was certain of, for it was from that spot that he had seen a soldier wounded in the foot medivac-ed out, and that soldier had been the only casualty of the day.

Daniel had a last question for him: "Did you receive any hostile fire at all any time that day?"

"No, sir," Beardslee replied.

But he had done some shooting. Under cross-examination by Latimer (and again the aging counsel might have been better served to ask no questions at all), he told how he and the squad he was with went down to Highway 521 and spotted ten or fifteen Vietnamese moving along the dirt road. "The platoon opened fire on them," Beardslee said.

Latimer: Did you open fire?
Beardslee: Yes, sir.
Latimer: Did you kill some?
Beardslee: I don't know. I may have.
Latimer: Well, how many bodies were there?
Beardslee: Ten or fifteen. Some got away.

But some of the dead, Beardslee thought, might well have been killed by gunships because "some of the bodies were already dead when we got there. They were pretty torn up."

Highway 521 was not the only place where Beardslee and his squad did some shooting. Inside the hamlet later, "we shot the livestock." He had not shot at civilians, though he had seen bodies lying around inside My Lai.

For Daniel, Beardslee's purpose as a witness was, like those before and many to follow, to testify to the existence of the bodies on the trail at the intersection, and to reiterate that there had been no hostile action by the civilians of My Lai. Daniel was not, at that point, ready to move on to the even larger slaughter at the irrigation ditch. But Latimer decided to bring the ditch in himself for the first time since Daniel's opening.

Latimer: Did you see a ditch?
Beardslee: Well, sir, we lunched by a ditch. I don't know whether it was *the* ditch.
Latimer: Did you see any bodies in that ditch?
Beardslee: No, sir. The gooks like to booby trap them, ditches and bodies and things, so we stayed well away.

And then Latimer made his final point, though it was one Daniel was perfectly willing to concede at this point—and, in fact, would even begin to ask the question for Latimer with later witnesses in this string.

Latimer: Did you ever see Lieutenant Calley?

Beardslee: No, sir.

Latimer: Do you know him?

Beardslee: [Looking across the court at Calley] I recognize him by his name tag.

Latimer: But you never saw him?

Beardslee: No, sir, not to my recollection.

If Latimer was through, Daniel had one more point to make—in an area that Latimer, not he, had originally opened up. The question concerned the CIB. In the moment before Beardslee left the stand, Daniel asked if he had indeed received that decoration after the battle of My Lai.

"I did not accept the CIB on this mission, sir," Beardslee said, "because we met no resistance and the CIB indicates combat action."

It was a strong point with which to leave the jury as the second day of testimony in the court-martial ended.

John Paul had been one of Medina's two radio operators at My Lai, and for Daniel he was just another witness in that initial cumulative train, saying, as the others before him had, that there had been no opposition at My Lai, no requests from the forward platoons for support, and that he too had seen "a group of fifteen or twenty Vietnamese strung along the trail. . .because they were dead." And he, too, identified Haeberle's pictures.

Daniel finished with Paul quickly and turned him over to the defense for cross-examination, this time not by Latimer but by Raby. As a questioner, Raby, unlike many other lawyers, did not drive home the points he wanted to make insistently and with an overpowering impact. Raby felt that his job was to question as briefly as possible—"If you're quick," he told me later, "you don't bore the jury and maybe they'll remember better." He would usually ask only a question or two on any point he wanted to make, so that the answers and the questions would stand starkly in contrast to the length and softness of the cross-examinations by others, particularly Latimer and Kay.

With Paul, Raby darted here and there, moving rapidly from

one subject to another. And Raby made points—though because he did not follow them sharply, they could have been lost in all the testimony that would follow in the months ahead. Paul noticed that the artillery preparation had been extremely near My Lai, perhaps only fifty meters away, far closer than was usual on an assault operation. And the enormous volume of rifle fire being directed at My Lai by the troops was right in line with Medina's standard orders. "Had not Captain Medina always said it was necessary to gain the fire edge?" Raby asked, and Paul agreed, and he agreed that Medina's directive was in line with the standard infantry order in Viet-Nam "to saturate the area with the highest volume of fire available to force the enemy to seek cover."

It was apparent where Raby was going—and what would become one of the major lines of defense. For Raby at least, there would be no denial that Calley had done what the government charged. But with that admission, an attempt would be made to remove Calley from the dock by showing that everyone else at My Lai was also killing indiscriminately that morning, and therefore what Calley did was not extraordinary but actually the rule. Raby would also try to show that the manner of the attack on My Lai, and its results, were not unusual but part of a common pattern of action in Viet-Nam, and thus not per se illegal. And Raby would try to pin the responsibility for what happened, if it were considered illegal, on someone else. He would pin it on higher officers who had set the policies Calley had followed; and he would pin it on Ernest Medina not only for giving direct orders to Calley but also for committing a little murder in his own right. Raby's aim, then, was at least symbolically to remove Calley from the dock and replace him with Medina, to turn the court-martial into a trial of Medina, and to turn the defense into the prosecution and the prosecution, if possible, into reactive defense.

Daniel, of course, knew exactly what Raby was trying to do, and as the questions were shot at Paul in Raby's abrasively belligerent manner, Daniel sat on the edge of his chair, his hands on the table, ready to spring up with an objection as soon as Raby tried to move Paul beyond the area of direct examination.

Raby moved there suddenly and matter-of-factly. Had any calls been received from the helicopter by the headquarters group? he asked. Yes, Paul said, a helicopter called and said "he was dropping smoke on bodies in the paddies and he asked us to move out and check them for weapons." The chopper pilot mentioned five bodies.

"Is it not true," Raby asked, "that at this time there were no elements of the first platoon in the area?"

"No, I don't remember seeing them," Paul said.

"Did you not tell me at the steel desk in my office not fifteen meters from here the other night that from your knowledge of the location that the shooting had been done by the third platoon or by helicopter?"

Before Paul could answer, Daniel was up. The jury was marched from the courtroom while he argued his objections. "We are," he said, "presenting evidence at this time of a limited nature on one specific act of which Lieutenant Calley is charged. How is it relevant to bring in acts of misconduct by other people?"

Kennedy was now to make a ruling that would broaden the scope of this trial far beyond the acts charged to Calley and to turn it, as much as was possible, into a broad inquiry into the events at My Lai. He peered over the edge of the bench at Daniel and told the prosecutor in a mild voice that once he had had his witnesses draw a line with white crayon on the plastic overlay on the aerial photograph. From the landing zone on the western edge of the hamlet to the Carter medivac, as he had done with Paul and the others, he had opened up their testimony so that the defense could ask them about anything they had observed along that route.

"We're entitled to ask about anything he observed," Latimer chimed in.

But Daniel was fighting hard. He did not want to have to try the whole of Charlie Company, everyone at My Lai, and if he had to do that, perhaps the whole Army in Viet-Nam. He felt, as he had always felt, that his best chance lay in restricting this trial as much as possible to a trial only of Calley and only of the acts for which Calley was charged. So he pressed his point that under law the defense was entitled only to cross-examine a witness on the areas that had been raised in the direct examination; Raby's line of questioning went beyond those bounds and ought to be stricken.

"The law," Kennedy said, "is not that narrow. I'm not really going to restrict them just to that much."

Again Latimer was up, leaning toward the microphone on the defense table. "Lieutenant Calley," he intoned portentously, "is charged with mass murder and we are entitled to go in and cross-examine government witnesses on anything and everything they know."

Daniel did not give up easily. "The defense," he snapped angrily, "is going to broaden this whole thing. They want to bring in the acts of others, acts committed in different places, acts committed at different times, acts of a different nature, acts committed by different people. If they want to do that, let them recall the witness as their own witness. But they can't do that by cross-examining our witnesses."

Raby gave Daniel a tight, triumphant smile from across the court. "The government opened the door with witness Paul by asking him about radio messages he had given and received. The government is trying to say that the events at My Lai are related only to Lieutenant Calley. We're going to show that this is not so."

Again Latimer had to intervene, and with indignation he shot, "I will not let Captain Daniels draw a white line where I must stop." As usual, he mispronounced Daniel's name, calling him Daniels. "The time, the place, the sequence, anything that ties in with My Lai should be permitted into this record and it should be permitted unlimited."

There was silence, all eyes on Kennedy. The judge made his momentous ruling: "Any witness can personally testify to what he saw or did anytime in the village. The entire transaction at My Lai has got to be disclosed in this proceeding."

Daniel made one last effort. "Will the defense be able to establish their case within the presentation of our case by the cross-examination of our witnesses?"

"Anything this witness saw or personally did in the village of My Lai," the judge said, "he can testify to."

The defense had won its point; the case had opened up and from then on the trial would be concerned with, and would hear in detail, the grisly stories of murder and slaughter committed not just by Calley but by many others that day.

The jury returned and Raby led Paul through the first account.

Raby: Were all the bodies there in that general area dead?
Paul: No, one was still alive.

Raby: Would you explain how you and the command group approached?
Paul: We approached and she was lying face down. We didn't physically check her out, we just assumed that she was dead. Just as we started away, she flinched, moved or something. Captain Medina said, "Oh my God, son of a bitch, she's got a grenade." He jumped and flinched.

Raby: Was Captain Medina carrying a weapon?
Paul: Yes.

Raby: Did he shoot it?
Paul: Yes, he did.

Raby: Do you consider a grenade a weapon of death?
Paul: Yes.

Raby: Do you consider a person with a grenade to be offering resistance?
Paul: Yes.

But that was not the end of the killing that Paul had seen. Raby took him to the Carter medivac and to his view of perhaps ten to twenty bodies on the trial, and Paul's admission that some of them might have been killed by miniguns from a helicopter (guns that fire a thousand rounds a minute).

Raby: Did any other acts of killing occur in your presence that you recall?

Paul: No.

Raby: Well, let me ask you, did you see a running boy?

Paul: Yes. I saw a young boy, about eight. He was running across in front of us, from right to left.

Raby: At the time you saw these people you were with the command group, is that right?

Paul: Yes.

Raby: And you did not see the accused?

Paul: No.

Raby: Tell us what happened to that boy who was running.

Paul: He was running across our front. A shot was fired from my rear. Immediately, the boy dropped.

Raby: Did Captain Medina say anything?

Paul: I do not recall Captain Medina saying anything.

Raby: Captain Medina was in close proximity and said nothing, made no comment?

Paul: No.

Raby had made his point and so, instead of pressing along this line, he turned to new areas, wringing from Paul the admission that as far as he knew, no call was ever received that morning from Colonel Barker, nor was one made to the colonel about setting up a center to evacuate refugees or to provide medical aid to wounded civilians. It hung, unspoken, the realization that no one had given a thought to what would happen to civilians caught in My Lai, civilians who might survive.

And then for days the trial fell into a pattern. The witnesses, all members of Charlie Company but none members of Calley's first platoon, marched in a parade to the stand and under Daniel's questioning traced their route from the LZ outside the hamlet to the Carter medivac. Each would describe how he had encountered no resistance. Each would describe the scene of the bodies, women and children, near the medivac. Each would examine the Haeberle photographs and agree that the group of bodies was the group he had seen.

And the cross-examination, most of it by Latimer, instead of striking out along the lines opened up by Paul, was desultory, devoted mainly to making the point that none of the witnesses had seen Calley, that there was firing all over the hamlet by just about everyone, and that there were bodies everywhere. "They were," one witness said, "scattered all over—in front, behind hootches, on the path, just everywhere."

With Gerald "Hot Rod" Heming, a black former demolition man from Mississippi, Latimer, with a disbelieving scorn, tried to shake his recollection of the accuracy of the Haeberle photograph. "What is there about the photograph of those bodies that refreshes your memory?"

With exasperation, Heming tried to explain: "How can you put something like that out of your mind, a group of people dead like that?"

Sergeant Leo Maroney, a career soldier with nineteen years in the Army, had been in charge of the mortar platoon, which fired not a round that day. It was from him that Daniel won the admission that not everyone was killing that day. He told how he had come upon two little girls "in a house that had been partly torn down. The kids were back in a corner of it. One was five or six and the other was seven or eight. We kept them with us until we pulled out of that place after lunch."

But Maroney had seen killing. "I saw one man killed," he told Latimer on cross-examination, "but I don't know who killed him." In response to Latimer's disbelief, Maroney told how there had been an old man with a beard at one point in the hamlet. One of the soldiers with the sergeant asked if he should kill him. "'If we don't kill him,'" Maroney said the soldier told him, "'somebody else will.' That man in my platoon shot him. But he did not kill him. Somebody else did, I don't know who."

Turning away, Latimer shot, "It was a massacre, wasn't it, that day!"

We had heard so far only of the bodies on the trial in the list of Calley's crimes. David Hein, under Daniel's questioning, took us to the ditch for the first time, with the casual mention that he had seen a ditch on the east side of the hamlet and "there were bodies in the ditch, just laying there." It was a flat statement that was allowed to lie there for a while without being followed.

Until the appearance of Gene Oilver, Jr., a former rifleman, no one had heard a single shot fired from the Vietnamese; no one had described combat or battle whose fury might have been the cause of the deaths at My Lai. But Oliver, a short, stocky man with sideburns, slicked-back dark hair, and a trim mustache, with a pearl stickpin gleaming in his tie, in a tight suit with vest, a shoe salesman who reminded almost everyone of an old-fashioned "drummer" touring the West with a sample case filled with ladies' undergarments, was the one man in a hundred and five who knew the enemy had been there. He was the one man who heard hostile fire. "I heard," he told Daniel who stared at him with surprise, "three AK-47 rounds go whistling over my head." But reluctantly Oliver admitted that that was the only sign of hostility he had encountered, and as far as he knew there had been no other resistance.

Oliver was the first chance Kay had to test his courtroom abilities, and he tried to make the most of that chance. He asked a question that both Latimer and Raby had used as a stock thrust: "Were you frightened when you landed?" Oliver replied that sure he "was scared. If you weren't scared you were crazy, and I was scared."

Kay took Oliver on the march south of My Lai toward Highway 521 in the third platoon's squad with Haeberle, Beardslee, and others. "What did you see as you went south?"

"One Viet Cong with a weapon," Oliver said. "And a lot of people in black pajamas running all over about two hundred meters away." There were, he said, several such groups, the largest with about six people. Oliver and the men he was with opened fire. Some of the people fell, but nobody bothered to go over to examine them. Then the group turned and headed back to My Lai, passing the group of bodies on the trail near the Carter medivac.

Kay: What did you do in the village?

Oliver: What you do on a search and destroy mission. Burn the hootches and kill the livestock.

Kay: Did you do any shooting?

Oliver: Yes, sir.

Kay: Did you see any dead Vietnamese in the village?

Oliver: Yes, sir.

Kay: How many?

Oliver: Most of them. All over.

Kay: I mean, how many dead Vietnamese did you see?

Oliver: Oh, I don't know. A lot.

Kay: More than thirty?

Oliver: Yes.

Kay: More than forty?

Oliver: Yes, but we didn't stop to count them

Kay took out a Haeberle picture showing a soldier in Oliver's squad burning a hootch and asked if Oliver could identify where that had taken place. Oliver shrugged, "You seen one hootch, you seen 'em all."

And from Oliver, over repeated objections by Daniel, Kay got onto the record that the mission to My Lai had been a search and destroy mission and that My Lai itself was within what was termed a free-fire zone—where Americans had a license to kill anything that moved, and where Vietnamese had a license to be killed. And he also got from Oliver what had been told by every witness—that this was the first combat assault the company had ever gone on.

Oliver, Kay crowed as the witness left the stand, would be called back for the defense later. And Oliver, as he passed the defense table, leaned over to wish Calley luck.

It was at the end of the first week of government testimony that the first detailed description of the dead in the irrigation ditch went into the record. Richard Pendleton, a slight, emaciated young man with long hair and a hawk face, had been a rifleman in the third platoon. He, too, had seen the dead near the Carter medivac, had gotten within five feet of that group.

Daniel: Did you go to the east of My Lai Four?

Pendleton: Yes.

Daniel: Did you see a ditch?

Pendleton: Yes, I did.

Daniel: Did you look into that ditch?

Pendleton: Yes, I did.

Daniel: What did you see?

Pendleton: I saw dead Vietnamese in that ditch.

Daniel: Can you describe what you saw?

Pendleton: There was a large mound of dead Vietnamese in the ditch

Daniel: Can you estimate how many?

Pendelton: It's hard to say. I'd say forty to fifty.

Daniel: Can you describe the ditch?

Pendleton: It was seven to ten feet deep, maybe ten to fifteen feet across. The bodies were all across it. There was one group in the middle and more on the sides. The bodies were on top of each other.

And so we had moved to the second of the mass executions at My Lai. There were, after the witnesses of the first week, no further doubts that a large number of Vietnamese—perhaps not the thirty the government had charged but a large number and close to that—had been slaughtered at the crossroads south of My Lai (4). Now, starting with Pendleton, Daniel would go on to develop the existence of the second and larger group at the irrigation ditch to the east.

We expected that he would follow the same pattern in establishing that massacre as he had with the first; he would call a dozen witnesses to tell what they had seen, all using the same language, all telling basically the same story, so that by the time the next element entered after a week, after such a blanket of fatigue and boredom—for, as we learned, it is possible to become bored even with horror when it is repeated again and again to the point where you know the testimony a step ahead of its recital—it would be greeted with a rush of relief and expectation and belief.

But as that second week began, it seemed that Daniel might, after all, begin to introduce some drama. He had finished for the moment with the ground troops, and now the helicopter pilots and crewmen were arriving to tell what they had seen from the air.

One of these pilots, if the stories he and others had told in the past were true, was one of the few authentic heroes of that March morning. Lieutenant Hugh C. Thompson, a warrant officer at the time of My Lai, had, so the stories went, seen the slaughter at the ditch from his chopper and had landed several times in an effort to rescue some of the wounded civilians, particularly the children. On one of these landings he had confronted Calley and threatened to have his door gunner, Larry Coburn, shoot Calley if he interfered with the rescue. For his actions at My Lai, Thompson had been awarded the Distinguished Flying Cross—though it had been given him not for rescuing civilians from marauding American troops but, the citation said, for landing in the middle of a battle between Americans and Viet Cong and, in disregard for his own life and safety, rescuing the wounded civilians.

But if we expected to hear of the dramatic confrontation between Thompson and Calley from Thompson, we were to be disappointed. Daniel had no intention of questioning him or Coburn about such a meeting. It was not yet time to bring Calley in; Thompson, Coburn, and the others from the choppers were being called only to tell of the bodies in the ditch and of their numbers, though there was drama enough in those descriptions.

Flying over My Lai at mid-morning, Thompson said, one of his crew members pointed out a ditch to the east of the hamlet. He dropped low over the ditch. "There were a lot of bodies in there." Thompson's voice was muffled and choked with emotion as though he were seeing it all again. "Women, kids, babies, old men. Some were dead, some were alive." Thompson was not sure how many bodies were in the ditch, though he thought there might have been between fifty and a hundred.

Since some seemed to be still alive, he landed near the ditch, the first of three landings he said he made that morning at My Lai. There were several Americans in the area and he motioned to "a colored NCO" to come forward and asked the man "if he knew if we could help them out. He said the only way to help them out was out of their misery." When Thompson took off moments later, one of his crew called out that the black NCO was "firing into the ditch."

Later, Thompson was back over the scene and "I saw a woman and a couple of kids in the doorway of the bunker" and troops advancing toward them. Thompson landed again and this time talked to another soldier, whom he did not identify except as being in charge of the advancing troops (Calley later admitted he was that soldier). "I asked him how we could get them out and he said the only way we could was with a grenade. I told him to hold his men there. Then I went over to the bunker. There were a lot more people than I thought, about ten old men, a woman, and a baby small enough to be carried." To help evacuate these people, Thompson called in two helicopter gunships hovering nearby.

Could Thompson describe the wounds on these people?

Thompson bowed his head and there were tears in his eyes. "They just had wounds. Some, I don't even think they were shot. There was one baby there that part of its head was missing."

A third time, still later, Thompson again landed near the ditch. "We had seen some people in the ditch were still alive and we wanted to see if we could help them out. We got a kid out of the ditch and got him up the aircraft. He was about the size of a six-year-old, muddy with blood all over him. We took him to a hospital."

It was a gruesome, devastating story of the events of that morning, of the slaughter of children and unarmed civilians. And it was confirmed in almost every detail by Thompson's door gunner, Larry Coburn, who added one detail of his own: As they had flown over the ditch he had seen two children alive; when they set down, one of those kids was dead and the other was the one they had lifted off to the hospital.

Instead of trying to cast doubt on that story—if he were to try to do anything on cross-examination—Latimer attempted to heap scorn on the decorations Thompson and Coburn, who won a Bronze Star for his part that day, had received. Those awards had already been criticized by the House sub-committee, which said, "If medals are to retain their significance as a reward for heroic action, they should not be dispensed under such questionable circumstances." Perhaps that was so, but if Thompson's actions that day were not heroic, then the meaning of heroism has totally disappeared, and Latimer's attempts to cast aspersion on Thompson failed utterly. And, in fact, at times seemed almost laughable as once again he revealed one his speech peculiarities, an inability to pronounce the word helicopter, calling it heel-i-o-copter.

Kay, questioning Coburn, made a further stab—directing his question at an area he attempted to develop with almost every government witness he questioned. He charged that Coburn's testimony should not be believed because Coburn was a pot smoker. And Coburn admitted that on occasion he did smoke marijuana, but "never while I was flying." And when Kay trapped him in what seemed to be an inconsistency, Coburn shot back, "Ever since it happened, I've been trying to push it out of may mind, to forget what happened."

The view of My Lai as a charnel house as seen from the air was a picture that was in the minds of others in the helicopters flying over.

Calvin Dean Hodde had been a door gunner that day and had made several low passes over the ditch. He was stunned by what he saw. "It looked like a bunch of people lying out in the open—with paint all over them, a bright red color."

First Lieutenant Jerry R. Culverhouse, a gunship pilot, said he saw the ditch with "seventy-five to more than a hundred bodies." Many of the dead were babies, and the water in the ditch was stained with blood. As he swooped low over the ditch he saw a black sergeant (David Mitchell was the name that rose in the mind) standing by the ditch and then he heard a burst of automatic fire. Banking his chopper over the scene, he saw that "the sergeant was standing on the eastern bank and still had his weapon near shoulder height."

Former Warrant Officer Dan R. Millians saw the same black sergeant firing into the ditch and remembered the shuddering impact as the bullets hit a Vietnamese.

Millians and former Lieutenant Brian Livingston added another element to the picture of My Lai—one that had little to do with Calley—and both helped knock down one defense contention. They described a group of more than a hundred Vietnamese fleeing along Highway 521, racing west toward Quang Ngai city from the infantry assault on My Lai. Sharks and other gunships swooped over the group and fired into it with their miniguns, killing a large number of the escaping refugees. When Kay attempted to link these killings to those at the ditch and the trail intersection, and so advance that original defense contention that the people at both places had been killed by artillery and gunships, Livingston and Millians continually refuted him. Livingston kept saying, "You're misconstruing what I said, sir." The choppers, both said, had killed only those people on the highway; they had killed none anywhere else.

And both added another intriguing scene. As the group along the highway fled west, the command and control helicopter in which Colonel Henderson was flying—one of three C-and-C choppers over the scene, the other two containing Colonel Barker and General Koster—suddenly set down right near the group and picked up two military-age males who were taken back to the fire base for interrogation.

And then the court-martial went into a long Thanksgiving recess. Daniel had now established the foundations of his case; there was no dispute any longer, if there ever had been any; that there had been no resistance at My Lai and there had been no combat that day, no battle; and everyone knew at least two large groups of Vietnamese civilians had been slaughtered at those two locations Daniel had specified.

Daniel was ready to make the next, and most important move.

7

"I Saw Calley Shooting"

The court-martial had been in progress for two weeks and, since the first day, Calley had not been directly linked to anything that had happened at My Lai. We would discover any day, somebody said one afternoon, that it was all a mistake; Calley hadn't even been at My Lai after all; he had been shacked up at Vung Tau with a five-dollar-a-night Vietnamese whore named Yvonne, revisiting the girl he had so romantically told about in an *Esquire* article, part of a series on his life, which had been published just as the trial was getting under way.

But nobody need have worried. Aubrey Daniel knew exactly what he was doing and where he was going. As the trial resumed on Tuesday afternoon after the Thanksgiving recess, he was ready to erect a skyscraper on top of his now unshakable foundation.

We had grown so used to hearing witnesses say that they had served in the second or third platoon, that when Roy Wood, a twenty-three-year-old former rifleman, told Daniel that he had been a member of the second squad of the first platoon, everyone in court leaned forward in expectation. But that, with Wood, was to remain unsatisfied. Wood proved only a link, the first step now in the direct chain that would lead inexorably to Calley. And with Wood it was evident that within hours in that courtroom Calley would be center stage.

Wood told the by now familiar story of the landing and the advance into My Lai. But now new elements began to enter. Meeting no opposition, his squad moved through the hedgerows into the hamlet. "I came to a hootch and a lady jumped out. I shot and wounded her, and she jumped in again and then came out with a baby and some others. There were about five people. We gathered the people together and sent them out."

Wood's squad continued its advance "and came on some cows and another hootch. There was a man, a woman, and two girls. We grabbed them out." They were about to shove this group ahead of them when "a guy from the second platoon came up and grabbed my rifle and said, 'Kill 'em all!' He shot them."

Ahead then was a group of ten or fifteen people moving along a path. "One was an old lady, that's all I remember." The group was moving off to the right, toward where, he said, Lieutenant Calley was supposed to be (a surmise that brought a quick and sustained objection from Latimer). But the impression was there now.

Latimer's cross-examination was brief. He brought out that Wood "was frightened all the time I was in Viet-Nam" and at My Lai had started firing as he entered the hamlet and "fired all the way through."

Latimer: Did you shoot chickens, pigs, and dogs?
Wood: Yes, sir.
Latimer: Did you shoot all you saw?
Wood: Not all I saw.
Latimer: Most of them?
Wood: Yes, most of them.
Latimer: And you never did see Lieutenant Calley that day?
Wood: No, I never saw Lieutenant Calley that day.

But there was that group of a dozen unarmed, unresisting Vietnamese civilians moving down the trail. Where were those people going? To whom were they being sent?

Daniel was now ready to bring Calley onto the scene at My Lai, ready to tell where that group was heading and to whom. Suddenly the jury was marched from the courtroom. Out of its hearing, Daniel told Kennedy that his next witness, Rennard

Doines, a rifleman in the first platoon's second squad, would testify that as he was moving through My Lai, he suddenly came upon Calley's radio operator, Charles Sledge. In a moment of extreme passion, Sledge told Doines that Roy Wood, Paul Meadlo, and Calley had just killed a large group of people, and then Doines had come upon those bodies. While such a statement from Sledge to Doines would normally be inadmissible as hearsay, on this occasion, Daniel contended, such a statement was "a spontaneous exclamation" and so would be admissible.

Kennedy was skeptical. "I don't think I'm going to grant your request, Captain Daniel," he said. "According to my reading of the law, that exclamation and statement by Sledge are not admissible. Mr. Doines can testify that he had a conversation with Sledge and that as a result of that conversation he returned and saw the bodies. But that's as far as he can go. I'm not going to permit him to say what Sledge said to him. You can, when Sledge testifies, have him testify that he had a conversation with Doines and what he said. But you can't have Mr. Doines tell it."

Blocked from that route, Daniel led Doines by another path. As he moved through the hamlet, Doines said, he and his squad were "gathering up prisoners. Most of them were in hootches. They were women and kids and old men. Most of them was trying to hide in their hootches. I gathered up ten or fifteen, most of them women and kids. One was a kind of young guy, but he was on crutches. We took them up the trail in the middle of the village."

"Did you see Lieutenant Calley?" Daniel asked.

There was a pause. Doines nodded. "He was right on the trail." There were other soldiers there, too, but "I don't know their names." This was a pattern that would constantly recur; nobody could remember anyone else by name as being anywhere in My Lai except for Calley and, perhaps, Meadlo. Doines turned his group of civilian prisoners, unarmed and unresisting, over to Calley and the other Americans and walked away.

Daniel: Did you see a man named Charles Sledge in the village?

Doines: Yes.

Daniel: Did you have a conversation with Charles Sledge?

Doines: Yes.

Daniel: What did you do after that conversation?

Doines: I went over to where the people was.

Daniel: Did you see them?

Doines: Yes, to the right of the trial.

Daniel: Can you describe them?

Doines: They was women and little kids.

Daniel: What were they doing?

Doines: They were lying on the ground, bleeding from all over. They was dead.

We had come one step closer to Calley.

And on cross-examination, Doines pulled another prop right out from under the defense—which seemed never to know, despite its opportunities for preparation, what a witness was going to say. "Was it not your understanding," Latimer demanded, "that you were to go through the village, kill all the people and move out to the next village and repeat the operation again?"

Daniel objected; Kennedy sustained the objection, then changed his mind. "You may answer that question, Mr. Doines."

Doines looked directly at Latimer and said, "No."

From Doines to Sidney Kye was the step from Calley with live civilians to dead civilians to Calley with a rifle in his hands. "I seen Lieutenant Calley once," Kye told Daniel. "He was standing and I don't know where. He was standing and there were GI's standing about with him."

"What was Calley doing?" Daniel asked.

"I saw Calley shooting."

"How did you know it was Calley?"

"He was my platoon leader."

Could the defense do anything with such a direct statement? It did not seem likely, for Kye, a soft-spoken black man with an Afro haircut, seemed certain of what he knew and what he didn't know. Raby tried to break him down. He got Kye to say that maybe he was off a little when he said his squad had picked up ten Vietnamese and sent them down the trail— maybe it had only been eight or nine. And Raby confused Kye enough so that Kye said he didn't know who was on his right or left or whether the soldiers were black or white during the sweep.

With scorn, Raby said, "And you said you recognized Lieutenant Calley firing after a five second observation from about sixty meters away, but you didn't know who was on your left or right though they were only six meters away." Then Raby snapped, "Did you hear any shots fired by Lieutenant Calley?"

Kye shook his head. "No, I didn't hear any shots. I just saw the smoke coming out of the muzzle of his rifle."

Raby: You could not see Lieutenant Calley's weapon, could you? You couldn't see where it was pointed. For all you know, he could have been pointing it straight into the air, isn't that so?

Kye: Yes.

Raby: And you don't know how many shots Lieutenant Calley fired, do you?

Kye: I couldn't say.

Raby: In other words, you don't know one way or another if Lieutenant Calley was .shooting. You merely presume he was.

Kye: Yes. But I saw smoke coming from the muzzle.

The case directly against Calley was mounting. We now had Calley with a smoking weapon. We would have more.

Robert Maples, a former machine gunner in the first platoon, followed Kye that Tuesday afternoon. He, too, told how as they advanced through My Lai, "we were grabbing up people. We went into hootches, got some of the people there and shot at them. One woman come up and showed me her arm, where she had been shot. She was elderly. I couldn't see how old she was. The guys pushed these people on up the trail, a few women, kids. We just moved through the village. We came to this hole or ditch or something. I was with [James] Bergthold. Calley was there at the ditch and he asked [Harry] Stanley to interpret for him. We came up. They had people standing by the hole. Calley and Meadlo were firing at the people. They were firing into the hole. I saw Meadlo firing into the hole."

Daniel: Where was Lieutenant Calley?
Maples: There. Firing.
Daniel: Where was his weapon?
Maples: Pointing into the hole.
Daniel: Did you have any conversation with Lieutenant Calley at that ditch?
Maples: Yes.
Daniel: What did he say?
Maples: He asked me to use my machine gun.
Daniel: At the ditch?
Maples: Yes.
Daniel: What did you say?
Maples: I refused.

And so, as court ended that afternoon, Calley had been branded by men from his own platoon as a killer. And with Maples a dent, and a major one, had been smashed into one of the major lines of Calley's defense—that all that happened at My Lai was in obedience to orders, that it was the duty of a soldier, including an officer like Calley, to follow orders without question. But Maples had refused a direct order from Calley to use his machine gun. And nothing had happened to Maples.

The defense, of course, recognized just how devastating a witness Maples was, the first of the really incriminating witnesses. Latimer tried to take him apart, but he did not fully succeed. Maples admitted that he was uncertain of locations or directions, but he was certain of what he had seen and what had happened. "I saw Lieutenant Calley and Meadlo shooting into the hole," he said several times. "The muzzles were down and I heard the firing."

How many people were in that hole and how many of them were dead? Latimer demanded.

Maples had no clear idea because "this hole"—as he persisted in calling the irrigation ditch—was about seventy-five yards to his right. "I never looked into the hole; I never got closer than seventy-five yards."

Latimer: Were they firing single shot or automatic?

Maples: I haven't any idea. Meadlo and Lieutenant Calley was both firing into that hole. I saw people go into that hole and no one come out. That's all I know.

Latimer: Well, you've changed your testimony, haven't you? Didn't you tell the Peers committee in January, 1970, that you never saw Calley pushing people into that hole?

Maples: I never paid it no mind. I just remembered now. I haven't changed my testimony. I remember Calley was pushing people into that hole. Over a period of time, you forget things and then you remember.

Latimer: And what else have you remembered that you saw?

Maples: I saw Meadlo crying.

Latimer: From seventy-five yards away?

Maples: Yes.

Latimer: You saw tears in his eyes?

Maples: Yes.

Latimer: From seventy-five yards, that's your estimate?

Maples: Yes. I saw tears in Meadlo's eyes.

Latimer: He had on his helmet and his gear and you saw tears in his eyes?

Maples: Yes.

Latimer: Do you remember anything else?

Maples: No.

Latimer: Well, tell me, what was so remarkable about Meadlo that made you remember him?

Maples: He was firing and crying.

Latimer: He was pointing his weapon away from you and yet you saw tears in his eyes?

Maples: Yes.

Latimer turned away with a shrug of disbelief.

*   *   *

The testimony mounted, the grisly details of slaughter piling on each other and burying Calley under their weight, labeling him a murderer and testifying to the fact that not everyone killed, not everyone obeyed orders at My Lai without a thought, as though an automaton.

Lenny Lagunoy came from Hawaii to tell of people, perhaps thirty or forty of them, being herded in a group and then of hearing shots from the direction they had gone. He told of Meadlo with his gun pointing into a ditch and crying, of Calley standing nearby (though he could not say what Calley was doing), of hearing more fire from that direction. And he told of a helicopter landing between his position out in the paddies and the ditch, of going to the chopper and being unable to understand what the pilot was saying, and then of Lieutenant Calley appearing, having a conversation he did not hear with the pilot and then returning to the ditch.

Charles Hall, a calm, self-assured blond man with a trim mustache from Columbus, Ohio, added a little more. As his squad moved through the hamlet, the only resistance he had encountered was "the same kind I would offer if someone had tried to stop me from eating breakfast and ordered me to walk down the street." He and his squad had gathered up thirty to forty people, mainly "very old men, women, young mothers, and very small children." As they were holding that group, "Calley came from the left with more people. We grouped the people together and marched them down the trail to the ditch."

Hall and machine gunner Gregory Olsen left their group at the ditch with Calley, Mitchell, and a couple of other soldiers, crossed the ditch, and went into the rice paddies where they set up their machine gun, forming a perimeter defensive line about fifty meters out. They watched a chopper land, saw Lagunoy go to it, saw him leave when Calley approached, saw Calley and the pilot talk, with the pilot "making strong gestures with his hand toward the ditch. Calley was listening with his head down toward the ground. Calley walked away toward the ditch and the helicopter took off. Then I saw Calley talking to Mitchell at the perimeter of the ditch. Then I heard slow, semi-automatic fire from the ditch."

A little later, Hall said he and Olsen and a few others were ordered back over the ditch. As they crossed it, "I looked back and saw people in the ditch. They were dead."

"How did you know they were dead?" Daniel asked.

"They weren't moving. There was a lot of blood coming from all over them. They were in piles and scattered. There were very old people, very young people and mothers. Blood was coming from everywhere. Everything was all blood."

In most respects, Olsen bore out Hall. A young man who had flown in from his home in Portland, Oregon, on the eve of his wedding, Olsen was a man who looked, and was, haunted by his memories of that morning. He was a machine gunner in the first platoon and had fired his weapon at "a Vietnamese man running away" soon after landing. "I fired a few bursts at him and then the gun jammed. So I don't know whether I hit him." As he moved through My Lai, Olsen fired his machine gun off and on. "I don't remember encountering any enemy fire. I shot at a few animals. My main concern was with the machine gun which was jamming all the time."

At first, Olsen saw few Vietnamese. Then, "at a juncture of two trails, one going north and south, the other going east and west, I saw a group of thirty or so Vietnamese. They were old women, young women, children, old men. They were being guarded by some GI's." What happened to these people at the southern edge of My Lai, Olsen did not know.

"The next thing I remember was approaching a ditch and I saw Lieutenant Calley standing by it. He was standing on the side closest to the village." The ditch "was about twenty-five meters from the village, but I haven't got a good memory for it." With Hall and Lagunoy, Olsen started across the ditch and "I saw approximately two dozen Vietnamese bodies in it to my right. The majority were women and some babies. I particularly remember a middle-aged Vietnamese dressed in white at my feet. He followed me with his eyes as I walked across the ditch. Some of the people appeared to be dead and others followed me with their eyes as I walked across the ditch."

Out in the paddies, Olsen saw the same scene described by Hall. He watched Calley return from the helicopter and meet Mitchell "at the point where I crossed the ditch. Mitchell stood at the ditch where I had crossed, raised his weapon to firing position and fired into the ditch. I heard the shots."

Olsen was unshakable on cross-examination. All that Raby could wring from him was that he had not personally seen Calley shoot anyone. Then Olsen went back to Portland to get married.

There had been excitement all that day around the courthouse. Paul David Meadlo had arrived. He had refused to testify at Mitchell's court-martial, taking the Fifth Amendment. But there were rumors that he would testify against Calley. He had, in the past, particularly on a television interview with Mike Wallace of the Columbia Broadcasting System a year earlier, told an appalling story of the slaughter by him and Calley, at Calley's direction, of hundreds at the trail intersection and the ditch, of the massacre of babies.

Some of the men in his platoon were to tell me and others of an incident the morning after My Lai when Meadlo's foot was blown off by a landmine. He had been carrying a minesweeper on a patrol from the night camp some distance from My Lai. According to a soldier who had been right behind him, Calley had been prodding Meadlo to hurry up. He had pushed him slightly and Meadlo had stumbled down a short rise; a mine had gone off, and with it Meadlo's foot. As he lay on the ground writhing in pain, waiting for a medivac, Meadlo had screamed at Calley, "God's had his vengeance on me for what we did yesterday; but He's going to have His vengeance on you, too, you'll see!"

In the years since that episode, Meadlo had become more and more embittered. For some time he had been unable to adjust to civilian life, unable to hold a job, obsessed by his memories of My Lai. And to some he had spoken of himself as the hand of God ensuring that retribution would fall on his former platoon leader.

Thus there was great anticipation as Meadlo, accompanied by his lawyer from Terre Haute, Indiana, Paul Kessler, limped into court and onto the witness stand. Dressed in a brown suit, white shirt, and brown tie, his complexion sallow and muddy, he seemed flabby and limp. Watching him, my wife thought he looked like a toad resting on a log, and it was an image everyone agreed was apt.

As Meadlo took the stand, the jury was out of the room. No one, then, was certain whether Meadlo would testify. There was for him a grant of immunity and Kennedy read it to him. "It is my view of the law," Kennedy said after he finished reading, "that there are only two possible tribunals that can try you for crimes growing out of My Lai, Mr. Meadlo. They would be, first, a Presidentially convoked military tribunal, and, second, a court-martial. And this grant of immunity covers both these areas."

But Meadlo would not testify.

And Raby was on his feet, too, challenging Kennedy's interpretation. There are, he said, other forums which might try Meadlo. He might have to face an international tribunal, for example. Or, Raby said, "Meadlo might be hijacked, for instance, and find himself in Cuba and so might face prosecution there" for the crimes he might testify to here under a grant of testimonial immunity.

Kennedy looked at him sarcastically. "Come on now, Major Raby, you don't really think the Cubans are going to worry about the Fifth Amendment, do you?"

But Raby fought through the rest of that morning to prevent a grant of immunity being given to Meadlo. As one reporter put it, "Baby, they don't want Meadlo testifying nohow."

Kessler carried forward Raby's arguments. Further, Kessler said, why should Meadlo, who might incriminate himself, be forced to testify against a fellow soldier? After all, Kessler said, "he had his foot blown off by these innocent civilians with whom we are concerned here."

Kessler raised other legal precedents and then claimed that the Army had no jurisdiction over Meadlo.

"If the Army can't try him," Kennedy snapped with growing impatience, "then he doesn't need any immunity because no one can try him."

"How about the sixty signatories to the Geneva Convention?" Kessler asked.

"The order signed by General Talbott is binding on the President," Kennedy responded, which, he said, would foreclose turning Meadlo over to an international tribunal on war crimes. Kennedy had reached the end of his patience. "If he doesn't answer, we can litigate all these issues in Federal District Court."

But Kessler was not finished; he had one more point he wanted to argue. "One witness cannot make or break this case. I plead with you, your honor, don't deprive him of his rights."

That was too much. "Wait one minute, Mr. Kessler," Kennedy said. "Isn't this the man who granted those interviews on television? He showed no reluctance at that time to tell in great and nauseous detail all he knew about My Lai. I'm satisfied that he has been granted a valid grant of immunity." Turning to Daniel, Kennedy directed him to begin questioning Meadlo. "Let's find out from the witness whether he's going to testify or not."

But all Meadlo would say was his name, his home, and that he knew Calley. Beyond that, he refused to answer any questions.

"If you continue to refuse," Kennedy warned, "I will refer this matter to the local United States prosecutor for prosecution."

Still Meadlo balked.

"I will turn you over to the MP's," Kennedy warned again. "I don't want to do anything that will harm you in any way, Mr. Meadlo, but I won't hesitate one second if I have to." He gave Meadlo a short recess to think it over.

Outside court in that recess, Kessler asserted that Meadlo would remain silent. "You bet your ass he's not going to testify," the lawyer declared. "The Army may have got his foot, but they're not going to get his ass."

Back in court, Meadlo again refused to testify, looking first to Kessler for advice. "Don't look at your lawyer, Mr. Meadlo," Kennedy said. "He's not going to help you. If anyone goes to jail, Mr. Meadlo, it's going to be you and not your lawyer."

When Meadlo remained mute, Kennedy finally turned to the MP's and told them to take Meadlo to the provost marshal's office. "He is not free to leave at this point."

Limping, Meadlo was led away by the military police. He was, however, held only part of the day and never turned over to a United States marshal because no marshal could be found. The next day, Kennedy let him fly back to Terre Haute. But he would be back at Fort Benning one winter day in January, a final link in Daniel's chain.

If Meadlo had been a temporary diversion, Dennis Conti, who took the stand the next morning, was a crucial character. He was the most incriminating witness against Calley to that point. A truck driver from Providence, Conti came to court in an open blue shirt and blue pants with no jacket. His black hair was long and combed over his low forehead; he had long bushy sideburns and a large mustache and a disingenuous expression. He spoke with a decided accent of the Boston-Providence area.

On the morning of March 16, 1968, he said, he had carried two weapons to My Lai—an M-79 grenade launcher and a minesweeper. Coming in on the first lift, he had jumped off his chopper and found himself alone and cut off in high elephant grass. "A farmer was running up ahead. A machine gun opened up on him and I used the launcher, but he was too far away."

Looking for the headquarters unit to which he was supposed to be assigned, Conti said he wandered into the hamlet. He saw a man up ahead and somebody opened up on him. "I don't know if he hit him. I was not firing myself, I had the grenade launcher." As he progressed, he saw a squad leader from the first platoon, Sergeant L. G. Bacon, and some other soldiers "at a hootch shooting a buffalo, you know, for sport."

And then he came upon Calley on the east-west trail with

some other soldiers. "As I came up, he said round up the people."

Daniel: What did you do?

Conti: So I did, rounded up the people. There were five or six, mostly women and children. They were unarmed and huddled together.

Daniel: What did you do with them?

Conti: I brought them back to Calley on the trail. There were others there. Thirty or forty. All women and children. I remember one old man. They were in their sixties to infants.

Daniel: What were they doing?

Conti: Just standing there.

Daniel: Who was with them?

Conti: The only GI I remember was Meadlo.

Daniel: What happened then?

Conti: Calley told me and Meadlo to take the people off and push them in a rice paddy. We took them out there, pushed them off the trail and made them squat down and bunch up so they couldn't get up and run. We stayed there and guarded them. At this time, I seen a young child running from a hootch toward us. He seen us and he took off. I dropped my gear and checked out a hootch with a woman and a child in it. There was an old woman in a bunker. I took her out and put her on the ground. Then I saw a man running away. I took the other woman and child to the group. The old woman wouldn't go, so I left her there.

Daniel: What was Meadlo doing at this time?

Conti: He was guarding the people.

Daniel: Where was he?

Conti: He was standing on the village side of the people.

Daniel: Then what happened?

Conti: Lieutenant Calley came out and said take care of these people. So we said, okay, so we stood there and watched them. He went away, then he came back and said, "I thought I told you to take care of these people." We said, "We are." He said, "I mean, kill them."

DENNIS I. CONTI

I was a little stunned and I didn't know what do do. He said, "Come around this side. We'll get on line and we'll fire into them."

I said, "No, I've got a grenade launcher. I'll watch the tree line." I stood behind them and they stood side by side. So they—Calley and Meadlo—got on line and fired directly into the people. There were bursts and single shots for two minutes. It was automatic. The people screamed and yelled and fell. I guess they tried to get up, too. They couldn't. That was it. The people were pretty well messed up. Lots of heads was shot off, pieces of heads and pieces of flesh flew off the sides and arms. They were all messed up. Meadlo fired a little bit and broke down. He was crying. He said he couldn't do any more. He couldn't kill any more people. He couldn't fire into the people any more. He gave me his weapon into my hands. I said I wouldn't. "If they're going to be killed, I'm not going to do it. Let Lieutenant Calley do it," I told him.

So I gave Meadlo back his weapon. At that time there was only a few kids still alive. Lieutenant Calley killed them one-by-one. Then I saw a group of five women and six kids—eleven in all—going to a tree line. "Get 'em! Get 'em! Kill 'em!" Calley told me. I waited until they got to the line and fired off four or five grenades. I don't know what happened.

Then Conti had wandered away. He came upon Herb Carter, sitting on the ground with a bullet through his foot, and asked Carter if he needed any help. "Then I left Carter and cut through the hootches again. I met a couple of GI's, had a smoke and there was some small talk. Then I heard some fire. It sounded like sixteen's, so I took off in that direction."

Conti headed toward the eastern edge of the village, went through it and into the open fields just beyond. He saw some soldiers shooting at a tree line. "I looked up and saw a dike. Lieutenant Calley and Sergeant Mitchell were on top firing. I moved to the left to see what they were shooting at. It was a ditch and there were people there, and Calley and Mitchell were firing down into them." The fire, Conti said, was both automatic and semi-automatic, single shots. "A lot of them, the people, were trying to get up and mostly they was just screaming and pretty bad shot up."

The people were lying in the ditch right beneath Calley and Mitchell, Conti said, and both men were "holding their weapons at their shoulders and I could see muzzle flashes. I seen a woman tried to get up. I seen Lieutenant Calley fire. He hit the side of her head and blew it off."

There was utter silence when Conti finished his recital. Daniel broke it by handing him Haeberle's photograph, Prosecution Exhibit 12. Conti identified it as the group Calley and Meadlo had killed at the trail. And at last the jury got a look at that picture as Daniel finally offered it as evidence. Each juror studied it closely and at length, each for more than a minute.

Conti was Kay's on cross-examination, and the effort was to destroy him utterly, to make him out such a liar and so characterless that nothing he said could be believed. Kay did not assault Conti's testimony, his descriptions of what he had seen at the trail and at the ditch. Instead, he spent most of the rest of that Friday morning and all the afternoon trying to picture Conti as a rapist, addicted to unnatural sex acts, who had spent all that day looking for a lay and not a fight, a pot-smoker, a goof-off, a coward, and a liar.

But Conti was imperturbable. He readily admitted, despite Kay's scorn, that he had dropped out of school in the tenth grade, and was equally bland and unconcerned as Kay tried to say that he was stupid in addition to all else.

Kay turned to Conti's military training, and again Conti seemed to have the best of it. "Did you receive instructions to obey orders?" Kay posed.

"Yes," Conti replied and then elaborated. "You obey any order given by an officer or NCO no matter how asinine it may be. In combat, you obey orders or you could be shot."

Well, had Conti then disobeyed orders in combat at My Lai? Conti shrugged.

Kay was constantly sneering. "Did you," he asked, "see any

dead bodies at My Lai?" Conti said that of course he had. "How many?"

"Quite a few."

"Were they sleeping or did they appear to be dead?" Kay snarled.

"Well," Conti said with insouciance, "They had holes in 'em, so I assumed they were dead."

What had Conti done that morning, Kay demanded, while he was wandering around looking for the headquarters element? Had he searched for mines with his minesweeper?

No, Conti said.

Did he fire his weapon?

No.

Did he see anyone he knew?

Yes, Herb Carter.

Anyone besides Carter?

Not that he could remember.

Kay switched. "Were you under medical treatment that day?"

Conti: No.

Kay: Isn't it a fact that you were taking penicillin for venereal disease?

Conti: No. . . . Oh, yeah, you're right. I was getting shots.

Kay: Isn't it a fact that the medic was carrying penicillin to give you that day on that mission?

Conti: Yeah, I guess you're right.

Kay: And weren't you under the influence of marijuana on March 16, 1968?

Conti: No.

Kay: Didn't you smoke it that day?

Conti: No.

Kay: Didn't you smoke it the night before?

Conti: No.

Kay: Didn't you smoke it before getting into the helicopters that morning?

Conti: No.

Kay: Weren't you a constant marijuana smoker?
Conti: No.

And so it went for hours, Kay asking questions designed not to elicit answers—which he knew Conti would not give—but rather to show that Conti had spent that day at My Lai seeking to gratify a proclivity for "unnatural and immoral behavior." Conti was never perturbed by any of the questions, always cool and self-assured.

Hadn't Conti threatened a Vietnamese woman, Kay demanded, hadn't he said he would kill her child if she refused "to give you a blow job?"

Conti: Of course not.
Kay: Did you ever open your pants in front of a woman in the village of My Lai?
Conti: No.
Kay: Isn't it a fact that you were going through My Lai that day looking for women?
Conti: No.
Kay: Didn't you carry a woman half-nude on your shoulders and throw her down and say that she was too dirty to rape? You did that, didn't you?
Conti: Oh yeah, but it wasn't at My Lai.

That had happened later in the day, at another hamlet near My Lai, Conti said. He and several other soldiers had captured a woman and three men and "strip-searched" them. The woman had lost her blouse during the search and he had carried her to the unit on his shoulder because she was unconscious.

Kay: Didn't you cuss Lieutenant Calley out because he stopped you from performing a perverse, unnatural sex act at My Lai?
Conti: No.
Kay: Do you remember you went into a hootch and started to rape a woman and Lieutenant Calley told you to get out? Do you deny that occurred?

Conti: Yes.

Kay: Didn't you go around and tell members of your platoon about the number of times you'd raped Vietnamese women?

Conti: No.

Kay: You didn't like Lieutenant Calley, did you, Mr. Conti?

Conti: I didn't dislike him; I didn't like him. He was just there.

Kay: As a matter of fact, you hated him, didn't you?

Conti: No.

Kay: Do you remember one night, you were on guard duty and had a M-79 and you shot all your ammunition so when it came time to go on patrol, you didn't have any ammunition left? You remember that night?

Conti: That's right. I didn't have any ammunition left.

Kay: Weren't you mad at Lieutenant Calley for reporting you?

Conti: I don't think so.

Kay: You threatened to shoot Lieutenant Calley, didn't you?

Conti: Oh, I deny that.

Kay: You deny that?

Conti: Yes, I do.

Kay: Mr. Conti, isn't it a fact that you'd like to see Lieutenant Calley hanged?

Conti: No.

It was a long and frustrating cross-examination. Kay certainly cast doubts on Conti's reputation and morality. But he did little to shake his story of My Lai. When Conti finally left the stand, the question that faced the jury was whether Conti had hated Calley so much, was so morally depraved, that nothing he said could be believed.

But Conti's story made a vivid impression on the spectators, and a lasting one, as his person did. "Conti," somebody said that night, "he was the only guy on the whole operation who knew exactly what he was there for."

"Yeah," somebody else said, "he invented the slogan, 'Make love, not war.'"

And Pye Chamberlain, the radio commentator, thought Conti had added a new word to the language—contilingus.

Daniel was now in his final push. Before advancing with those who would corroborate and expand what Conti had said, though, he backed up briefly and tried with some success to destroy another of the defense contentions (at the same time, though he didn't realize it,giving Raby a chance to make one of those points about the conduct of war by Americans that he would make whenever the opportunity arose).

Major Charles D. Lane, an Army pathologist, came to the stand, examined Haeberle's picture of the bodies on the trail, and declared that all were dead and "there are no wounds that are inconsistent with small arms fire." And so much, from a medical expert, for the defense claim that the deaths had been caused by artillery and gunships.

Raby, in cross-examination, quickly made the one point he wanted and, as was his wont, did not press it. In his questioning of Major Lane, it was brought out that the M-16 bullet when it hits explodes into a multitude of fragments that destroy all the tissue over a wide area. Such bullets are similar to dum-dum or filed bullets. And they are all outlawed by the Geneva Conventions because of their mutilating effect on the human body.

It hung there, not followed up and not commented upon. Maybe Calley shot these people, but he shot them with weapons issued by the United States government and those weapons, like so much else about American policy in the war in Viet-Nam, were a crime, a violation of the Geneva Conventions on humane warfare.

Lane was a brief diversion. Then it was back to tying the final chains around Calley. Charles Sledge, a stocky black man from Sardis, Mississippi, was to tell of the final crimes. He had been Calley's radio operator.

Again, in its initial stages, it was just the "usual" tale of the march through an unresisting hamlet with killing everywhere. Almost immediately after the landing, Sledge said, "we came to a well in the paddies. A man stuck his hands up. Sergeant [Isaiah] Cowan yelled, 'Shoot the so-and-so!' I fired once and my M-16 jammed. [Daniel] Simone shot him and we moved up. We came on some huts and a woman and children. They were just standing there. They had no weapons. The people were from one to forty or fifty. There was a water buffalo in a stable and he had been wounded. I shot once to put him out of his misery, but he didn't fall. We moved out and came on Lieutenant Calley about a third of the way through the village, in the vicinity of the north-south trail."

Calley told Sledge to stay with him and together they moved south, coming upon some troops who had gathered about thirty or forty Vietnamese, mainly women and children and a few old men. The people were standing silently by the trail, a few squatting. Meadlo and some other soldiers were gathered around. Harry Stanley and Ronald Grzesik, two soldiers who spoke a little Vietnamese, went over to talk to the people, Sledge said; all said there were no VC in the hamlet, they were not VC.

What happened then?

"Calley told Meadlo to waste 'em, and we started moving on."

"When Calley told Meadlo to 'waste 'em,' what did Meadlo do?" Daniel asked.

"He started shooting into the people."

"What did they do?"

"A few of them started falling. I turned my head back and looked for only a second. I heard short bursts. I heard screams. Then I didn't look back no more. I walked along the east-west trail to the east."

Together with Calley and another RTO (radio-telephone operator), Sledge passed the eastern edge of the hamlet and went into the rice paddies. "Someone yelled that Sergeant Mitchell had some people over at a ditch."

"What did you do?"

"We went over to the ditch. It was outside the village. Sergeant Mitchell was standing there, smoking. There were

CHARLES SLEDGE

soldiers and Vietnamese people, about twenty or thirty, standing around in a bunch at the ditch—women, children, some old men."

"What happened then?"

"Lieutenant Calley walked over to Sergeant Mitchell. They walked back and started shoving the people into the ditch with their rifles."

"What did you do?"

"Nothing. I looked away." Then, Sledge said, Mitchell and Calley started firing into the ditch, their rifles in an underarm position. They were on automatic fire and were sweeping their rifles back and forth, only four or five feet from the people who "were screaming and falling."

A few minutes later, Sledge said, a helicopter landed in the paddies to the east of them. The pilot called out that he wanted to see whoever was in charge. Calley walked over, talked to the pilot, and then returned, saying to Sledge, "He doesn't like the way I'm running this show, but I'm the boss here."

Sledge would take us farther up the ditch, farther than just the trail and the ditch, though.

"We went up the ditch," he said, "and we came upon a priest almost at the end of the ditch. At least I think he was a priest; he was dressed in white robes. Lieutenant Calley started to ask him some questions and the priest, he would fold his hands and bow his head and say, 'No Viet, no Viet.' Calley asked him a few more questions and he kept saying, 'No Viet.' Then Lieutenant Calley hit him with the butt of his rifle."

"Where did he hit him?"

"Across the mouth. His mouth was bleeding and then he fell back a little and folded his hands and, sort of like pleading. Lieutenant Calley took his rifle and point-blank pulled the trigger right in his face and blew half his head off. The priest fell. Half his head was blown away."

Then, Sledge said, "someone hollered, 'There's a child getting away! There's a child running back toward the village!' Lieutenant Calley ran back and grabbed the baby by one arm. I don't know whether it was a boy or a girl. He picked it up by one arm and threw it into the ditch, and shot it. He flung it into the ditch, the deep end of it. The child was maybe one or two. Lieutenant Calley fired one shot."

What was Sledge doing all this time?

"I didn't do anything. I was twenty or thirty feet away." All he did was to tell Calley right after the shooting of the child that the captain was calling over the radio and that a chopper pilot had reported that something was not right and that Calley should report to Medina.

So all of Calley's crimes were now on the record, recreated in the testimony of those who had seen him commit them.

How would Raby try to knock down Sledge's testimony, at least that of the two individual murders which were as damning as anything said about the lieutenant yet, for there he had killed not an anonymous group but individuals face to face and alone.

What Raby did was try to cast doubt on how believable Sledge was. After all, Raby noted, he had been convicted in 1964, when he was seventeen, of being a Peeping Tom in Mississippi and sent to prison—a black man convicted of peeping on a white woman in Mississippi.

But for the direct testimony, Raby could do little to shake Sledge. Sledge admitted that he had placed little stress on Calley's statement after the meeting with Thompson, for Calley was always bragging about the fact that he was the boss. And Sledge said that he hadn't seen Calley firing at the trail intersection. Sledge, too, did not know for sure that the man at the ditch was a priest; he only assumed it because he was wearing white robes. "Is it not true," Raby asked, "that from the position of the man's hands when he was shot, you couldn't know whether he was reaching into his robes?" That was true, Sledge admitted.

Suddenly Raby turned dramatically and announced, "I request permission at this point to adopt Mr. Sledge as a defense witness."

Why? Here was a man whom Raby had attempted to make out a liar and now he wanted him as his own. With the jury out of the room, Raby amplified. "I want to explore two areas with him"—both dealing with events later that day at the night lager, or bivouac, when some prisoners were interrogated in the presence of the Vietnamese National Police. "This was part and parcel of Task Force Barker's operation and mission." The second point would deal with Medina's methods of interrogation and the captain's state of mind on both March 15 and March 16.

Daniel resisted. "If you want to ask him about these things, call him as your own witness when the defense begins its case. That's the proper time. Not in the middle of the presentation of our case."

Kennedy sided with Daniel for a change. Raby could not adopt Sledge at this point; if he wanted him later, he could recall him as a defense witness (as it turned out, Sledge was never recalled; other witnesses made these points).

There was little more for Sledge to say. On redirect, he told Daniel that Calley had questioned the monk for three or four minutes, had been standing directly in front of him, and the monk had made no hostile move then and Sledge had seen no weapon on him. He also said that Calley had fired at the child immediately after throwing it into the ditch, without any hesitation.

"Devastating . . . boy, that was a tough one. That's what's known as being taken by surprise." Thus did Richard Kay react to the appearance of Thomas Turner, a twenty-four-year-old University of Nebraska student and one-time member of the first platoon of Charlie Company. A tall, stolid, heavy-set young man with glasses, a slight mod cut to his clothes, Turner gave the impression of doing his duty reluctantly but doing it because it was his duty. Only Daniel knew what to expect when Turner appeared. The former soldier had never talked to anyone before, not the Criminal Investigation Division (CID), not any of the investigating committees; not the defense; most reporters who had done any work on My Lai were unaware of his existence until he turned up as a defense witness at the

Mitchell trial, and there his testimony had dealt only with Conti's reputation as a liar.

There was nothing to indicate where Turner would take us at first; he went through the by now stale story of his journey through the hamlet to the ditch. And then his testimony leapt with destructive impact at Calley. "I looked in," he said, "and saw a pile of bodies. They were lying there and they were covered with blood."

Had he seen any Americans at the ditch?

Yes, Turner replied, "Lieutenant Calley and Paul Meadlo were standing on the dike. Lieutenant Calley was firing into another group of Vietnamese kneeling in the ditch. He was about five feet away from them."

Turner passed Meadlo and Calley, heading north. "As I began walking by there, Lieutenant Calley was firing into the second group. He continued firing as I walked past. Then he changed clips. He fired for approximately ten seconds and then changed clips and started firing again. Paul Meadlo was firing, too, as I walked passed. Both of them were firing semi-automatic."

Was anyone else shooting into the ditch?

"Yes, other people were firing, but I don't remember who."

What were the people doing?

"There was constant firing and the people were squatting in the ditch. Some were screaming and crying."

Turner continued past and was joined by Conti and Simone. For more than an hour, the three of them sat on a dike north of the irrigation ditch. Simone and Conti, Turner said, were facing out eastward toward a tree line, in a perimeter defense, watching for possible enemy action.

But not Turner. He sat on that dike, he said, and stared back at the ditch. What did he see? "Small groups of people were being brought up and were being placed in the ditch and Lieutenant Calley was firing. There were several groups. I would estimate between ninety and a hundred people."

For an hour to an hour and a half, Turner said, he sat there and watched Calley execute group after group of Vietnamese brought to him by other soldiers.

When finally the shooting stopped, Calley started to move toward Turner's position. As he approached, "a young Vietnamese woman was coming out with her hands raised. Lieutenant Calley shot her several times. She fell over into a rice paddy, about seventy-five yards from the ditch." Calley, he said, was alone at this time.

Latimer was incensed. As soon as Turner was finished with his direct testimony, Latimer demanded that the jury be removed from the courtroom, and when it was gone he practically shouted in anger, his voice showing emotion for a change, rather than his usual deadening drone. "This testimony about the shooting of the woman is a surprise charge and a peripheral one, and I demand that it be stricken from the record and the jury so advised."

That was not all that enraged Latimer, who had been visibly more and more disturbed from the moment Turner appeared in the courtroom. "This witness," he declared, "has refused to talk to the defense. He never made a statement to the CID and he refused to talk to the defense. We had no idea as to what he would testify. The government, your honor, has consistently misled the defense throughout this trial. It had been claiming that there was one large group of people killed at the ditch. Now it is claiming that there were at least two groups and maybe more. And now the government is bringing in a new charge of murder. It is charging Lieutenant Calley with shooting that woman at the ditch. We are being misled. We had a bill of particulars of the government, we demanded when this trial began a bill of particulars and that has been violated. As soon as the government knew what Mr. Turner would testify, it should have filed an amended bill of particulars so that we could have been prepared.

"It did not and, accordingly, your honor, the defense moves for a mistrial."

After a brief recess for Kennedy and Daniel to consider Latimer's motion, Latimer expanded on his charge of duplicity. "The first notice of Mr. Turner's appearance," he said, "came with receipt of the transcript of the Mitchell trial just a couple of days ago." But that gave no indication what Turner would say here, and so "the type of testimony that Mr. Turner has given here, which was totally unexpected by the defense, that type of testimony is just devastating. It's crucial and critical. Consider the impact on the accused at this time. There has been introduced into evidence a separate and distinct count of murder."

Kennedy interjected mildly, "But, Mr. Latimer, I didn't hear any objection from the defense at the time it was given."

"I wasn't alerted to it," Latimer complained. And that testimony, he added, hurts the defense irreparably. Those witnesses Turner claimed were sitting with him on the dike had already testified and so couldn't be questioned now about Turner's testimony.

"You have the right to recall all those mentioned for cross-examination," Kennedy reminded him. (Daniel Simone was subpoenaed by the defense, appeared just before the Christmas recess at the courthouse but refused to testify, and Latimer decided not to press him; Simone went home for Christmas and never returned to Fort Benning.)

But that wasn't enough. Latimer demanded that the testimony about the woman be "stricken from the record. All this is very prejudicial to the defense. Your honor originally ruled to limit the government so that we could defend against specific charges. This testimony is not within the confines of these pleadings. To permit this evidence to stand would be a travesty and very prejudicial and a miscarriage of justice."

Daniel rose. Was the defense, he demanded, charging that the government was "unfair"?

Not Daniel personally, Latimer amended. The prosecutor "is lilywhite and has never been unfair. It is just that the prosecutor has the tools that are inherently unfair. It is the system that is unfair."

Now Daniel responded. True, there was no charge against Calley for murdering the woman, "but the government would contend that despite the fact that this offense is not charged, the testimony is admissible because it goes to the state of mind of the accused and to the intent to kill. His state of mind holds true throughout the episode at the ditch. His intent was to kill everybody there and that is what we are showing. Turner's testimony shows that discrepancies which seemed to exist in other witnesses' testimony about the killings at the ditch were not really discrepancies."

"If ever there was a case," Raby interposed, "where the government desired to have its cake and eat it too, this is it." Turner, Raby said, presented a fatal variance in the bill of particulars. "The government intentionally put on a witness that violated the bill of particulars. It is up to this august court to strike that evidence."

"Now wait a minute, Major Raby," Kennedy said, his patience nearly at an end. "You had your notice that this man existed and would testify when he testified at the Mitchell trial. You should have raised these questions before Turner testified and not after."

Now Daniel got back some of his own. "Your honor ruled," he said, staring at Raby with a slight smile of triumph, "that anything that happened at My Lai Four was relevant. And Mr. Turner's testimony is certainly relevant."

Kennedy thought for a moment, then ruled. "As far as the defense argument that the government had exceeded the bill of particulars, I'm going to hold the government accountable to one bill of particulars, the one it filed. Therefore, while the testimony about the killing of the woman is admissible to show Lieutenant Calley's mood and mind that morning, nevertheless, I'm going to strike it."

Daniel was incredulous. "You're going to strike it even though it's admissible?"

"The law to the contrary notwithstanding." Then he turned to Raby and Latimer and said he would rule on their motion for a mistrial in the morning.

Overnight, Kennedy did his homework, and when court reconvened, he pointed out discrepancies in Turner's testimony when compared with that of other prosecution witnesses, "but these are facts for the jury to decide." The whole testimony, he admitted, is very confusing, but he thought it was within the limits of the government's bill of particulars and while he would strike Turner's testimony about the killing of the woman, he would not strike the rest of that testimony and he would deny the motion for a mistrial.

"By your ruling," Raby said testily, "the burden of proof has been shifted to us."

"That's a nice argument, Major Raby," the judge smiled, "but it just isn't true."

And so the flurry which had the court in a turmoil for a few hours—for nobody wanted a mistrial, nobody wanted to go through the whole thing again—was over. The jury, with no idea what had happened—as it never knew what happened when it was sent from court—was back and Turner was back on the stand, ready to face a bitter cross-examination by Latimer.

It was not one of the aging judge's better performances. He knew little about Turner or what his vulnerable spots were, and he floundered, trying in vain to bewilder, trap, fluster the stolid, unflusterable witness.

There was nothing in Turner's background, despite Latimer's efforts to find something there. He was an average young man born in North Platte, Nebraska, who had left college to enlist in the Army and when his service was over had returned to college.

The only weakness the groping Latimer could see was that Turner was represented by an attorney, a law professor at the University of Nebraska, and that through this attorney he had initially sought a grant of immunity. So Latimer attacked there. He asked, as though it were a crime equivalent to murder, "Did you or your attorney originally attempt to get immunity?"

Turner: Yes, but we abandoned that.

Latimer: What offense did you commit that you needed immunity for?

Turner: I didn't commit any offense.

Latimer: Did you shoot anyone at My Lai?

Turner: No, I did not.
Latimer: Well, did you do any shooting at all?
Turner: Yes, at animals.
Latimer: Did you shoot all the way through that village?
Turner: No. I stopped somewhere in the middle.
Latimer: Well, were you just running around like animals?
Turner: Yes, that's right.
Latimer: How come, with all that shooting every whichway, you didn't shoot some of your buddies?
Turner: I don't know.

Latimer tried to assault Turner's story from every angle, but to no avail. He scorned Turner for claiming not to know the names of other soldiers he had seen firing into the ditch or the names of soldiers who, for an hour and a half, he had watched march group after group of Vietnamese to Calley at the ditch to be executed. "You can't identify any single solitary American soldier bringing those groups?"

"No," Turner replied in even tones. "I don't remember their names."

"You have good vision with glasses, but you remember Calley's name and Meadlo's name and then a curtain comes down over your mind. You don't have amnesia, do you?"

Hunting desperately for something with which to discredit Turner, Latimer at the end fired blindly.

Latimer: Are you a conscientious objector?
Turner: No, I'm not.
Latimer: Were you opposed to the war before you went to Viet-Nam?
Turner: No, I wasn't.
Latimer: How about after you came back?
Turner: After I came back? No.
Latimer: And you are still not opposed to the war?
Turner: I am now, yes.

Part of Turner's shattering impact when he left the stand was the futile blundering of the defense in trying to break him, and succeeding not one bit. He was certainly as important as

THOMAS TURNER

anyone, he cleared up discrepancies, but by its very manner toward him, the defense made him more important and in the eyes of the jury even more damaging.

As he left the courtroom, though, Turner stopped at Calley's chair and leaned over, whispering something in his ear. Someone just behind them thought he heard Turner say, "Hang tough," but no one was quite sure, and Calley himself said outside court later that he had heard the words indistinctly and did not know either.

If Turner had thrown the defense into enormous distress, James Joseph Dursi was to turn that distress into near panic. A tall, husky man from Brooklyn with dark hair and a trim mustache, in a well-fitting mod suit, Dursi was a salesman for Western Electric who was waiting to hear whether an application to become a New York City policeman had been accepted.

Daniel moved through the preliminaries with Dursi quickly; no one really wanted to hear that story again. But Dursi seemed in no hurry; he spoke slowly, remembered and recited the names of those who had been with him when he landed at My Lai, whom he had seen in the first few minutes. Sergeant Mitchell led Dursi's squad into the hamlet, where they found civilians, most of whom were in hootches with the breakfast fires going. "We gathered up about fifteen people, mainly children, women, and old men."

As they moved these prisoners along a trail inside the hamlet, Dursi saw Conti and Meadlo. "They had a group and Carter and I had another." Meadlo was holding his group, which Dursi estimated at twenty to thirty people, in a paddy near the trail. "He had them standing by a rice dike."

What was Meadlo doing?

"He had been sitting down on the dike playing with the kids, giving them things, you know, C-rations from his pack. He did that a lot when we went into villages."

Suddenly, Dursi said, Calley appeared and "asked Meadlo if he could take care of that group." Meadlo said he could and Calley left. "A couple of minutes later, Calley returned and yelled, 'Why haven't you wasted them yet?' Meadlo stood there looking astonished."

What had Dursi done?

"I moved my people out, down the trail. I heard M-16 automatic and semi-automatic fire from behind."

Where was Calley?

"He was on the trail, ten to fifteen feet from Meadlo."

Dursi did not remain to see what happened. "I moved my people around a small bend in the trail and came to a ditch bordering the east side of the village. I stopped my people there." Dursi waited there with his group for several minutes, and then "Calley came to where I was standing with my people, in front of the ditch. Calley came first and he was followed by Meadlo. Meadlo was all broke up. He was crying."

What happened then?

"Lieutenant Calley said, 'Meadlo, we've got another job to do.' He said, 'Kill the people in the ditch.' "

What did you do?

"We pushed them into the ditch with our rifles. We pushed them and some of those in the front jumped in. Some of the people started to cry and yell. Meadlo was crying and pushing the people. Then Lieutenant Calley gave an order to shoot. I can't remember his exact words, just to start firing or something. And Calley and Meadlo started firing into the ditch."

Did you fire when Lieutenant Calley ordered you to?

"No. I just stood there. Meadlo turned to me after a couple of minutes and said, 'Shoot! Why don't you shoot! Why don't you fire!' He was crying and yelling. I said, 'I can't! I won't!' And the people were screaming and crying and yelling. They kept firing for a couple of minutes, mostly automatic and semi-automatic."

Where was Calley's weapon?

"Lieutenant Calley's weapon was pointing down into the ditch. Meadlo's—well, I remember Meadlo changing magazines. They kept firing continuously for three or four minutes." minutes."

What were the people in the ditch doing when they were firing?

"The people were lying on top of each other. Mothers were trying to protect their children. At that point, Lieutenant Calley told me to move across the ditch before I got sick. I went across the ditch to the right at a bend. I saw the people. There was lots of blood, people were wounded, shot in the chest, in the arms, in the head."

Daniel had two more questions. Both attacked what he knew would be the heart of the defense.

Daniel: Did Lieutenant Calley order you to fire?
Dursi: Yes, sir.
Daniel: Why did you not fire?
Dursi: I couldn't go through with it.

And so another witness—the seventh—had described Calley as a cold-blooded murderer.

And Dursi was another who had refused to talk to the defense before the court-martial. Latimer angrily attacked him for this, as he had attacked Turner on the same grounds. "Did you," he demanded, "say that all that defense lawyers do is twist what you say and make fools of you?"

"Yes," Dursi answered. "I'm just here to tell the truth. I'm not a professional witness. I've seen how lawyers try to mix you up and confuse you. I saw fools made of Dennis Conti and his testimony twisted."

"And so," Latimer sneered, "you were afraid to talk to the defense."

"My story I told is damaging to Lieutenant Calley," Dursi said. "I know this."

"So you wouldn't even talk to anyone on the defense team, would you? Nobody asked you about specifics, you were just asked to relate your story and you refused, isn't that correct?"

"Yes, sir. I'm not a professional witness and statements can be twisted."

Despite his efforts, it is doubtful whether Latimer was able to persuade the jury that the reason Dursi wouldn't talk was that

JAMES DURSI

he had something to hide. So Latimer sought elsewhere to shake his testimony, but instead many of Dursi's answers hurt the defense.

When Latimer asked him whether it wasn't true that he had been ordered to destroy everything in My Lai, Dursi said, "No. We were told to gather the people together and move them to a central location while a search went on. We were told it might be a suspected VC stronghold and we might have to shoot, but we weren't told to shoot at unarmed civilians. We were not told to fire at unarmed civilians."

Latimer groped. Perhaps he could do something about this emerging image of Calley as an almost bestial executioner. What was Calley's tone of voice, Latimer asked, when he told Dursi to move across the ditch after the soldier had refused to fire?

"He told me in a sympathetic tone, as though he actually felt what I felt. He told me to get away across the ditch before I felt sick."

Rather than helping Calley, that answer, at least to some, presented Calley in an even worse aura—a killer so inured to his killing that he could stop in the middle, express concern for the stomach of one of his men, and then go back to the slaughter. One reporter, in disgust, wrote a mock lead for his overnight story (one, of course, he never sent): "A witness today described how Lieutenant Calley called a recess in his slaughter of women and children, showing a kind side to his nature, so that one of his troopers could puke."

Latimer made one final stab at discrediting Dursi. "Didn't you kill a woman and a child at My Lai that day yourself?"

"Yes, but—"

"I don't want to hear your explanations. Just answer yes or no."

"Yes. But let me explain."

Latimer would not. But Daniel did when he took Dursi on a redirect examination. "As I was moving away from the ditch," Dursi explained, "after I crossed it, I saw some movement in the elephant grass. I turned and saw what I thought was a person crouching with a rifle. I yelled, 'Stop!' But the person continued running. I yelled stop again, and the person continued running. I fired and saw something fly away. The person was still running. I fired two more times and then went over to investigate. I found a chogi stick. It seems that the first shot went through the woman's shoulder and killed a baby she was carrying. The other shots killed her."

Dursi left the stand. There was silence. No one came through the door. Kennedy looked questioningly at Daniel.

"The government rests, your honor," Daniel said.

It was 4:09 on Tuesday, December 8, 1970. It had taken twelve days of testimony and thirty-five witnesses to present the case against Calley.

That afternoon, in the press room, an unofficial poll was taken of the reporters at the trial. On the basis of the government's evidence, what did the reporters think the verdict would be—not their own choice, but what they thought the jury would decide?

Almost all thought the jury would convict Calley. But only two thought he would be found guilty of premeditated murder, and two thought he would be acquitted. The vast majority, feeling that no military jury would hand out the stiffest penalty to one of its own, felt Calley would be found guilty of manslaughter—which just goes to show how wrong reporters can be.

8
Of Booby-Trapped Babies

But Daniel's case was not yet over. There were still a couple of witnesses to be heard who could not or would not appear during those first few weeks. Just before he rested, Daniel had informed the court that he had issued arrest warrants for two former soldiers in Calley's platoon who had been subpoenaed and had refused to honor those subpoenas and, in fact, had faded from sight. Though he did not mention the names, they were Ronald Grzesik and Harry Stanley, both of whom spoke some Vietnamese and had on occasion done some translating for the platoon. And Daniel was still hopeful that he could persuade Meadlo to testify.

Because of the difficulties in rounding up these witnesses, Kennedy gave Daniel permission to reopen his case briefly if he could get them to Fort Benning no later than the day court reconvened after a Christmas recess.

And so the prosecution had one more day with its direct evidence. Both Grzesik and Stanley were found. Stanley, however, took the money given for his fare to Fort Benning from his home in Chicago and disappeared again. Grzesik bowed and made the trip from his home in Holyoke, Massachusetts. And Paul Meadlo at last agreed to talk for the record.

On January 11, the first day of court after Christmas, Daniel had his last go-round.

Ronald David Christopher Grzesik was a bored young man who knew what he knew, or what he was willing to talk about,

148

and what he didn't know or wouldn't talk about. When he took the witness stand, he had made up his mind just how much he would testify to, no matter what the pressure. And there were moments when, in his answers to questions from both government and defense, it was apparent what contempt he had for the whole process that had brought him from his home and from his job as a die maker to this trial.

And so once again we heard Daniel lead a witness through the early stages of the attack and the round-up of Vietnamese civilians. What were the Vietnamese doing?

"How do I know what they were doing?" Grzesik said. "They were in a hootch and we told them to come out."

"Did they resist?"

"Well, they didn't understand our language, so they didn't immediately come out."

Moving the people ahead of them and searching the hamlet, they ran into another group of Vietnamese being held by some soldiers; Grzesik didn't know their names, "they were just U.S. soldiers."

Later, he saw Mitchell standing by a hootch shooting some cows.

"What did you do?" Daniel asked.

"I shot some cows."

Then, at the eastern edge of the hamlet, Grzesik ran into Meadlo.

Grzesik: Meadlo was sitting on a small dike. He was crying. I went over to him and he was very upset. I tried to talk with him.

Daniel: Did you ask any questions?

Grzesik: I must have.

Latimer: Objection to this line of questioning, your honor.

Kennedy: Objection sustained.

So Daniel took Grzesik directly to the irrigation ditch and asked, "Who was there?"

Grzesik: Several people.

Daniel: Can you give their names?

Grzesik: I don't think so.

Daniel: Well, what did you see in that ditch?

Grzesik: Inside the ditch there were bodies.

Daniel: Do you know how many?

Grzesik: Thirty-five to fifty.

Daniel: What were they doing?

Grzesik: They appeared to be dead.

Daniel: Why did they appear to be dead?

Grzesik: Well, they had multiple wounds. I just glanced into the ditch for five or ten seconds, but they were all grouped within fifteen or twenty feet.

Daniel: Did you see Lieutenant Calley?

Grzesik: Yes.

Daniel: Under what circumstance?

Grzesik: Well, Lieutenant Calley—I walked past the ditch. I was called back by someone, I don't recall who. I had a discussion with Lieutenant Calley. He said to take the fire team back into the village and help the second platoon search.

Daniel: Did Lieutenant Calley say anything before he gave you that order?

Grzesik: He said, "Finish them off." I refused.

Daniel: What did you refuse to do?

Grzesik: To finish them off.

Daniel: What did he mean? Who did he mean to finish off?

Grzesik: I don't know what he meant or who he meant by them.

Daniel: What was his reaction when you refused?

Grzesik: I wasn't paying any attention to his reaction. I was paying attention to staying alive.

So Grzesik refused to "finish them off"—whoever "them" might be—and went back into My Lai with his fire team to help the search and destruction. And in the hamlet he saw a little more of the events of the day. "I saw an individual with a camera on the north-south trail. He was near a group of people—Vietnamese men, women, and children. There were about fifteen of them, I guess, the youngest about four, though some of the women may have had babies. There were other people around, some U.S. soldiers. Some of my fire team. Some other men from other platoons. I passed by and heard some shots from the rear. So I turned around. The people had been shot by the soldiers." This, however, was not the group of thirty charged to Calley; it was another group altogether.

Then Grzesik moved south along the trail, reaching the southern edge of the hamlet in time to see Carter being treated for his foot wound and then medivac-ed. A little farther along, he saw "a group of bodies. I didn't inspect them, but it looked like they had multiple wounds."

When Latimer rose to begin his cross-examination, Grzesik looked at him and sighed, and throughout the questioning, he seemed to sigh and take deep breaths frequently, as though annoyed or bored by the whole process.

Latimer tried to trap him in inconsistencies between his statements in court and those he had given to CID and the Inspector General, but Grzesik mildly pointed out that he had never signed those other statements. And as Latimer kept probing, Grzesik kept repeating, "Look, I don't remember. It was three years ago."

But Latimer went after the inconsistencies and he thought he had Grzesik on several in the CID statement.

Latimer: Didn't you tell the CID that you saw the group in the hamlet being guarded by two Negro soldiers?

Grzesik: I don't remember, sir.

Latimer: Didn't you tell Billy Thompson of the CID that you came upon two Negro soldiers who you can't identify guarding ten or twelve Vietnamese and one of the Negroes attempted to tear the blouse off a girl?

Grzesik: When I made this statement to the CID, Thompson was sitting across the table from me in a Holyoke motel and saying, "Did you see this?" and when I said, "Negative," he practically called me a liar. I don't know about that statement you're holding and I don't believe I saw any massacre.

Latimer then pulled out a statement made to Colonel William Wilson of the Inspector General's office in which Grzesik supposedly had said that he had seen "possibly one" atrocity at My Lai. But again Grzesik said he didn't remember saying that; he couldn't deny it, he just didn't remember it. "I don't know," he said. "By this time we'd had a couple of drinks already, so I don't know whether I said that." And Grzesik added, "We just kept filling the glasses—well, the officer was filling the glasses. We were in the same room."

Judge Kennedy was perturbed. "What kind of beverage were you drinking?"

"Alcoholic beverages," Grzesik answered.

"What kind?" the judge persisted.

"Gin, I believe."

The more Latimer tried to prod, the more Grzesik gave a stock reply: "I don't remember . . . " "I don't recall . . . " "That was three years ago."

It was all too much for Latimer. Finally he said sarcastically, "You just don't recall anything, do you?"

And Grzesik replied wearily, "It was two, three years ago. I went through—lord knows how many of these things I went through."

And Ronald Grzesik went home to Holyoke. He had added a little humor, a little sarcasm, another lesson in disobedience to orders and how to get away with it. Whether he had been worth waiting a month for, worth breaking into the defense case for, was a question.

But Paul Meadlo *was* worth the wait and the delay.

Once again accompanied by his lawyer, Paul Kessler, Meadlo arrived in court, wearing this time a green short-sleeved crew-neck shirt and green pants, his whole manner emotionless, almost dead—and his voice, for the most part, equally lifeless. As Meadlo took the witness stand, two United States marshals, a representative of the Department of Justice, and an assistant U.S. Attorney took seats just inside the railing in the main arena. If Meadlo refused to testify this time, they were ready to take him away in custody.

Calley watched Meadlo from the moment he entered the courtroom all the way to the stand, his eyes never leaving his former trooper, staring at him intently.

Meadlo sat down. Judge Kennedy looked down on him and told him he had been granted testimonial immunity by the Department of Justice in a grant signed by Deputy Attorney General Will B. Wilson. That meant, the judge explained, that no testimony he gave here could ever be used against him, nor could that testimony be used to develop other evidence that might lead to his prosecution. Meadlo listened, his head cocked toward the judge.

When Kennedy finished, Kessler rose. The judge waved him away in annoyance. "Mr. Kessler," he said, "I'm not going to hear any further arguments from you. Either he testifies or he doesn't." Kennedy looked at Meadlo. "Are you going to testify?" Kessler tried to interrupt. "Mr. Kessler," Kennedy snapped, "if you have anything to say, you can be heard in the United States District Court." Kennedy turned again to Meadlo. "Mr. Meadlo, are you going to testify this time?"

"Yes."

One could hear a sigh, the breath of released tension, swirl through the courtroom.

Daniel led Meadlo quickly to his sweep into My Lai in Mitchell's squad. "There was a lot of fire going on and we was all scared."

Daniel, as he had done with almost every one of his major witnesses, crossed to a spot between the defense table and Meadlo, blocking with his back Calley's view of the witness. Now the horror and tragedy of Meadlo's day at My Lai spewed forth.

Daniel: What did you do in the village?

Meadlo: We just gathered up the people and led them to a designated area.

Daniel: How many people did you gather up?

Meadlo: Between thirty and fifty. Men, women, and children.

Daniel: What kind of children?

Meadlo: They was just children.

Daniel: Where did you get these people?

Meadlo: Some of them was in hootches and some was in rice paddies when we gathered them up.

Daniel: Why did you gather them up?

Meadlo: We suspected them of being Viet Cong. And [he said this with the first real emotion he had shown] as far as I'm concerned, they're still Viet Cong.

Meadlo led the people to a clearing he thought was in the center of the hamlet, though he couldn't be sure. "There were thirty or forty people, some of them was already there. Conti and myself guarded them."

Daniel: What did you do when you got there?

Meadlo: Just guarded them.

Daniel: Did you see Lieutenant Calley?

Meadlo: Yes.

Daniel: What did he do?

Meadlo: He came up to me and he said, "You know what to do with them, Meadlo," and I assumed he wanted me to guard them. That's what I did.

Daniel: What were the people doing?

Meadlo: They was just standing there.

For ten or fifteen minutes, Meadlo guarded that group—men, women, and children. "It's hard to say how old the children were. Some was walking and some was not walking, they was babies." He did not know what to do next.

Then Calley returned.

Meadlo: He said, "How come they're not dead?" I said, "I didn't know we were supposed to kill them." He said, "I want them dead." He backed off twenty or thirty feet and started shooting into the people—the Viet Cong—shooting automatic. He was beside me. He burned four or five magazines. I burned off a few, about three. I helped shoot 'em.

Daniel: What were the people doing after you shot them?

Meadlo: They were lying down.

Daniel: Why were they lying down?

Meadlo: They was mortally wounded.

Daniel: How were you feeling at that time?

Meadlo: I was mortally upset, scared, because of the briefing we had the day before.

Daniel: Were you crying?
Meadlo: I imagine I was.

Once that group had been executed, nobody remained there
long. Conti, Meadlo said, had done no firing and disappeared.
Calley, too, went off someplace. For a while Meadlo was alone,
just wandering. He ran into Grzesik, had a short talk with him,
and then "just started gathering up more people, from the
hootches and the huts. I had seven or eight people, women and
children." He moved them east to a "ravine." There he saw
Calley, Sledge, Grzesik, Dursi, Mitchell, and two other soldiers.

Daniel: Were there any Vietnamese there?
Meadlo: Yes, there was Viet Cong there. About seventy-five
to a hundred, standing outside the ravine.

Meadlo added his group to that one.

Meadlo: Then Lieutenant Calley said to me, "We've got
another job to do, Meadlo."
Daniel: What happened then?
Meadlo: He started shoving them off and shooting them in
the ravine.
Daniel: How many times did he shoot?
Meadlo: I can't remember.
Daniel: Did you shoot?
Meadlo: Yes. I shot the Viet Cong. He ordered me to help
kill the people. I started shoving them off and shooting.
Daniel: How long did you fire?
Meadlo: I don't know.
Daniel: Did you change magazines?
Meadlo: Yes.
Daniel: Did Lieutenant Calley change magazines?
Meadlo: Yes.
Daniel: How many times did he change magazines?
Meadlo: Ten to fifteen times.
Daniel: How many bullets in a magazine?
Meadlo: Twenty, normally.
Daniel: How was Lieutenant Calley armed?

Meadlo: He had a M-16.

Daniel: What were the people doing after you and Lieutenant Calley shot them?

Meadlo: The people was just lying there, with blood all over them.

Daniel: What was the condition of the people?

Meadlo: I can't say what their condition was. I didn't get down in the ditch and check them out.

Daniel: Were they wounded?

Meadlo: They had wounds in the head, in the body, in the chest, in the stomach.

Daniel: Where were you when you shot at those people?

Meadlo: We was standing on top of the ravine and shooting down.

Daniel: Did you miss?

Meadlo: On automatic? Yes.

Daniel: Did Lieutenant Calley miss?

Meadlo: On automatic? Yes.

Daniel: Was anyone still alive when you stopped firing?

Meadlo: I couldn't tell whether they was mortally wounded. I didn't check them out.

Was anyone else firing at the ditch? Meadlo said yes, and ticked off Harry Stanley, Dennis Conti, Daniel Simone. And Dursi? No, not Dursi. Dursi didn't fire at the ditch.

When Daniel finished with direct examination, there was a brief recess, and as Meadlo left the stand, Calley stood up and greeted him. They shood hands, warily it seemed, and together with the defense lawyers walked out and down to the defense chambers.

What would Latimer do with Meadlo? Would he attack him—certainly as damaging a witness as had appeared, as damaging as Turner or Dursi or Sledge or Conti or any other. But there was a danger in attacking Meadlo head-on; after all, he was a wounded veteran, his foot blown off by a landmine. So Latimer decided to be relatively gentle with him.

He started with orders, and the defense contention that orders were behind it all and excuse for it all. What had Meadlo

PAUL DAVID MEADLO

learned about orders? "During a combat operation," he said, "if you disobey an order you could be shot on the spot or court-martialed." He had never, Meadlo said, been given any instruction on illegal and legal orders. As far as he knew, an order was an order and had to be obeyed, and that had been beaten into him from the moment he went into the Army. "During basic training, if you disobeyed an order, if you were slow in obeying orders, they'd slap you on the head, drop-kick you in the chest and other rinky-dink stuff like that. You're trained to obey your officers. If an officer tells you to go out and stand on your head in the middle of the highway, you do it."

So Meadlo was conditioned, even before My Lai, to act as an automaton; he was not bright enough to question that role, and it was his impression that such was the role of the American soldier.

Latimer moved to an area he was then in the midst of exploring with his own witnesses—Captain Medina's briefing the night before the attack, a briefing that he was claiming had so conditioned Charlie Company that slaughter was inevitable. Meadlo went along with that. Medina, he said, had told the troops "there was a VC organization in the village and everybody there is Viet Cong or VC sympathizers, and we was supposed to search it and destroy it, and that includes women and children, animals and livestock. We was supposed to destroy it, burn it." And so they went into My Lai. "I was scared and really expected a big fight, really expected all hell to break out."

But unlike others, Meadlo said he "did not go in firing." It was not until he reached the center of My Lai that he started to fire his rifle.

Latimer: And then you started firing into that group you had rounded up?
Meadlo: I didn't start—
Latimer: You did start firing into that group, didn't you?
Meadlo: Yes.
Latimer: You killed men, women, and children?

Meadlo: Yes.

Latimer: You were ordered to do so?

Meadlo: Yes.

Latimer: Why did you carry out that order?

Meadlo: I was ordered to. And I was emotionally upset. . . . And we were supposed to get satisfaction from this village for all the men we'd lost. They was all VC and VC sympathizers and I still believe they was all Viet Cong and Viet Cong sympathizers.

Latimer: Did you see Captain Medina?

Meadlo: Yes. And he didn't say anything and did not even try to put a stop to it. So I figured we was doing the right thing.

Latimer: What was your impression of Lieutenant Calley at this place where he gave you these orders?

Meadlo: I thought the man was doing his duty and doing his job.

Daniel objected to that, but Latimer rejoined, "I'm trying to find out whether he's acting like a Chicago gangster mowing down everyone in sight or whether he's acting like a man doing his job or like a lunatic or something, and I have a right to ask those questions on this line." Kennedy agreed, and Latimer had one more question.

"Was Lieutenant Calley violent and in a sense raving around?"

"No," Meadlo said.

Daniel did not get Meadlo for redirect until the next morning, and then he was sharp and pointed, his questions firing out in quick order, giving Meadlo little chance to think. It was as though Daniel had switched roles and was now the cross-examiner, leading and directing his witness—not, as Latimer was later to complain, in an attempt to destroy his credibility but rather to reinforce it and strengthen his testimony.

And that is what he did. He showed that Meadlo was confused as to exactly what Medina had ordered the troops to do in My Lai; "I just remember him saying destroy." But he remembered enough to expect to meet an armed enemy in battle.

And orders were what Daniel probed.

Daniel: Why didn't you fire when you got on line?

Meadlo: I don't know. There was a lot of firing going on and I couldn't tell whether it was incoming or outgoing.

Daniel: Weren't you ordered to fire into that village?

Meadlo: I don't remember whether the orders was to fire when we hit the ground.

Daniel: Wasn't everyone else firing?

Meadlo: I don't know.

Daniel: When did you first see a Vietnamese?

Meadlo: Right after we landed. In an open field.

Daniel: Did you fire?

Meadlo: No.

Daniel: Why not?

Meadlo: I didn't have my orders to fire.

Daniel: Was he a resident of the village?

Meadlo: He was a Viet Cong, yes.

Daniel: Then why didn't you fire?

Meadlo: I didn't have my orders to fire.

Daniel: Didn't you get orders to kill him from Medina?

Meadlo: No. And besides, he was being guarded.

(Even Daniel laughed about that.)

Daniel: When did you see the next Vietnamese?

Meadlo: In the village. He was thirty to fifty years old.

Daniel: Did you shoot him?

Meadlo: Yes.

Daniel: Why?

Meadlo: I was ordered to by Sergeant Mitchell, I believe. And, besides, why take chances?

Daniel: Then you gathered up people. Why?

Meadlo: That was my orders. It ain't my reason to say why.

Daniel: When Lieutenant Calley came up and said, "Take care of these people," why did you continue to guard them?

Meadlo: I figured he just wanted me to guard them.

Daniel: Why didn't you shoot them?

Meadlo: I figured maybe he wanted to hold them for interrogation.

Daniel: What did you do?

Meadlo: I held my M-16 on them.

Daniel: Why?

Meadlo: Because they might attack.

Daniel: They were children and babies?

Meadlo: Yes.

Daniel: And they might attack? Children and babies?

Meadlo: They might have had a fully loaded grenade on them. The mothers might have throwed them at us.

Daniel: Babies?

Meadlo: Yes.

Daniel: Then why didn't you shoot them?

Meadlo: I didn't have no orders to kill them right then.

Daniel: Why didn't you fire first when Lieutenant Calley said, "I want them dead"?

Meadlo: Because Lieutenant Calley started firing first. I don't know why I didn't fire first.

Daniel: What were the people doing when Lieutenant Calley arrived?

Meadlo: They was sitting down.

Daniel: The women, the children, and babies were sitting down?

Meadlo: Yes.

Daniel: Did they attack you?

Meadlo: I assumed at every minute that they would counterbalance. I thought they had some sort of chain or a little string they had to give a little pull and they blow us up, things like that.

Daniel: What did you do?

Meadlo: I just watched them. I was scared all the time.

Daniel: How many people did you take to the ditch?

Meadlo: Seven or eight people.

Daniel: Why didn't you shoot these people rather than take them with you?

Meadlo: I assumed we was going to hold them for interrogation.

Daniel: Why didn't you kill them?

Meadlo: I didn't have my orders to kill them. It ain't my

reason to figure what they was going to do with them. It was just natural procedure to hold them for questioning.

Daniel: Captain Medina's orders did not change that standard operating procedure for these seven or eight people, to hold them for interrogation?

Meadlo: No.

Daniel: What changed the order?

Meadlo: Lieutenant Calley said, "We've got another job to do, Meadlo."

Daniel: You said you were under emotional strain. Can you describe that strain?

Meadlo: Just I was scared and frightened.

Daniel: At what?

Meadlo: At carrying out the orders.

Daniel: Why?

Meadlo: Because nobody really wants to take a human being's life.

Daniel: But they were Viet Cong, weren't they?

Meadlo: Yes, they were Viet Cong.

Daniel: And it was your job?

Meadlo: It was my job, yes.

Daniel: What were the children in the ditch doing?

Meadlo: I don't know.

Daniel: Were the babies in their mother's arms?

Meadlo: I guess so.

Daniel: And the babies moved to attack?

Meadlo: I expected at any moment they were about to make a counterbalance.

Daniel: Had they made any move to attack?

Meadlo: No.

Daniel: When you left the ditch, were any of the people standing?

Meadlo: Not that I remember.

Daniel: Did you see anyone who was not shot?

Meadlo: I can't say. I didn't get down and check them out.

Daniel: Did you see anyone who wasn't shot?

Meadlo: There might have been a few. I didn't check 'em out.

Daniel: Now, Mr. Meadlo, one last question: Did Lieutenant Calley or did Captain Medina order you to kill?

Meadlo: I took my orders from Lieutenant Calley. But—

Daniel: That's all.

But Judge Kennedy let Meadlo finish, and Meadlo said, "But Captain Medina was there before the ditch and I assumed everything was okay because if it wasn't I assumed he would put a stop to it. And he didn't so I assumed it was all right. With all the bodies lying around, why didn't he put a stop to all the killings?"

It would have been a dramatic end, but both Latimer and the jurors had a few things they wanted to know. Latimer, as usual, did not help his cause, for Meadlo in response to a question said he did not remember Medina telling the troops to kill all the men, women, and children, just "to search and destroy."

And when he was asked by Kennedy, for a juror, why he had not searched the captured Vietnamese, he replied, "You mean the Viet Cong, sir. Maybe if we searched them they would have had a booby trap rigged up or something."

Then Paul David Meadlo limped out of court, alone again with his memories and his conscience. And as he left, one could not but wonder if either the United States or Meadlo himself had been served other than ill by his term as a soldier.

That was Aubrey Daniel's case against Calley. It was as direct and deadly as any case could be.

Part Three:
Calley on Trial
-The Defense

9
Fun and Games

There had been Meadlo and Turner and Dursi and Conti and the other dramatic witnesses; but there had also been the long stretches of tedium, with repetition and what seemed meaningless detail on detail put in the record only because the law required it. And so much of the time a deadly miasma had settled over the courtroom, over some of the participants and over much of the press which sat day after day listening. The tale of horror that first sickens the stomach, brings ice to the back of the neck, and chills the mind loses its power on its fifth or sixth retelling; the mind develops mechanisms to withstand the shock of constant recital of brutality and cruelty, and a cynical black humor begins to greet tales of man's depravity. For some in the court, the fascination was no longer the recital in the court but the reaction to it by others, the contests to see who could develop the sickest joke, invent the most bizarre witticism. Nerves were strung tight, frayed by the constant tension, by constant horror. Disputes erupted as real wrongs were magnified and imagined wrongs became dominant. The byplay became an attempt to restore some sanity, some means of living with, and in, an otherwise unlivable situation.

This trial was filled with it all.

There were the regulars, those who came to court every day and whom we watched and about whom we speculated. There were a couple of retired officers who sat stoically watching it all and rarely making a comment.

There was Dorothy Kennedy, the judge's wife, who seemed

to enjoy as much as he the banter with the press in court and our company outside. Sometimes alone, and sometimes with one or both of her daughters—one married to an officer in Viet-Nam and the other engaged to a soldier who was there—but never with their son, who wasn't at Fort Benning anyway and who disagreed strenuously with the judge about the length of his hair, Dorothy Kennedy would arrive in court almost every day and watch her husband at work, and watch the press at work, and always have a kind word for someone.

Daniel's wife and Raby's, a small, slim, attractive woman, were often in court together. Mrs. Raby rarely had a word to say. Mrs. Daniel beamed with pride at her husband's performance, as did his father, who seemed to appear at all the right moments, from the opening statement through the testimony of Calley and Medina to the final summations. Shirley Daniel was slightly pregnant when the trial began. In the last weeks, it seemed a race as to which would come first, the baby or the verdict; the verdict won, the baby arriving two weeks later.

And we watched Anne Moore, Calley's girlfriend, a Red Cross hospital worker at Fort Benning. She came to court almost every day and sat without emotion—and without a word to anyone who approached her, other than friends. In the dullness of the testimony, the speculation about this sharp-featured, slim girl (who, for some reason, always seemed to be written about as pretty) began to fascinate some. Was the high reddish-blond hairdo she wore a wig or her own hair, a speculation made rifer because when she wore her hair down a few times, it seemed darker and not as voluminous. What do you call her when you write about her? Calley's fiancée? Calley's girlfriend? What? Was the fact that she seemed always to remain in the background, slightly away from him when they were together, a sign that all was not well with them? Was there any truth to the story that as soon as the court-martial was over, they would break up? It was all meaningless, but it passed the time.

If we watched Anne, we watched all the girls who came to

court, and speculated about them, about their reasons for spending their time in that small courtroom listening to tales of death and destruction. We had been told, of course, of the thousands of letters (or was it a hundred, or just a few? Nobody really knew for sure) that Calley had gotten from girls, some with pictures of themselves and some even with pictures of themselves in the nude, offering everything from marriage to a one-night stand (so they could brag later that they had slept with a killer, and the most famous killer of his time? Well, there is that kind, they show up every time there's an infamous trial). And there were the girls who came to court almost every day, often different girls, bearing cookies and cakes and other treats for Calley in the hope of meeting him, and perhaps more.

There were some, of course, who surprised us. There were the two schoolteachers from Columbus who showed up in the pressroom one day, taking the day off from their classes in hopes of getting a seat at the trial and then reporting back to the students the next day what it had all been like. That day, unfortunately for them, they lost out in the public drawing for seats at seven in the morning and so they walked over to the pressroom hoping to talk some reporter into turning over his seat to them. No chance. But they hung around anyway and spent a couple of hours talking to my wife, Arlene. As it turned out, they were really less interested in Calley than in the press anyway, and at a break, when the reporters trooped in to file their stories, the two teachers stared with huge eyes, poked each other, and nearly swooned when they recognized some of the television reporters. "Why there's Robert Goralski! And that's Bruce Morton!" It made Goralski's day and Morton's, if it left a slightly less joyous taste in the mouths of those of us who wrote for a living.

And then there was Joanne, who for more than a month was an object of constant fascination, semi-amour—and in-formation. A tall, dark divorcée of mixed Indian background, she had driven to Fort Benning from New Mexico (where, she said, she was studying for a doctorate in anthropology) with her two children, installing herself and them in a motel near the fort. She wanted to witness, and become part of, what she thought was the most crucial and decisive trial of our time.

Joanne became, someone said later, the first press groupie in history. She seemed to date a different reporter every night (and had the gift of being able to drink most of them under the table), then complained the following night about the lack of amorous advances by those she had been with previously. Even in court she practiced her techniques, some days wearing a low-cut blouse with some of the buttons undone, other days wearing a tight sweater without a bra. Her skirts were long but buttoned, and she would sit in court unbuttoning those buttons all the way up her thigh while some poor reporter sitting behind her would stare in utter fascination, distracted and almost forgetting what was happening in the well of the court.

But if Joanne was a press groupie, she soon became closer to Calley than to reporters. One afternoon she stayed after court to meet him and moved in from there. Soon she was sitting in his seats in the front row of the spectator section. She told a reporter one day that she "found all men fascinating and sexual," but looked at Calley in a different way. And she complained to Arlene that she was always losing her scarfs, "and it costs so damn much money to replace them." Arlene said she had the same problem, losing scarfs, in subways and taxis, and had considered putting her name on them as one way out. "Oh, I couldn't do that," Joanne said. "What would happen when the fellow's wife came home and found it?"

With her slit skirts hiked up her thigh, with her braless blouses, Joanne drew stares and knew it, both in and out of court. Calley's included. But she always maintained that there was nothing but friendship between the lieutenant and her—and he said the same thing. They were just friends who spent a lot of time together, at her bungalow and at his two-bedroom apartment, but during those times they just talked and he played with her children. Before any reporter had been in Calley's apartment, we had detailed descriptions of it—and of him in his private life—from Joanne. And from her Calley learned much about us and our feelings about him and his case.

Joanne would often come to the pressroom during recesses, listen to our conversations or try to draw some of us out, and a little later we would see her talking to Calley, sometimes nodding in the direction of the reporter she had been talking to minutes before.

But much was forgiven Joanne just because she was a woman and a diversion when we needed one and because she added sex and her own type of glamour to a scene that was totally lacking in either. (For at least three of us, however, that was not true: Homer Bigart of *The New York Times* had married just before the trial and was spending his honeymoon with his new wife at a Ramada Inn in Phenix City; I got married the first week of the trial and Arlene was with me for much of the time at the Heritage Inn in Columbus; Tony Heffernan of Reuters got married, too, during the trial and had his wife with him; and some others, like Roger Peterson of American Broadcasting Company, brought their wives down on a couple of occasions.)

But like most things, Joanne was transitory; one day she was gone and although her name came up now and again, she did not return.

If we bore and even enjoyed Joanne, the same could not be said for another of our diversions—John Sack, the *Esquire* writer-editor who had become Calley's authorized autobiographer, collaborating with the lieutenant on his life story, having taken most of it down on tape (but not all of it; Calley would later testify that he had never told Sack or anyone except his lawyer and one of his psychiatrists his story of March 16 at My Lai). Sack would sit like a lord surveying his fiefdom in one of the five front-row seats assigned for Calley's personal use each day (disappearing only after Calley testified, not to return). He would scribble odd notes on a pad (stream-of-consciousness impressions of the trial, some of those who watched him said). And he would hand out Calley's seats at his own whim to those he considered deserving. Sometimes a couple of reporters would be given those choice locations;

sometimes it would be one of the television artists; sometimes he would be joined by an *Esquire* editor down from New York or an editor from the book publisher who was going to come out with Calley's autobiography when the trial was over. At one point his guests were Stanley Kramer, the Hollywood director-producer, and an associate. Kramer sat for a couple of days watching impassively through camera-like eyes, aloof and unapproachable. When Sack was asked by one reporter which of his guests was Kramer, Sack turned coy and refused to say, claiming it would violate the director's privacy.

Outside court, Sack would scurry off to the defense chambers with Calley and his attorneys, listen to their discussions, and offer his own opinions. His confidence in those attorneys was unbounded; whenever anyone criticized their performance, he was quick to defend them. And when Daniel tried to subpoena his tapes of his discussions with Calley in an effort to find out if Calley had talked to Sack about My Lai and what he had said, so that he would be prepared for cross-examination, Sack hired Richard Kay as his lawyer (and both of them seemed excessively petulant when no one seemed to care much, after a while, about the latest development in the fight to keep those tapes out of Daniel's hands and keep Sack from going to jail for contempt).

In the corridors at recesses, Sack would hover over Calley, fending off the approaches of other reporters who tried to get a comment or two from the lieutenant. Calley, Sack's manner indicated, was private property and he had posted a "no poaching" sign. That did not stop Sack, though, from berating those reporters he thought had dealt uncharitably or harshly with Calley in their stories. Sack's anger was usually in evidence in the corridors of the courthouse, with Calley a little distance away, watching.

For a while I was the focus of Sack's wrath and of his protective instincts. Both he and Calley had become upset when I had mentioned to other reporters Calley's smiling during a particularly disturbing part of Daniel's opening remarks, and when that description appeared in almost every paper around the country and on the television newscasts. (Calley said later that he wanted to shake my hand so I'd find it didn't have slime all over it; he was right; we shook hands and it didn't.) Both Calley and Sack seemed put out at me for my book, *One Morning in the War*, and Sack, to a greater extent than Calley, had taken offense about some of the things I was writing about Calley and the court-martial in *The New York Times Week in Review* section each Sunday. Early one afternoon in mid-December, Sack approached me just outside the courtroom door and chastised me for having given the world a totally false picture of Calley, for having made much of the world (that part of it, anyway, that read and or was influenced by *The New York Times*) think that Calley was a cold-eyed little killer. "If you knew Rusty," Sack said, "you'd know he just isn't like that at all. He's a bright, sensitive guy."

"Maybe so, John," I said, "but how the hell am I supposed to know? The only things I can write are the things I observe. I haven't talked to Calley during this trial. You've got a corner on him and nobody can get near him."

"He'll talk to reporters," Sack said.

"All right, when can I talk with him?"

"Well, he won't talk to you. But he'll talk to reporters who are friendly to him. And he has."

There were more than twenty reporters standing around listening to us. I looked at them. "Has anybody here talked to Calley?"

Nobody had. And when they began to press Sack about setting up an interview with Calley, Sack would have nothing to do with it and just walked away.

Later there were some changes. By February, after Sack was gone, we had all loosened up. We had been living together too long and too intimately for strangeness to continue, and Calley made friends with one or two reporters (though when they wrote about talks with him, he dropped them quickly, claiming they had violated his confidence). And he was open to brief conversations in the halls. "Where's that good-looking wife of yours?" he asked me one day after Arlene had gone back to

New York to start rehearsals for a new play. After that we had some brief but inconsequential talks. Later, when the jury was out, he began to invite some reporters to his apartment in the evenings for drinks. But that was all later, when Sack was no longer in evidence.

For Sack had become the *bête noire* of most of the newsmen at Fort Benning. When some of them would complain about their own papers' preventing them from writing some of the things they wanted to say, Sack would gloat that he was no longer a reporter but was now a writer, and that was why he had given up reporting. That did not endear him to the working newsmen.

And often he was in the pressroom, seemingly just to use the phone or stand around. But the story spread that he was listening to everything everyone said and then reporting back to Calley (Joanne could get away with that, being a woman; Sack could not). One reporter from one of the news weeklies became so angry at Sack that he announced he was going to circulate a petition barring Sack from the pressroom. Nothing ever came of that.

When Sack was in the midst of his battle with Daniel over possession of his Calley tapes, a number of reporters found themselves facing a dilemma. The freedom of the press to gather news and not reveal raw files seemed at issue. But Sack had been proclaiming up to then that he was not a newsman (a statement that both Daniel and Judge Kennedy threw back in his face with no little delight). And above that, there was the manner in which he had alienated so many news reporters. "This is the first time in my life," one reporter said at the time, "that I wouldn't sign a petition defending the rights of another reporter—if that's what Sack is."

But the trial and its effects existed not only around the courtroom; for those of us who were covering the court-martial, it was impossible to escape them even when we were away from Fort Benning. Instinctively, people in Columbus and Phenix City spotted us as outsiders, and if we were outsiders, we must be newsmen covering the Calley trial. Wherever we went, there was certain to be someone who would want to talk about it—and to argue with us and condemn us. Most of the local people were blindly and vociferously pro-Calley, and we were all considered the opposition. We would be stopped in the streets and told how we were responsible for crucifying Calley. In restaurants there were usually people at nearby tables to tell us that Calley had only done his duty. "They trained him to kill, didn't they?" one woman slashed at me one evening. "He did what they trained him to do, didn't he, so why should they be trying him now?"

And there was a night in a restaurant when a man at the next table spent more than an hour trying to start an argument with me about Calley. He defended the lieutenant on every ground he could think of and finally used his own experience as the clincher. "I put the final inspection approval on the *Enola Gay*," he declared. (That was the bomber that dropped the first atomic bomb on Hiroshima.) "And I'm proud of it."

There were some, though, who came to look kindly on some of us. Sarah, an assistant at the desk in the motel where many of us stayed, had been cold and distant when we first arrived. She told us pointedly that she was pro-Calley and "couldn't understand why they're persecuting that poor little old boy." She would take our money, but she wanted us to know that she wished we weren't there and it would be a happy day when we were all gone and things were back to normal.

But finally, when the trial was at last over and many of us were checking out for the final time, it was with tears in her eyes that Sarah said good-by. She still believed in Calley, but "we've grown to love you all."

10
"I Merely Say"

There was Calley, on the government's evidence a calculating mass executioner, marching from place to place, killing everything in his path and ordering those around him to kill while all his victims went to their deaths without resistance, with only screams and pleas for mercy. There was Calley, on so much direct evidence, the killer of the innocent, the murderer of old men, of women, of children, not driven by battle and combat, for there had been none, but driven, it seemed, only by a lust for blood.

Was there any conceivable way the defense could mitigate the evidence, could alter the picture, to create a portrait of this baby-faced lieutenant as only a soldier and not a murderer? It was apparent from the lines developed by Latimer in his cross-examination of government witnesses that he was going to rely heavily on the defense of orders. But would that be enough? Calley had not been a private, not an enlisted man, but an officer with a responsibility to lead, to guide, to understand, and to set an example.

It would be up to Latimer to say if there would be more. His opening statement would, or should, reveal the outlines of the case he would make for Calley. That opening statement was something everyone in the court had been anticipating, initially with some excitement but, as time went by, with almost a sense of dread. But then Latimer did have a reputation, and so no one was completely ready to write him off before his case even began. At least, it was thought, he would make a ringing statement on Calley's behalf. He would surely try to match the example of Daniel's finely tuned and eloquent opening, or even to top it. He was supposed to have the flair for courtroom dramatics that would lend itself to such a gambit. And then there was the year and more he had had to prepare for that moment, a year in which he must surely have spent some time sketching the outlines of what he would say and filling in those outlines with eloquence and rhetoric.

So there was at least some sense of electricity in the courtroom on Thursday morning, December 10, 1970, when Latimer, a fashion plate as ever in his trim gray suit, royal blue shirt, and darker blue tie, rose to open the case for the defense. Every seat was filled and almost everyone was leaning forward prepared to be entertained, amused, horrified, played to and, at least partially, persuaded for the next several hours. We would, we were sure, hear sarcasm, fervor, anger, every histrionic trick in Latimer's well-stocked repertoire.

It was not to be; Latimer did not seem up to the task, as he had not seemed up to so much before, and those who had seriously questioned his abilities were confirmed in their judgment.

He spoke not from a prepared text but from a few rough notes. He stumbled. He rambled. His voice droned and was often so muted that he was hard to hear or follow. There was almost no emotion. And when he finished, his listeners looked at each other and sadly shook their heads.

"It is now," he began, "the accused's turn to come forward with evidence and paint a picture of his acts and conduct from the standpoint of a platoon commander in charge of a very difficult and confusing operation. While the burden is on the government to establish every element of the charges and specifications, the defense will present testimony which we believe will cause you to return a finding in his favor.

"To remove all doubt and speculation, I can assure you that the accused will testify in his own defense, thereby giving you a full account of his actions, conduct, and behavior. Only in this way can you determine his guilt or innocence from all the facts and circumstances. In that connection, we will bring before the court the following facts and circumstances:

"He and his platoon were inadequately trained and instructed for this type of combat. The unit was understrength and it was the first time that some of them were tested under fire, in an assault operation which they were led to believe would be bitterly resisted. The accused had knowledge of many atrocities committed by the enemy against the Americans and South Vietnamese servicemen and civilians in the area. Many of the soldiers operating in the Quang Ngai area had been killed and others ruined for life by having their hands and legs blown off. The unit had on previous occasions been repulsed in its attacks in this area with disastrous consequences. Resentment and anger were engendered in the hearts and minds of the survivors by the means and methods used by the enemy and its sympathizers. The use of mines, booby traps, sniper fire, and ambushes aided by civilians of all ages and sexes had taken its toll. That area was openly known as a Viet Cong-controlled area and a deathtrap for American servicemen.

"Shortly before the My Lai operation, American units, operating on a search and clear mission involving villages in this very area, had permitted civilians to pass through their lines—to be shot in the back by those who passed through or with their assistance.

"The afternoon of the day before the attack, funeral services had been held for at least three members of the unit who had been killed in the Pinkville area. The nature of the services was such that a feeling of revenge and reprisal was created. That evening, the company commander held a briefing. He informed the members that at long last they were going to close with the enemy and have an opportunity to get even for the loss and ruination of their buddies; that the villages were being defended by the Forty-Eighth Viet Cong Battalion, which was one of the best units of the Viet Cong forces; that the mission was to search and destroy My Lai Four, Five, Six, with the ultimate objective being My Lai One. The company commander further stated that he had just received intelligence information that all civilians had left the area and that if there were any occupants remaining they would be Viet Cong or Viet Cong sympathizers. He ordered the village burned, the livestock killed, the wells contaminated and every living thing in the hamlet killed. No instructions were given on the handling of civilians.

"When the operation commenced, it was carried on by reconnaissance by fire and civilians were killed as the boys walked through the area; that the men became confused due to fear, with the result that all assault units killed civilians because of that and the briefing and the belief that anyone they encountered were Viet Cong. During the actual operation, other orders were issued, which will explain some of the events appearing in the prosecutor's area.

"Higher commanders were in the area, whether on the ground or in the air, and knew or could see what was transpiring on the ground, but not until lunch break were there any orders to cease firing.

"The evidence will further show that persons were shot and killed by helicopters right at the ditch before the troops arrived and the Viet Cong personnel, Viet Cong of military age, were killed right at the edge of the ditch. Yes, and that the Viet Cong personnel was in the area.

"Much of the evidence of the prosecution will be disputed, challenged, or rendered unbelievable by the defense testimony.

"I will not discuss Lieutenant Calley's personalized testimony because his life is at stake and I prefer to have him relate it to you first without it being diluted by me.

"I merely say that the orders were to kill every living thing."

Latimer had taken his opportunity and let it collapse. He had rambled, droned on for only nine minutes. He had barely outlined the defense that could, perhaps, win freedom for Calley. He had not even mentioned what would develop for a time as one of the major areas of defense—Calley's mental capacity and responsibility. He had not, at least in his statement, challenged Daniel's basic contentions.

And though asserting that Calley was not the only killer, he had as much as admitted that Calley was, as the government charged, a murderer and that a massacre of enormous scope had taken place at My Lai.

11
An Oscar for Raby

It was Raby's day and if he had ever had acting pretentions, he now made the most of them. The case for Calley began, after Latimer sat down, with the reading of depositions taken in Viet-Nam, in Quang Ngai Province, by Raby during an evidence-finding trip there a year earlier (accompanied by Daniel). Now Raby took the witness stand, to enact the part of those Vietnamese witnesses, complete to the use of broken, halting, falsetto pidgin English in response to questions read by Brooks Doyle, enacting the part of Raby (though he made no attempt to imitate the manner of the major), and to cross-examination read by John Partin, pretending to be Daniel.

Those depositions—four from Vietnamese and one from a helicopter door gunner now confined with a nervous disorder to a veterans hospital in Montana—took most of the day, during which Calley sat yawning and looking bored (a reaction duplicated by almost everyone else in the courtroom). What emerged was, at least partially, a portrait of the attack on My Lai along the lines the prosecution had, to some extent, presented; it was a report the prosecution did not challenge, and that the defense contended was excuse for Calley's action.

General Nguyen Van Toan, commander of the 2nd Division of the Army of the Republic of Viet-Nam (ARVN), declared that Son My village had been Communist-controlled, that the area was a free-fire zone filled with booby traps and mines, that the people had all been told on several occasions to move to resettlement camps by the government, and that all who remained "were Viet Cong or Viet Cong sympathizers or associated with Viet Cong families." Toan's belief was seconded by Linh Ta Vien, assistant director of the census grievance committee for the Son Tinh District, on the basis of what people had told him—he had last been to Son My, he said, in 1959.

If neither Toan nor Vien had any direct knowledge of what had happened at My Lai, two other Vietnamese did—Sergeant Duong Minh and Sergeant Nguyen Dinh Phu. Both had been interpreters assigned to the American forces, Minh to intelligence for the 11th Brigade and Phu to Medina and Charlie Company.

Minh had gone to My Lai with an intelligence officer, Lieutenant (later Captain) Dennis H. Johnson, and together they had, he said, remained with Medina's company command post as it moved through the hamlet. "I saw people killed," Minh-Raby said. "I ask Lieutenant Johnson why people were killed, why houses burned, all the animals, chickens, pigs, cows, and others were killed. He say he couldn't answer. I ask the captain, who look Spanish, why the soldiers kill all the people, why they burn all houses, why they kill all animals like cows, chickens, pigs, and water buffalo. He say he has been ordered to do these things."

Minh remembered this operation above all the others he had been on because "so many people were killed in this hamlet. People who were killed were women and children and old people. Almost all were killed by small arms."

Phu, almost to the letter, agreed with everything Minh said.

Daniel Hill had given a story which went along with some of Latimer's contention—and which had been disputed by the testimony of others in the air that morning. He said that some of the people were killed by helicopters and that he had seen three to five bodies in the vicinity of the trail intersection and several bodies in the ditch before the troops reached those areas. And he said he had seen at least one Vietnamese near the ditch running with a weapon in his hands.

There was a final question, aimed at what had been, we at

home had been consistently told for years, the heart of American policy in rural Viet-Nam. "Did you ever hear of pacification?"

"No," Hill said.

"Did you ever hear of the saying, win their hearts and minds?"

"No, I never heard that. But I heard that if you get them by the balls, the hearts and minds will follow."

The depositions were over, Raby had had his fun and games for the day, enjoying himself immensely. Now the defense witnesses would begin to appear.

But from these depositions, and from what followed, it seemed that, as had been so apparent during the government's case, the defense was striking blindly into every area it could think of, not opting for a particular line or strategy. The defense was confused and often contradictory. There were admissions that soldiers had done the killings and claims that the killings had been done by helicopters and artillery. There was the attempt to put all the blame on Medina, and there was an attempt to put it on officers even higher than Medina.

If, throughout the trial, the defense constantly berated Daniel for what it said was his technique of not following a consistent line of prosecution, and that was a necessary requirement, what could then be said for the defense? It could not seem to focus on a consistent line even with its first depositions. And its confusions and aimlessness would grow ever more apparent as it led its parade of witnesses through stories of the day at My Lai and the night before at LZ-Dotti.

12
'The Party's Over'

A week—and twenty witnesses—later, Daniel rose wearily and echoed the sentiments of nearly everyone in the courtroom. "There are," he said to Kennedy, "a hundred and five members of the company. We've now had some twenty here for the defense. Does the defense intend to call them all to tell the same story? When is evidence merely cumulative?"

Kennedy sighed and nodded. "I hope today," he said, "at least in this area. I hope they don't intend to call every member of the company to testify about that briefing. I agree that after a while it is merely cumulative."

If Daniel had taken us down that trail from the LZ on the western edge of My Lai to the intersection of the trails and the Carter medivac to the point where we could have traced it foot by foot and stone by stone in our sleep, at least his witnesses had the virtue of having seen the bodies and of having established that murder had indeed been done. Each had been a block upon which he built with his next witness. And when he felt he had made his point strongly enough, he advanced to the next area of his case.

But most of Latimer's witnesses—there were, of course, some exceptions—were called to testify only (as Daniel's first had about the trail) about the briefing they had been given the night before the attack by Captain Medina, about the orders he had given them and how they had been followed. There was little variance in what they said, or what they remembered hearing, or their impressions of that briefing. Latimer's aim was apparent—had been apparent all along, even before those witnesses appeared. He would try to shift this to a trial of Medina rather than Calley, shift the responsibility for the murders at My Lai from Calley to Medina, blame everything that happened on orders, make Calley again the forgotten man in the courtroom.

It was, though, one thing—as anyone who knew anything about the Army ought to have been aware—to have enlisted men talk about orders and obeying them, and another thing entirely to discuss those same orders in relation to an officer. Enlisted men were supposed to follow orders without question, at least most orders. But a man had bars on his shoulders because he was considered able to think, to reason, to lead, and his reaction to orders was not, or should not have been, the same as an enlisted man's. All the enlisted men in the company could talk about their orders and how they followed them, and still it would not excuse Calley, an officer.

And Daniel—growing more assured all the time—managed in a variety of ways to soften the impact of the testimony on orders by almost every witness, to turn the focus back on Calley and even sharpen it, to bring out clearly and constantly Calley's own responsibility and actions. At first, it might have seemed a contest. But as Daniel grew and more and more dominated the scene, it soon turned into a repetitious and sterile exercise serving little useful purpose for either side.

Even with the first defense witness, even before the tale of that briefing began to spin, Daniel wiped out several defense contentions in a cross-examination of Captain George White, who had been a platoon leader in Alpha Company of Task Force Barker. White described how attacks by his company against Son My village—against the area around what the Army called My Lai (1) and not My Lai (4)—had been turned back with heavy casualties, inflicted perhaps by civilians the unit had let pass through its lines. (This evidence, the defense said, showed there were no innocent civilians in the area, that everyone was a potential enemy—which might have been true but did not justify the indiscriminate executions of the unarmed, even if captured enemy, which was something the defense did not seem to grasp.)

Kay tried to push White as hard as possible into saying the troops, because of such actions, had grown to fear civilians— which, of course, was true—and so could be excused for shooting them down. And Kay tried to get White to list by name those Americans in his company who had been killed and wounded in those earlier assaults against Son My.

Daniel, of course, objected and Kennedy ruled that the list of names was irrelevant unless Kay could show that Calley had known all those men and what effect knowledge of their deaths and wounds had had on him. "You mean," Kay whined, in the hurt voice he so often assumed, "the names of individual American boys killed—that's not important?"

Kennedy flushed and his voice hardened. "Now listen, Mr. Kay, you know better than that!"

Kay's head dropped and he murmured an apology.

Then Daniel turned White, as he was to turn so many defense witnesses, into a government witness with a few sharp questions. On March 16, Alpha Company had been in a blocking position to the north of My Lai, designated the unit to trap any fleeing enemy moving toward the Batangan Peninsula and its sanctuary from American attack. White had told Kay that no provisions had been made during his briefing to evacuate or care for large numbers of civilians. Daniel carried that a little farther.

Daniel: There were no orders to kill numbers of civilians, were there?

White: No, sir.

Daniel: Your orders weren't to kill them?

White: No. (Then White told of stopping a man and a ten-year-old boy without shooting them.)

Daniel: You knew that the man and the little boy were not armed?

White: That's correct.

Daniel: And that's why you didn't fire?

White: Correct.

Daniel: Had you fired, would that have been a contradiction of the orders you had?

White: In my opinion, yes. We could see they didn't have a weapon. There was no sense in firing on them. This was a blocking position, but it did not mean that you had to fire on everyone who came up to you.

But then White had not been at the briefing for Charlie Company. Maybe something different happened there that led to different, and more tragic, results. The Reverend Carl Edward Cresswell of Emporia, Kansas, had been a military chaplain with the Americal Division. On March 15, 1968, he had paid a courtesy call on Lieutenant Colonel Frank Barker and found him and his executive officer, Major Charles C. Calhoun, poring over a map of Son My and discussing the operation for the next day. Barker explained, Cresswell said, that the attack would be launched the next morning and "if they received fire they were going to level it." Cresswell said he complained to Barker, saying, "I didn't know we made war that way."

Barker replied, "It's a tough war."

What Cresswell heard from Barker was what, in more explicit detail, the twenty and more men of Charlie Company called by Latimer said they heard from Medina that same night. First there had been a brief memorial service for fallen comrades, particularly Sergeant Charles Cox, who had been killed a day earlier by a mine. Then Medina had come before the entire company, gathered outside his command post, and told the men about the operation the next day and what would be expected of them.

Gene Oliver, stickpin and all, reappeared for the defense and said he remembered that Medina had said the mission "was supposed to be a combat assault into the Pinkville area. It was a search and destroy mission. Destroy, that's the word. We were supposed to level the place. I remember the statement, If there was one hot round caught, we were supposed to level that place. Captain Medina said, 'I know for a fact there are no civilians there.' He said, 'Kill the enemy.' That was it. We were supposed to destroy everything—chickens, pigs, rice, everything that could be of use to the enemy."

Elmer G. Haywood remembered that Medina had said, "There are no innocent civilians in My Lai. It was a free-fire zone."

Sergeant L. G. Bacon, a squad leader in Calley's platoon, added a few more details. He recalled Medina saying that they were going to the Pinkville area and that the 48th Viet Cong Battalion was there. They were "to kill all the VC and all the VC suspects, all the NVA [North Vietnamese Army] and all the NVA suspects, destroy all the food, villages, and animals." To him, a sympathizer "meant some person who was helping the VC to destroy me or kill me. A VC could be a woman or a child, and a VC was trying to kill me and was my enemy." He had, he said, "been taught never to trust a child or a woman or an old person."

Charles West was a little more colorful. A squad leader in the third platoon, West said, "We was on a search and destroy mission; we was to completely overrun the village, leave nothing walking, crawling, or growing. We was to kill all the livestock. We was to leave no living thing when we left."

In an understated way, Salvatore LaMartina, a twenty-four-year-old former rifleman from New Orleans, summed up the reactions of many. A man with long flowing locks, a long mustache, a psychedelic blouse, bell bottom trousers, and brown boots, LaMartina even drew a chuckle from the jury when he said he was now a welder. Examined by Raby, he said, "We were told we had a search and destroy mission and to go into the village and kill anything that breathed."

Raby: Did you obey your orders?
LaMartina: Yes, sir.
Raby: What were your orders?
LaMartina: Kill anything that breathed.
Raby: Were the troops on your right and left obeying the orders?
LaMartina: Yes, sir. Everyone was shooting.

Thomas John Kinch thought he remembered almost exactly what Medina had said. "Medina started out with words similar to, you all know what happened in a mine field a couple of miles from here. Well, tomorrow you're going to have a chance to get back at them." Medina ended his talk, Kinch said, by saying, "When he came through the next day he didn't want to see anything living but GI's."

And so the pattern was clear. With these witnesses—and with many more interspersed among them—the defense raised its major contention. Medina had ordered the men to leave nothing standing. And everyone had obeyed those orders.

But it wasn't quite that way, and that was what Daniel brought out on cross-examination. Not everyone had taken his impression of Medina's orders literally. Almost every witness remembered, by the time Daniel was through, that Medina had specifically mentioned that they were going against the 48th Viet Cong Battalion, that no civilians were expected to be in My Lai, and that Medina had made no reference to women and children (though Medina himself would contradict this).

Even those witnesses who seemed most convincing for the defense—that all that happened was the result of Medina's orders, orders they were obeying as they were supposed to, and obviously so was Calley—proved something less than that when Daniel finished with them. Some said they had seen no dead at all in My Lai, or only a handful as they wandered through the hamlet—and in light of the other testimony that had reverberated throughout the trial, even the jury looked skeptical at such answers.

And then some of the witnesses turned out to be, under Daniel's handling, more damaging to the defense than they had been helpful with their recollections of Medina's briefing. Elmer Haywood remembered, as Daniel prodded him, that he had seen Calley come from the direction of the ditch, talk to a helicopter pilot, and then return to the ditch. Though he said he had not seen Calley in the area again, he had seen "Conti and Meadlo firing into the ditch. They had people with them and they pushed them in. I assumed they were firing at them."

"Was it your impression that everything was to be killed?" Daniel asked.

"Yes," Haywood replied.

"But you didn't kill all the women and children you gathered up?"

"No."

Sergeant Bacon didn't shoot everyone either, though when Daniel tried to get him to explain why, he could only say, "I don't know, sir." He had gathered up large groups and then "told the men to take these people to Lieutenant Calley." What happened to them after that, he didn't know and hadn't tried to find out.

"You disobeyed Captain Medina's orders, didn't you?" Daniel asked.

When Kay objected to that question, Kennedy overruled him, telling Bacon he could "answer if you mean by disobeying not killing everyone in the village."

Bacon thought for a moment and said, "Sir, I don't know. I can't say yes and I can't say no."

"You didn't kill all those people that you had, did you?" Daniel snapped.

"No, sir."

And there were some witnesses who added a further dimension to the picture of the slaughter at My Lai. That dimension, though, was just one in the entire portrait; if it helped the defense at all it was only by showing that Calley was not the only killer; but if the defense had tried to cast aspersions on some prosecution witnesses because they had killed at My Lai and so were not to be believed, what could be said for defense witnesses who had killed too? When such witnesses left the court, there was a kind of head-shaking among observers and the question was asked: Why had Latimer called them in the first place—they had helped his case hardly at all.

Charlie West, the tall, black, former squad leader from Chicago, was called apparently to give credence to several defense theories—that Medina's orders had been obeyed by everyone, and that some prosecution witnesses, Conti in particular, could not be believed because they were pot smokers. And on direct examination West made these points. But what he did basically was discredit himself in the process.

His squad had swept through My Lai, he said, behind the first and second platoons, though staying mainly in the northern part of the hamlet. At one point, he said, he had met Calley and told him, "'I think your people are moving too much into our area and not searching enough.' So he said okay and moved his people out." (Calley was to deny any such encounter.)

West's squad then "encountered about ten people. We stopped and apprehended them. One of the guys said what are we supposed to do with them?"

"What did you do with them?" Latimer asked.

"Well, I said, we are supposed to kill every living thing. But I tried to call my platoon leader, Lieutenant LaCross. While I was doing that, some of the guys opened up. I turned around once the people were wounded and figured I might as well shoot, too, because that was our mission. They were wounded and wasn't no one to help them, so I shot them, too. We killed about ten persons."

Daniel was not about to let that stand unchallenged, as though what West had done was just common and unquestioned practice.

Daniel: When did you encounter the people that you shot?

West: I shot?

Daniel: You testified on direct examination that you shot them.

West: All right. I'll go for that.

Daniel: When did you encounter them?

West: When I saw 'em, they was coming up the trail. I don't know whether they was walking or not. When I encountered them, they was just there.

Daniel: How many were children?

West: I don't know.

Daniel: More than one?

West: Yes.

Daniel: More than two?

West: Yes.

Daniel: Were some of them young girls?

West: I don't know.

Daniel: Isn't it a fact that one of your men tried to molest one of those young girls?

West: He tore her blouse off, if you call that molest.

Daniel: Who fired first at this group?

West: I don't know.

Daniel: Those people weren't armed, were they?

West: I didn't see any weapons on them.

Daniel: Then why did he fire at them?

West: Why? I figured he thought it was his orders to kill everything in the village.

Daniel: Was it also his orders to tear her blouse off?

West didn't have to answer that; Daniel had made his point and withdrew the question as soon as Latimer rose to object.

But Daniel was not through with West. Systematically, he took him apart. He pressed West on his own part in the killing. "The reason I fired was because the people were already wounded and I figured it was our orders to kill every living thing and besides I figured we ain't going to leave them here dying and I figured we'd put them out of their misery."

There was no need to press any farther with this; the point had been made. But Daniel was to score more points, for West proceeded to say that he had not killed all the prisoners he captured. "We more or less took it on ourselves to try and catch them to interrogate them rather than kill them." And when the shooting had stopped, he was holding more than thirty unharmed prisoners.

West, of course, had shown—but then so had so many others—that Calley was not the only killer at My Lai that day, not the only mass killer. (But was there another officer, rather than an enlisted man, who had acted as mass executioner? There was never any evidence of that.) People were being killed everywhere in My Lai and an awful lot of people were doing the killing, men from the first and the second and the third platoons.

The indiscriminate wave of killing was the core of testimony by others, too. Both Salvatore LaMartina and Leonard Gonzalez, members of Brooks's second platoon, told how they had left My Lai and gone to a hamlet a little distance north. With them was a soldier named Gary D. Roshevitz, carrying an M-79 grenade launcher.

Kay: Did you see any bodies shot?

Gonzalez: Right, sir.

Kay: Women and children?

Gonzalez: Right, sir, women and children, about twenty-five of them in the northeastern part of My Lai Four.

Kay: Did you see any other bodies?

Gonzalez: Right, sir. About ten of them, in that place north of My Lai. They were all women and they were all nude.

Kay: Were there any soldiers from your platoon there?

Gonzalez: Right, sir. Roshevitz, he was there. He had an M-79. Those women, they died from a canister round from his M-79.

In the macabre aura of the trial, that was good for a few laughs over the next few days—ten women, stripped and killed by one canister round of a grenade launcher.

The defense wanted it both ways, and every way. It wanted to show that the slaughter had been indiscriminate and almost unanimous, and then it wanted to show there had been no slaughter at all. For that, there was Sergeant Isaiah Cowan. If Charles West managed to destroy his own credibility, Cowan went even farther—he came close to destroying himself as a useful member of the Army, and he probably did as much as anyone who testified for Calley to hurt the lieutenant.

Cowan had been Calley's platoon sergeant, and thus the man on whom the lieutenant should have leaned to run his men. In his direct testimony, Cowan talked about the briefing: they were going on "a search and destroy mission and the onliest thing we would find there would be VC and VC sympathizers. We would sweep through the village and everything there we was to kill it, to destroy the village."

Throughout his testimony, Cowan never talked about the Vietnamese as people: they were always "personnel." "I saw one personnel, sir," he would say. And throughout the entire hamlet, though he had been in the rear ranks following the first platoon on its sweep, he had seen only five bodies, scattered and not in a group. He had never seen Calley shoot anyone and, in fact, the first time he saw Calley after the initial landing at My Lai was at the eastern edge of the hamlet.

Daniel took that testimony and chopped it and Cowan into fish bait, drawing from Cowan implications that the sergeant obviously did not want to state directly for the record. Cowan had been Calley's platoon sergeant for nearly three months, Daniel drew from him immediately, had felt loyalty to him, and "would not like to see him convicted."

In fact, Cowan didn't want anything to happen to any of the soldiers who had been in his platoon. A career noncom with eighteen years of service, he found himself caught in a trap. Anything he said about the conduct of his men would reflect on his performance as their sergeant, and so he was determined to say as little as he could. He consistently maintained that he had seen nobody that he could remember all through the hamlet until he came upon Calley an hour or an hour and a half after the landing.

When he encountered the lieutenant, Calley was on a trail with "ten or fifteen personnel" and a large number of men of the first platoon. The lieutenant, Cowan said, was interrogating "the personnel"—although no Vietnamese interpreter was there, Stanley and Grzesik, the two troopers who spoke some Vietnamese, were not there, and Calley himself did not speak any Vietnamese. The personnel, Cowan admitted, consisted of "males, females, and keeds, all the way up."

Daniel: How close were you to Lieutenant Calley?
Cowan: I don't know.
Daniel: Did you have any conversation with him?

Cowan: I don't recall having any conversation with him.

Daniel: Well, what did you do?

Cowan: This was a control problem. The men had stopped at or near the edge of the village and were all bunched up. The VC could have been preparing a counterattack and one mortar would have killed all my men. I immediately moved them out and spread them out.

Daniel: Did you discuss this with Lieutenant Calley?

Cowan: I couldn't stop at this critical point. I immediately moved the men out to a perimeter to keep the VC from running into our position if they made a counterattack.

Daniel: You made this decision on your own? Even though Lieutenant Calley was there and the men were with him?

Cowan: Yes, sir. He was interrogating the personnel.

Daniel: So you moved the men away without even checking with Lieutenant Calley?

Cowan: Yes, sir.

It was an appalling picture, a picture of an incompetent officer risking the lives of his men without thought, letting them gather in a group where they could be wiped out with ease—risking their lives, that is, unless he knew there was no danger of any enemy action.

But then Cowan's opinion of Calley as an officer was not exactly a secret. It was there, of course, by implication in his testimony. In the past, Cowan had told others that Calley was the worst officer he had ever served under in all his years in the Army. And he had told Medina a little later that "either Calley goes or I go"—Calley was shifted to command of the weapons platoon.

If the picture Cowan left was of an aimless operation, confusion and aimlessness were also the brunt of the testimony of Michael Bernhardt. But his was a tale of confusion and aimlessness not just at My Lai but throughout his experience in Viet-Nam.

When Latimer asked him to describe the combat missions he had taken part in while in Viet-Nam, Bernhardt, a bright, sardonic, and often cynical young man, not much taller than Calley, said, "I wouldn't know exactly how to describe the missions. We didn't know what we were doing most of the time. It seems to me that we were just walking around trying to draw fire."

Bernhardt agreed with others about what Medina had said the morning of March 16 would bring and what they should do—which seemed the only reason he had been called to testify. But he gave a new and insightful view of that briefing and his interpretation of it. "I had expected that the village might be deserted when we got there. I didn't expect to encounter the enemy, that's for certain."

"You didn't believe Captain Medina?" Latimer asked aghast.

"Nope."

It remained for the jury, through a question by Salem, to find out why Bernhardt had not believed what Medina said about a battle at My Lai.

"We never met the enemy head on, not if we could help it," the young former soldier, now a student, boat maker, and surveyor in Tarpon Springs, Florida, explained. "Most of our casualties were from mine fields and booby traps. I didn't think it would pay the enemy to have a World War Two battle. They were doing too well without it."

Was My Lai an aberration, as so many claimed, the orders far from ordinary and the results an isolated, horrifying, and not-repeated incident in Viet-Nam? Thomas John Kinch was called by the defense to show that My Lai was anything but unusual, that the orders he had heard Medina give on March 15 were not extraordinary or surprising.

He was, of course, Raby's witness—for this was the area that Raby drove after whenever he could; that My Lai was part of a common pattern in Viet-Nam, the results of overall American policy. Raby began immediately to ask him whether he had ever before that March 15 received orders to kill unarmed persons. Daniel quickly objected and the jury was sent from the room while the issue was argued.

What Raby obviously wanted with Kinch's story was to show that if such orders and their execution were common in Viet-Nam, then they were no longer illegal on the ground that a common action or pattern in a war ceases to become illegal just because it becomes universal policy. "The men," Latimer argued, "were being led to believe that orders are legal when they are repeated over and over. If I were a soldier and told to kill unarmed civilians, I might resist the first time. But after a while, I might begin to think it was standard practice and the way higher officers conducted this war."

Before he ruled on whether to let the jury hear Kinch's story, Kennedy wanted to hear it himself. And so Kinch told how late in February, 1968, before being assigned as a replacement to Charlie Company, he had been stationed at LZ-Charlie Brown near Duc Pho. One day he was ordered by a Lieutenant Lowe, who had just taken command of his weapons squad, to go down to a village south of Duc Pho, "where we had been several times before, and kill all the men, women, and children. Before we got down there, we talked Lieutenant Lowe into killing just the young men of military age. When we got to the village, I saw a young man leaning on a fishing net. I told him to get out of the village. He smiled and I said it again, urgently. But he just smiled. Then I heard Lowe and Sergeant Palmer coming around a hootch. So I yelled, 'I've got a young gook here.' Lowe said, 'Haven't you killed him yet?' And he ordered me to kill him. So I shot him."

Kinch and his squad went over to another village and later in the afternoon returned to the original one. "I saw the body with its arm cut off. They said it would be said he'd jumped me and I shot him in self-defense. That he'd had a grenade and it blew his arm off."

When Kinch finished, Kennedy looked at Raby, Latimer, and the defense table quizzically, with a certain surprise. "Are you sure you want to get this testimony in? Because if you are, I'll let it in."

"Yes," Raby said.

"Now, listen. The original order was to kill everyone. These men talked the lieutenant out of it."

"All right," Raby said grimly, "we'll withdraw this testimony."

"You have to make up your own mind," Kennedy said. "I'll let it in if you want it."

"No, no," Raby said. "You've just given trial counsel a base to argue from on this witness's testimony."

"Come now, Major Raby," Kennedy smiled, "he's not stupid. He'd figure this out for himself."

So the jury never did hear from Kinch how orders to kill, to massacre, were not all that uncommon; nor did the jury hear how on one occasion, at least, the soldiers had rebelled and talked their officer into rescinding that order.

But in some of his testimony, Kinch did help the defense turn the light back on Medina once again. He had seen Medina kill the woman in the field—as had Bernhardt and others. He, too, had seen the young boy killed near the group of bodies at the trail intersection, near the Carter medivac. "I heard screams," he said. "I noticed a boy running toward us. The boy was screaming and running toward us. An automatic weapon opened up and the boy fell to the ground. He got up again and the automatic weapon opened up again. He fell to the ground and didn't get up this time."

That boy, Kinch said, he could remember distinctly not just because of what had happened but because of the red shirt he was wearing. That recollection showed, perhaps, how elusive is the human memory. Others who saw the same killing remembered the boy in different ways, as wearing only a pair of light-colored pants or as wearing black pajamas.

And according to Kinch, Medina knew exactly what was happening in My Lai that day. He had been "about ten to twenty feet from him all day," Kinch said. "I followed him throughout the whole village." If Kinch had seen twenty bodies and maybe more at the trail intersection, then so had Medina. If Kinch had seen perhaps fifty or more bodies in the ditch, then so had Medina. If Kinch had seen bodies all through the hamlet, then so had Medina.

And Kinch, too, said he had heard Medina on the radio. "Was there a message relating to body count?" he was asked.

"Yes, sir. It was late afternoon when that happened. Someone had called down on Captain Medina's radio and asked for a body count and Captain Medina replied, 'Three hundred and ten.'"

There had been another call to Medina earlier that day, too, Kinch said. He was standing about ten feet away when the captain took a message from another helicopter. He heard Medina say, "I don't know. I'll have to call forward and find out."

What did Medina do?

"He called forward and said, 'The party's over. That's enough shooting for the day.'"

As the trial recessed for a long Christmas holiday—with Judge Kennedy leaning across the bench and wishing particular holiday cheer to Calley—the main thrust of the defense seemed all too clear. It was to put Medina in the dock. Could that possibly succeed? Would proving Medina's culpability do anything to wash away what Calley had done himself, or even to mitigate it? Whether it would or not, it seemed the best the defense could hope at that moment.

13
The Missing Witness

He would have seemed a crucial witness, would Herb Carter.
Yet he was the absent man. Each day, as each witness
described his wanderings through My Lai, the point of
reference both in time and place was Herb Carter's medivac.
Each day, as the witnesses came through the courtroom door
on the way to the stand, we looked for the chunky black figure
of Carter, but it was never he. Questions of both Daniel and the
defense were fruitless; there was no indication that Carter
would be called. And then the rumor started that Carter had
not been called by either side because nobody knew where he
was and both sides were looking for him.

Late on the night of December 14, through a series of
telephone calls, I was on the phone with Herb Carter, who said
he was then broke and living with some friends in Palo Alto,
California. During that long, rambling talk, Carter said he was
anxious to testify, almost demanding to testify, but that no one
had been in touch with him.

"Why do you want to testify, Herb?" I asked him.

Carter told me that he thought Calley was getting a raw deal,
was being railroaded. Despite what he had seen Calley do—he
had been helping Dursi guard one of the groups near the trail
intersection when Calley had approached Meadlo and Conti
who were holding another group—he thought it was wrong to
go after Calley alone. He wanted to testify that the night before
the attack, he had been on his way back to his bunker from the
ammo depot where he had been collecting a supply of grenades

(he was a tunnel rat and thought he would need extras), and he had heard Barker and Medina talking. "They had found out there wasn't going to be no enemy there," Carter told me, "but that wasn't going to change the orders nohow."

After I finished talking to him, I called both Daniel and Raby and gave them Carter's address and telephone number.

The next day, though, it seemed that neither the government nor the defense wanted any part of Herb Carter. In Viet-Nam he had been accused of committing a number of atrocities himself in the weeks before My Lai. And he had changed, or embellished, his story of My Lai several times. If he stayed with the story he had told me, he could hurt both sides, perhaps more than he could help either.

It seemed to me, though, that since Carter had become such a prominent figure in the testimony, he ought to have a chance to tell what he knew or thought he knew. I decided to put a little pressure on to get Carter to court. That afternoon I told Bob Goralski of NBC where Carter was and how to locate him and what to say to him. An NBC camera crew went to Palo Alto and that night on NBC's Nightly News, there was Herb Carter, shabbily dressed, repeating the bare outlines of what he had told me—that the troops had attacked and slaughtered an innocent village and that higher officers had known it would happen and had done nothing to stop it.

Judge Kennedy saw that telecast and the next morning, unaware of my part in the arrangements (Goralski did not tell him and so, to this day, Kennedy still does not know that I set up the Carter imbroglio), he called Goralski into his office, chewed him out, and lectured him about breaking ground rules by having his organization interview witnesses connected with the case.

Then, in open court, Kennedy lectured the entire press. First, he said that he had seen Carter on the telecast and he asked both Daniel and Latimer, "Let me inquire now, does either side plan on calling this Herbert Carter as a witness?"

"The government does not," Daniel said.

"I don't know," Latimer said. "The best I can say is I'm on

dead center. Maybe yes, maybe no. He was interviewed originally by the CID. But nobody from the defense has ever talked to him." That was not quite so. After my phone call to Raby, Brooks Doyle had called Carter and had a long interview with him.

Then Kennedy looked at the thirty reporters in the room. "There is a direct danger to either side and to these proceedings if interviews are given by prospective witnesses," he said. "I was highly suspicious of the press when this case started. But I have seen that you are content to report the facts as they unfold in the courtroom. While I can't take any action personally against you for legal violations, and I can't rely on the Justic Department to take legal action against the news media for contempt, let me say this: if any media interviews any witness and reports on it, that media will be barred from this courtroom and from Fort Benning."

But the question remained: Would Herb Carter testify?

Soon after the Christmas recess, he arrived at Fort Benning under subpoena as a witness for the defense. No longer was he seedy. He was groomed and almost psychedelic in his new clothes. "How do you like these threads?" he demanded when he saw me. He had arrived in a Cadillac limousine from Atlanta, from Fort McPherson, where he had just testified at one of the interminable pretrial hearings for Ernest Medina. And there he had thrown the court into something of a panic, calling the judge, "Baby," preening about the courtroom, effusively admiring F. Lee Bailey's mink coat, and in general just having a good time.

He was not going to change at Fort Benning. He came to the door of the pressroom and called me out. As lawyers—Daniel, Raby, Latimer, Partin, Kay—strolled past, as Colonel Kennedy wandered by, Carter and I stood in the corridor talking, his eyes wide and bloodshot, his hair Afro, his whole manner as though he were floating several inches off the ground.

"Hey, Herb," I said, "you're looking good. You got a job?"

Two jobs, it seemed. He was, Carter said, working in a VD program in California, trying to track down carriers, and he was also, he said, managing the rock group, Sly and the Family Stone.

Then Carter, in direct violation of Kennedy's ruling, began to tell me what he would say when he got on the stand.

That might not be easy, I told him. After all, there were court rules, he would have to respond to questions he was asked. He might not be able to say what he wanted in just the way he wanted to say it.

Carter looked at me. "They ain't gonna stop me," he said. "I'm gonna tell them white mother-fuckers just how it was, and ain't no white mother-fucker going to stop me. Baby, you know it."

There was practically no one in the courthouse who didn't hear Carter then, as he repeated the story he had told me on the phone and his certainty that nobody was going to shut him up once he got on the witness stand.

He never did get on that witness stand. When court reconvened, he went back to the witness room to await the call. It never came. And when court ended that evening, they gave Herb Carter a ticket back to California.

14

"What Else Did Conti Say?"

Latimer had said, early in December, that he hoped "to have the troops out of the trenches by Christmas." That was about in line with everything else that attorney did and said during the court-martial. We were a long way from home when Christmas arrived, and when the recess was over—after the final government spurt with Grzesik and Meadlo—the defense once again droned on. There was the continued fitful attempt to pin the responsibility on Medina, but Daniel continued to chop away at that, with varying degrees of success.

Part of the defense problem—in addition to the problem of the facts about the defendant—seemed to be a lack of preparation, a lack of knowledge of what the witnesses, its own witnesses, were going to say. This was true of both Latimer and Kay, particularly of Kay. He seemed constantly surprised at the answers he got even to the simplest questions; rarely was he ready for his witness's response. When the answer was not what he seemed to expect, his face assumed a hurt look (while Daniel donned a sardonic smile and Kennedy a look of resignation and the spectators exchanged glances). And his lack of preparation seemed even more woeful when Daniel, with a few sharp questions, managed to dilute whatever impact his witness might have had.

There was Tommy Moss, for example, the first witness to say he remembered a specific mention of women and children by Medina at the briefing. Someone, Moss said, had asked a question about women, and Medina had said that any women "would be VC and VC sympathizers and that everyone was to be killed."

But Moss, Daniel brought out, had not shot women and children at My Lai even though he had had the opportunity.

Kay wanted to make another point, that the killings at My Lai were part of a pattern throughout Son My during the operation. So he took Moss to the night lager, or bivouac, where prisoners were being questioned and where, it developed, a couple of them were shot to death by Vietnamese National Police when they had answered the wrong way or not at all.

"Did you see Captain Medina at the interrogation?" Kay asked.

"No," Moss replied.

"Did you see Captain Kotouc?"

Moss looked at Kay startled. "I don't know who you're talking about."

And Kay called Charles Hall back to cast doubt on Conti's truthfulness and character, and thus on his testimony. Hall had met Conti on a trail in My Lai in the morning and Conti had said that something had just happened with Calley. Kay asked him to relate the incident.

"He came up," Hall said, "and related what had just happened with one of the villagers—one of the women. He was attempting to have oral sex with this woman and had intimidated this woman's children. At that moment, Lieutenant Calley had come down the trail and stopped him."

Judge Kennedy leaned over the bench toward Hall. "He said," the judge asked with a kind of amazement, "that he was attempting to have 'oral sex'?"

"Yes, sir," Hall said.

"That was the word he used, 'oral sex'?" Kennedy persisted.

"Not exactly."

"What did he say exactly?"

"He said he was attempting to have a blow job from this woman."

Kay strutted back to the defense table at this response. Conti was obviously a morally depraved young man who was taking revenge on Calley for interrupting his pleasures that morning by telling lies that would send Calley to prison or the gallows.

Daniel did not seem worried. He got up and walked casually toward Hall. "Was that all the substance of the conversation between Conti and Lieutenant Calley?"

Before Hall could respond, Kay was on his feet objecting, claiming there was no reason to get into any further conversation, that it would be irrelevant and just hearsay.

"You opened it up," Daniel said. "We have a right to know what the rest of that conversation was."

"It's irrelevant," Kay said.

Kennedy looked from one to the other. "I'm not quite sure what this is all about," he said. "I suppose you both know what he's going to say."

Daniel nodded.

Not Kay. He looked at Kennedy and said, "I don't, your honor."

Kennedy stared at him with disgust. "Well, Mr. Kay, then suppose we all find out."

Daniel asked again, "What else did Conti say?"

And Hall replied; "Conti went on to say after he went down the trail that Calley had these people wasted anyway."

Nowhere was the ineptness and lack of preparation better displayed than with the calling of Vernardo Simpson. A twenty-three-year-old black student at Jackson State College in Jackson, Mississippi, Simpson had been a rifleman in the second platoon that March morning at My Lai. He told me and several other reporters on a number of occasions before the trial that he had killed perhaps twenty Vietnamese, including two babies, at the direct order—to kill or be court-martialed and perhaps shot himself—of Lieutenant Brooks (since Brooks was dead, no charges could be leveled against him). Latimer was obviously calling Simpson to show that others had given orders similar to Calley's, so why pick on Calley? Of course, no one had ever said that Brooks himself had slaughtered a hundred or more people in a mass execution or two, only that he had given such orders.)

Simpson refused to testify at Calley's trail, standing on his Fifth Amendment rights, and Kennedy, after studying briefs submitted by Simpson's lawyer, upheld that stand.

But Latimer seemed intent on getting Simpson's testimony onto the record, and he asked for immunity, similar to that granted Meadlo, Grzesik, and others. The immunity orders were prepared, but whether granted or not no one knew, for Simpson was never recalled.

That he was called in the first place was something of a shock to me. A couple of months earlier, when I spoke with him in the course of making a film on My Lai, it was apparent to me that if Simpson were called as a witness at Calley's trial it would only be as a government witness. Simpson had told me, "Oh, yes, I saw Lieutenant Calley . . . they had this massive ditch. I think it was about, oh, I think it was about fifty people at a time. They would put two machine guns on each side and put two people with automatic rifles and he said, 'Shoot 'em!' So he just killed all of 'em, all fifty of 'em, and they would make another pile of 'em and put 'em in the ditch and then another fifty and shoot them and do them the same way."

This was one time Daniel seemed almost disappointed not to have a crack at cross-examination of a defense witness.

Actually, if the defense had wanted to press the issue of orders, given by other officers and by Medina, it should have called Gary Crossley—only no one on the defense side seemed even aware of his existence. For Crossley had told me that he and his squad had rounded up a group of Vietnamese and "we phoned Captain Medina and we asked him what to do. He said that they were the enemy. This is a search and destroy mission and we were to carry out our orders."

Crossley waited at home in San Marcos, Texas; nobody ever called him.

But still the defense kept trying to spread the circle of guilt, the circle of blame, spiraling beyond Calley to Medina and beyond Medina higher and higher. It was to take the focus from Calley and put it on Medina, if not Medina, then Barker, if not Barker, then Henderson, if not Henderson, then Koster— and why not go even higher?

Nicholas Capezza, now a New York City housing patrolman, had been Medina's senior medic. At Kay's urging, he tried to explain that higher officers knew what was going on, had even been at the scene, and had done nothing. But when Kay confidently asked him whether Medina had received more than one radio transmission at the area of the Carter medivac, Capezza replied, "No, I don't think so." And the one message he remembered was one Medina was receiving, from whom he didn't know.

But Kay tried again. Had Capezza seen a chopper land other than the medivac? Yes, Capezza said, he had. What had Medina done?

"Captain Medina approached the chopper and saluted the officer who got out. His salute was returned"—indicating that the officer had been of higher rank. The two talked for about five minutes and then the other officer got back in his helicopter and left.

"Did you recognize that officer?" Kay asked, watching with obvious anticipation of a name.

"No," Capezza said, "I don't know who he was." Kay looked disappointed—he should not have been, not if he had talked to his witness before.

And Kay's disappointment must have been compounded when Daniel had his go at Capezza. It was through Daniel that Capezza remembered a second radio transmission.

Daniel: Is it not true that after the first transmission, Medina called Calley and asked what was going on?
Capezza: Yes.
Daniel: Did you hear that transmission?
Capezza: Part of it.
Daniel: What was said?
Capezza: Medina asked for a body count of civilians.

When Capezza left the courtroom, he smiled at Calley and patted him on the shoulder.

Now Kay was going to put Barker on the scene, and Christopher Garbow, copilot of Barker's helicopter, would do it. Or that was Kay's intention. But Garbow, while he remembered landing to take Carter back to base, also remembered that Barker was not in the chopper at the time. And though he remembered landing in the same area a second time, "I can't remember whether Barker left the chopper or whether anyone came up. I can't remember anything of what happened."

Under cross-examination, Garbow turned out to be something of a government witness. He had seen no armed Viet Cong while flying over My Lai, and he was flying at a thousand to fifteen hundred feet, "the magic altitude to keep you out of range of small arms fire and still be able to see the ground." And on the ground, near the medivac, he had seen the bodies on the trail.

The Daniel proceded to give a *coup de grace* to the defense contention that in a free-fire zone such as Son My everything was fair game and nobody had any compunction about shooting everything and anything. He drew Garbow into a discussion of a free-fire zone and the statement that in one you could fire at "targets of opportunity," meaning anything that moved. But Garbow had his own feelings about that. "It would depend on the circumstances, sir, whether you would fire at unarmed personnel. That's a moral question. I myself would never shoot at an unarmed woman or child. But I guess they could be classified as targets of opportunity."

With Dean C. Lind, the pilot in Garbow's chopper, there was a little better luck in placing high officers at My Lai, and showing they had knowledge of what was happening. Lind remembered that at LZ-Dotti after the medivac, "I was about to shut down when I was asked to take off again. I went back to the My Lai area with a senior officer. I think it was Colonel

Barker. I dropped him off and he was on the ground about five minutes. Then we went back to Dotti."

"Did he talk to anyone on the ground?" Kay asked.

"Right, sir."

"Who?"

"An officer. But I don't know his name."

Medina? It turned out not to be. On cross-examination, Daniel showed that the landing with Barker had not been at My Lai but east, where Bravo Company was operating.

Nevertheless, Lind had a feeling that things were not right. There was a conversation in the back seat of his chopper at LZ-Dotti. Barker was there and so, too, he thought, was Henderson, but he couldn't be sure of that. He had not heard the conversation, it was a feeling he had, just an opinion he had formed, "just what I'd seen at My Lai, but I can't remember the substance." It was all too vague.

But Henderson was in the air over My Lai. Martin Adcock, his RTO, was with him in a chopper, and had been with him when Henderson landed along Highway 521 and picked up two suspects to take back to LZ-Dotti for questioning. And he had seen bodies in the ditch, which, perhaps, was a better point for the government—though it would indicate that Henderson too knew what was happening. "We were in a slow bank and I saw the group in the ditch. They were a mixed group, men, women, and children."

Was General Koster there too? He was, indeed. Sergeant Dennis R. Vasquez, an artillery captain at the time of My Lai, had flown over the area with Barker. At one point in the morning, their helicopter had returned to LZ-Dotti when another chopper landed and out stepped General Koster and General Young. They went into the tactical operations center for a conversation with Barker, but Vasquez did not hear what was said.

But Vasquez put a measure of blame on Henderson too. For he had been at a high officers' briefing the night before the attack. Henderson, who had replaced Brigadier General Andy

Lipscomb as brigade commander that day (he had been executive officer of the brigade at the time), was there and had made "comments on the lack of aggressiveness in the past on missions. Colonel Henderson said we had not closed in fast enough, waiting too long for artillery and air strikes, which let the enemy escape. In the past we had almost accomplished our mission but we had not been aggressive enough. He wanted us to close in fast and be more aggressive."

And then Vasquez gave a final twist of the knife to what had on occasion been broached as a defense theory behind the deaths. No shells, he said, had fallen on the hamlet. They had all landed right where they were supposed to, along the outskirts of the hamlet in the landing zone.

So the defense had almost had its day. All its military witnesses had been heard. It was not much of a case. The defense had tried to put the blame on higher officers, and on lower-ranking soldiers. It had tried to show that the killings were indiscriminate and committed by everyone, or that there had been no killing, or that the killings had been the result of artillery and gunships. It had tried to show that the people of My Lai were all enemies who had killed Americans. It had tried to show that it was all the result of men acting like good soldiers and obeying orders.

It had not succeeded fully in any of these attempts, and it had failed utterly in some of them.

With all its witnesses, it had done nothing to erase the stigma of Calley as killer. No matter what others had done, there was still the picture of Calley with a rifle in his hands, still Calley giving orders to kill.

Perhaps Calley as a witness could give us some better explanations. Or perhaps there was even another reason.

15
Who Else but Calley?

Almost from the day the first word about My Lai reached the public, there had been people saying that if the charges were true, if Calley had really done all that, then he must be crazy; the slaughter of innocent, unresisting old men, women, and children, lined up and executed, could only be the work of a madman.

But there had been no indication that questions as to Calley's sanity, and thus his responsibility for his acts, would be raised at the court-martial. Daniel had never raised the question during the government's case. Latimer did not mention it in his opening remarks. Indeed, Calley himself had long maintained, sharply and flatly, that there was no question about his mental balance. Thus, while there was always speculation about the sanity question and wonderment that the defense didn't at least probe a little in that direction, that seemed about the limit of the discussion.

But we were wrong. The question of sanity, or at least of partial mental responsibility, apparently was something that had intrigued Latimer from the beginning, though he gave no public intimation that he would try to thread his way through the maze.

It seemed, though, a logical way for him to go, for the military definition of sanity, just like the civilian definitions, had become more sophisticated and subtle through the years. No longer did it say that the accused was insane only if his faculties were so impaired that he did not know the difference between right and wrong or was acting under an irresistible impulse. According to the *Manual for Courts-Martial,* "A person is not mentally responsible in a criminal sense for an offense unless he was, at the time, so far free of mental defect, disease or derangement as to be able concerning the particular act charged both to distinguish right from wrong and to adhere to the right." The ability to adhere to the right, then, became crucial when talking about a general lack of mental responsibility.

Then there were degrees. Concerning partial mental responsibility, the manual says: "A mental condition, not amounting to a general lack of mental responsibility, which produces a lack of mental ability, at the time of the offense, to possess actual knowledge or to entertain a specific intent or a premeditated design to kill, is a defense to an offense having one of these states of mind as an element. For example, if premeditated murder is charged and the court finds that, as a result of mental impairment, not amounting to a general lack of mental responsibility, the accused at the time of the offense lacked the mental ability to entertain a premeditated design to kill, the court must find the accused not guilty of premeditated murder, but it may find him guilty of the included offense of unpremeditated murder as a premeditated design to kill is not an element of the latter."

Thus, if the defense wanted to raise the issue of mental capacity as a defense, it could do it in one of two ways. It could claim that Calley could not adhere to the right and therefore was guilty of no crime no matter what he did. Or it could claim that because of a mental impairment he had a partial mental responsibility and so could not premeditate murder; his crime, then, was mitigated and if he was guilty of anything it was of a lesser offense.

And if the defense raised such claims, it would be up to Daniel to prove them false. Like everything else in the trial, and in the American system of justice, the burden of proof was on the government. "The accused is presumed initially to be sane," the manual says. "When, however, some evidence which could reasonably tend to show that the accused is insane or was insane at the time of his alleged offense is introduced . . . then the sanity of the accused is an essential issue. The burden of proving the sanity of the accused, like every other fact necessary to establish the offense alleged, is always on the prosecution."

If these areas, then, seemed natural for the defense, the court was constantly assured by Latimer that they would not be raised. So when the first word of a psychiatrist entered the trial, the morning it reconvened after Christmas, it was no little shock. Latimer filed a request for compensation for three psychiatrists, compensation to come from paying them extra witness fees.

Kennedy looked at him balefully. "I'm not going to negotiate with these psychiatrists as to how much money they get for appearing," he said. Then he stared grimly at Latimer. "Now, let me understand you, Mr. Latimer. Are you now going to raise an insanity issue in this case? Over a year ago, I asked the defense whether there was any question as to the mental capacity or ability of Lieutenant Calley. I was told there was not. If there was some question, I would have had no recourse then but to have had him sent to a sanity hearing to make a determination. Are you now going to raise that issue?"

Latimer tried to soothe Kennedy's ire. "No, your honor. I'm not going to raise the question of insanity. But we want to go into the mental conditions that are in existence in the stresses and strains of combat, orders and what people can stand."

"Please the court," Daniel interposed. "If the defense starts to talk insanity, then we're going to have to convene a sanity board at Walter Reed Hospital to make a complete examination of Lieutenant Calley. Such an examination would take three or four weeks, and I think we ought to know now if we're going to have to do that."

Latimer assured Kennedy and Daniel that such a thing would not be necessary. Again he reiterated that Calley's sanity would not be called into question; he was bringing his psychiatrists only for a limited purpose.

Whether, as had happened so often, Latimer did not know his own witnesses and so was surprised by them, or whether it was something else again, the sanity question arose when the first of his three psychiatrists, exactly a week later, arrived to testify.

The three were: Dr. David G. Crane, in private practice in Indianapolis, Indiana, and on the faculty of the Indiana University Medical School. A former Army psychiatrist in Viet-Nam, he had volunteered to help the defense at no pay. He had never talked to Calley and would testify on the basis of his knowledge of soldiers in combat and, in relation to Calley, on the basis of a "hypothetical statement of fact."

Dr. Wilbur A. Hamman, in private practice in Arlington, Virginia, and a psychiatrist on the maximum security ward at Washington's St. Elizabeth's Hospital, had, like Crane, volunteered to help after reading about the case and becoming fascinated by it. He had been to Viet-Nam for a week to help in the Duffy court-martial, the case of another soldier accused of murdering Vietnamese civilians. Latimer had accepted Hamman's offer of help, and during the Christmas recess the doctor had seen Calley for four lengthy sessions, and would see him a couple of times more before he took the stand.

And then there was Dr. Albert A. LaVerne, a New York psychiatrist who was on leave as senior psychiatrist at New York University-Bellevue Medical Center. LaVerne had entered the case a year earlier; soon after charges against Calley were filed.

LaVerne was the first to testify. He had some interesting theories—that marijuana, especially the quality of pot grown in Viet-Nam, which he claimed was seventeen times more potent than the domestic grades, could have a long-lasting and debilitating effect not just on the user but even on those who only breathed the fumes as others smoked. Though the effect would not be psychotic, it could produce severe impairment of judgment and behavior and a distortion of perception. "One of the most dramatic effects," LaVerne says, "is delusion. Another is hallucination. And another is a paranoid reaction, for example, becoming hostile toward a friend."

LaVerne had also developed some theories about stress, including stress in combat, on individuals. And he had developed some experimental techniques to test his suppositions.

LaVerne's theories seemed to present some possibilities for Calley's defense. There was, of course, the factor of stress in war and how it might have affected Calley. And there was the contention that a number of men in Calley's platoon smoked marijuana habitually. Their smoking might have distorted their perceptions, and Calley might have come under the influence of pot by breathing the fumes the night before My Lai. During the fall of 1970, on three occasions, LaVerne interviewed Calley and put him through his tests.

When LaVerne was ready to take the stand, Daniel was not all that anxious to hear him; he had not had government psychiatrists examine Calley. And he was particularly not anxious for the jury to hear this testimony. "I don't know what they're going to say," he said, "so I think we ought to hear them out of the presence of the jury to see just what is going to be said."

Latimer thought this a waste of time. "One of them will not get into the area of partial responsibility or insanity at all. Another will testify solely hypothetically. And the third can't raise the issue because he couldn't have made a thorough examination of Lieutenant Calley."

But Kennedy was cautious. "I know how verbose these psychiatrists are," he sighed, "and I don't want to listen to them twice. However, I suppose I have no choice." He would hear them with the jury absent and "if there is any indication at all that Lieutenant Calley suffers from even a character disorder, that impairs his judgment at all, I'm going to let the government have a sanity board."

But when LaVerne took the stand on January 18, it seemed that maybe Latimer was right after all, the discussion would be only academic. LaVerne, his lips constantly pursing in what seemed a nervous mannerism, gave a long lecture under Latimer's questioning, complete with charts and a model of the brain, about marijuana and stress, and described his experiments with Calley.

When the question of marijuana was raised, Kennedy asked, "The defense does not contend that Lieutenant Calley smoked marijuana or that he was exposed to its fumes, does it?"

"Lieutenant Calley was not a smoker of marijuana," Latimer said, "but he might have been exposed to it the night before by being in a tent where it was smoked."

"Then all this is only to discredit Conti and not relating to Calley?" Daniel said.

"That's right," Latimer said, "and others, too."

And LaVerne continued his lecture. Exposure to Oriental varieties of marijuana, he said, even if the pot is never smoked, "produces aberrations in judgment, performance and the ability to perform duties." He knew of a case where a man under the influence of Vietnamese marijuana had shot at the grass thinking it was a Viet Cong.

If Calley had been exposed to marijuana, LaVerne said, he and others so exposed might have acted irrationally at My Lai.

In his experiments he had put Calley in a small room, about the size of a closet—two by six by eight feet—and there "recreated the combat situation." In the stress of combat, LaVerne said, anoxia occurs, that is, the brain receives less oxygen, resulting in an impairment of judgment and motor abilities. He had recreated the anoxia of combat "by burning a quantity of tobacco to consume the oxygen in the room." The results were enough to show that Calley "is prone to nonspecific stress syndrome. He would go into simple actions and thought, but he couldn't engage in complex thoughts."

(Calley, describing the experiment later, said he had almost asphyxiated in that closet and all he had wanted was to get out. As for LaVerne, Calley said, "He's nuts.")

That seemed to be all Latimer wanted LaVerne for—if so, it wasn't much.

But Daniel wasn't so sure what might come out in front of the jury and so he probed LaVerne deeply (having stayed up for a number of nights reading everything he could about psychiatry to prepare)—and in this questioning and later questioning of both LaVerne and the two other psychiatrists, Daniel reached a peak, displaying what even Judge Kennedy was later to describe as "brilliance."

Did Dr. LaVerne have any views on Lieutenant Calley's sanity?

He did. Calley "was perfectly sane." He knew right from wrong, was aware, "but he could not analyze complex decisions because he could not think them through as a result of the stress of combat," which is present, perhaps, in most soldiers in Viet-Nam. But, added LaVerne, Calley "was absolutely sane. He suffered no character disorder or personality disorder or behavioral disorder."

And, in response to another question by Daniel, he said that Calley "had the capacity to form an intent to kill. He was a perfectly normal American soldier in his ability to form an intent to kill."

If that seemed to end that, Daniel was not quite sure, for there had been some disturbing elements in some of LaVerne's replies. He dug deeper into LaVerne's analysis of Calley and his interviews with the lieutenant. For a while the picture formed was that of "a normal personality of a twenty-six-year-old officer undergoing a great crisis in life with an ability to withstand crises. He had great idealism, for what was right and wrong. He had pride in being an officer in the Army and never said anything against anyone in the Army. He is a relatively strong person who could withstand the stresses he was under since he was charged. I was surprised that he was able to stand up so well."

Then what kind of impairment did LaVerne's tests show? As anoxia set in, LaVerne said, Calley showed a slowing down of his abilities. "He showed aberrations on almost everything. I then felt he'd be a candidate for a combat stress-syndrome."

Anything else?

It seemed that as Calley's reactions slowed down, LaVerne had gone to him. "I would say, 'What's wrong, Bill?' He'd say, 'Call me Rusty.' I kept calling him Bill," to which Calley reacted with some annoyance.

As Daniel pressed forward, some ominous words and signs began to appear. LaVerne tried a marijuana experiment on Calley and "he became hostile toward me. That I had gotten him into a trap. He gesticulated. The marijuana was beginning to have an impairment of the brain. He had a paranoid reaction. He said, 'Everybody was taking advantage of me, what everybody's been doing for the last year.'"

A little more and Daniel had LaVerne at a crucial point—and it was apparent that he had followed the wisest course by demanding LaVerne be heard out of the jury's hearing.

Daniel: Was Lieutenant Calley's judgment impaired beyond normal limits on March 16, 1968?

LaVerne: What do you mean by "normal limits"?

Kennedy: Was his judgment impaired on March sixteenth?

LaVerne: Yes, sir.

Kennedy: How?

LaVerne: He could not challenge the legality or illegality of the orders given by Captain Medina. Captain Medina had become a father figure to him.

Daniel: Did he suffer from an irresistible impulse?

LaVerne: He was compelled to carry out that order without challenging that order. But I would not call it an irresistible impulse.

Daniel: Could he disobey that order?

LaVerne: No, he could not disobey that order. He was like an automaton, a robot. When the order came to stop shooting, the party's over, he stopped. But I would not classify it as an irresistible impulse because it went on for several hours.

As Daniel made LaVerne more and more uneasy, the doctor had more and more to say—and Latimer, too, began to squirm uncomfortably. Calley, LaVerne declared, could not make complex decisions because he could not weigh their component parts on that March morning; he could not make complex judgments; he was suffering from "combat psychological stress" and possibly the results of unwitting inhalation of marijuana fumes. He was deranged but not insane.

Daniel: Was he conscious of his actions?

LaVerne: Yes, absolutely.

Daniel: Morally?

LaVerne: You mean did he know right from wrong? Yes, he knew right from wrong.

What happened, LaVerne said, was that the order given by Captain Medina "became the focus and the trigger for all his behavior in carrying out those orders. He had to carry out the orders—the first to start shooting and the second to stop." That was so, LaVerne said, because Calley "does not have the characteristics or traits of a premeditated murderer. He does not have the propensity for such a crime as is supposed to have happened for several hours on March sixteenth."

Daniel: Was Lieutenant Calley psychotic?

LaVerne: No.

Daniel: Was Lieutenant Calley neurotic?

LaVerne: No.

Daniel: Did Lieutenant Calley know right from wrong?

LaVerne: Yes.

Daniel: Could Lieutenant Calley adhere to the right?

LaVerne: He had a compulsion to carry out his orders, to do his duty as an officer.

Daniel: Isn't that characteristic of a soldier?

LaVerne: Who else has done what Lieutenant Calley is alleged to have done?

There was no question now but that the issue of Calley's mental capacity had been raised. "The ball's in your court, Captain Daniel," Judge Kennedy said. "Do you want a sanity board?"

"I'm ready to proceed."

"And what does that mean?"

"Let's hear the other defense psychiatrists."

"I don't think I'm going to give you that opportunity." The judge stared at Daniel. "The issue of sanity has obviously been raised at this point and it would be reversible error for me not to instruct the jury on it."

Daniel sighed. "I move this matter be referred to a sanity board."

Outside the courtroom in the corridors, Calley was enraged. He chain-smoked cigarettes, paced up and down, and railed. "I think it's unwarranted and unnecessary. I don't think we're trying to say I was insane. So I don't like it."

But there was nothing he could do about it. A few days later he was on his way north, to Walter Reed Hospital and the sanity board.

16
Only God's to Blame

It was a month, not until February 18, before everyone was back at Fort Benning. The sanity board at Walter Reed had found Calley to be normal in every respect, and the doctors who had so found would later tell about those findings. But Latimer's three psychiatrists were prepared to challenge that. It had been decided to attack frontally, using now as a defense the idea that Calley was not mentally or emotionally responsible for his actions on March 16 at My Lai.

The views of LaVerne and Crane would be based on a "hypothetical statement of fact." There was nothing unique in this idea; it is often used in courts, especially for psychiatrists to develop theories and generalizations about someone's stability and mental capacity when there has been no opportunity to personally examine the subject of that statement. Though Calley was available, Crane had not talked to him and LaVerne, even though he had examined Calley, would also base his responses on the hypothetical.

There is one thing about a hypothetical statement, though, and that is that everything in it is assumed to be true. If something is not true, then any opinions based on it are inadmissible. And so the hypothetical statement read to the court could be assumed by everyone to be the facts of what had happened at My Lai as Calley knew them, and the facts about his own life, for he was the subject of that *vita*.

What was not known when the hypothetical was read—it only developed later—was that the defense had taken almost verbatim the summary findings of the Walter Reed sanity board and used them as the hypothetical.

"Doctor," it began, "assume you are confronted with the following factual situation: Composite of pertinent information from the accused and other record sources indicate that First Lieutenant Calley is a 27-year-old single male with four and a half years of active duty who grew up in Miami, Florida. He has been retained on active duty since 6 September 1969, beyond his normal duty tour, for the purposes of general court-martial."

What followed was a rambling summary of Calley's early life with its repeated failures, through his enlistment in the Army, his graduation from OCS, and his assignment to Charlie Company in Hawaii.

". . . his first assignment found him a platoon leader in a company commanded by Capt. Ernest Medina. Part of the preparation for Viet-Nam was the reading of many afteraction reports. He felt that during the weeks in Hawaii various social and duty experiences built up a good group feeling in the company. He was trained in basic combat training and in officer candidate school that orders must be obeyed and that in combat it is mandatory that an officer carries out the orders of his superior officer and that one does the job one is told to do. In December 1967, the unit moved to RVN and joined the 23rd Infantry (Americal) Division.

"Assume further that Lieutenant Calley, in South Viet-Nam, obtained additional indoctrination and training with regard to the enemy that he would face. That as part of this training he was directed to treat all South Vietnamese with great caution since men, women of all ages including old men and women and small children have proved to be as dangerous an enemy as the fullgrown military age men, and that women fight alongside their men and that the children and old men and women participate by supplying shelter and food to the fighting men, that old men and women set booby traps and lay mines, that instances are on record of very small children having been made into walking booby traps and resulting in the death and maiming of many Americans.

"After the orderliness of OCS and garrison, he was shocked at the confusion of actual combat. The company was on a number of operations in the next few months. In February 1969, the Tet offensive began. Casualties were sustained from mines and his radio telephone operator, with whom he had been very close, was killed by a sniper. There were 18 dead and wounded casualties in the company from a minefield while he was on a brief in-country R & R. He felt grieved and hurt at being absent. The unit operated in Quang Ngai Province, RVN, in an area which Lieutenant Calley was told was one of the most heavily mined and booby trapped areas in Viet-Nam. Testimony indicates some units suffered more than 90 per cent of their casualties from mines or bobby traps and many soldiers, and the accused, felt that the local populace was responsible. He felt increasingly frustrated at the difficulty of identifying the enemy in this Vietnamese environment and described his men as increasingly hostile to civilians. They were unable to destroy the enemy because they were never able to find them. He describes grief at the loss of men, anger and frustration at the situation and constant fear for the lives and safety of his men and himself.

"Some days later, the company was to go on a search and destroy mission which was the first time this sort of mission had been ordered. On 15 March 1968, he attended briefings by the company commander concerning an operation to be held the next day. Assume that testimony of witnesses indicates that Captain Medina told the accused and other company personnel to expect to encounter a VC battalion, that the villagers had been warned to leave the area and that only VC and VC sympathizers would remain in the village; and that the mission was termed a search and destroy mission. Numerous soldiers have testified that Captain Medina's briefing caused them to believe that every living thing in the village was to be killed, and this included men, women, and children. Others, however, testified that they interpreted Captain Medina's orders differently and that they personally did not kill unarmed people. Lieutenant Calley came out of the briefing with the opinion that all enemy encountered during the operation were to be destroyed and that everyone remaining in the area were enemy, that the unit was to sweep rapidly through the area, destroy all the enemy so as not to have them in the rear. That his acts on 16 March 1968 were done as a matter of carrying out the directions and orders of the briefing on 15 March 1968, and he cannot recall than anyone questioned the legality of the orders at the briefing. That he himself believed his actions proper and in keeping with his orders and duties.

"On 16 March 1968, helicopters landed the three platoons of C Company on the west side of My Lai (4). The 1st and 2nd platoons had to be rearranged to comply with the assault plan, then swept eastward through the hamlet. The area had been prepared by artillery and helicopter barrage. There was light resistance to the operation. Twice Lieutenant Calley was called on the radio by the company commander, criticizing him for not moving his platoon faster. Lieutenant Calley ordered Paul Meadlo, a soldier in his platoon, to shoot, and took part himself in shooting some detained Vietnamese on two occasions, once about the center of the hamlet and once at the eastern edge of it in an irrigation ditch or depression. Lieutenant Calley believed he was following orders to destroy all living things in the village. He described various other persons as taking part in the destruction of people and animals. He also alleges that he had to stop one soldier from sexually molesting a Vietnamese female. Lieutenant Calley states that he did not feel as if he was killing humans but rather that they were the enemy with whom one could not speak or reason. After lunch the company went on with its mission. During the events of the morning up to about noon, Lieutenant Calley claimed he was 'hyper' or 'psyched up.' Lieutenant Calley will testify that at the lunch he was feeling fully alert and not fatigued. He had no head injuries, took no drugs or marijuana before or during the operation, had no 'blackouts,' no period of amnesia, and experienced no know change in consciousness.

"After the incidents of 16 March 1968, Lieutenant Calley continued as a platoon leader for some months. He extended for six months in Viet-Nam and spent part of that time as an Sp-5. Assume also that Lieutenant Calley is given the proverb, 'People who live in glass houses should not throw rocks' during an examination at Walter Reed Army Medical Center, he interpreted it, 'You can't throw rocks at other people or they will throw rocks at you.'

"Based on the hypothetical statement of facts related to you, given your qualifications in psychiatry, your knowledge and experience of the conditions in Viet-Nam in the year 1968, or approximately at that time, do you have an opinion as to the mental capacity of Lieutenant Calley on 16 March 1968 to plan, think out or contrive which would result in taking the lives of inhabitants of My Lai (4)?

". . . do you have an opinion as to Lieutenant Calley's intelligence, understanding and judgment on 16 March 1968, which would enable him to fully comprehend the act of taking the lives of the inhabitants of My Lai (4), without apparent reason or excuse?

". . . do you have an opinion as to Lieutenant Calley's intelligence, understanding and judgment on 16 March 1968 to make a reasoned decision concerning the legal consequences of the orders of his company commander?

". . . do you have an opinion as to the mental capacity of Lieutenant Calley on 16 March 1968 to form a specific intent to kill someone and consideration of the act intended?"

With that hypothetical statement read to Crane and LaVerne, it seemed that we had finally reached a crisis. Another change in the defense's posture, and a major one. If the hypothetical statement was true—as it must be if the answers of the psychiatrists were to be relevant and admissible— then the defense had finally decided to admit that the government's charges were totally true, that Calley had indeed murdered as the government said he had murdered. But it was now to do what it had said originally it would not do—use Calley's mental capacity on that date as its main defense, in essence, plead not guilty by reason of insanity or plead for mitigation by reason of diminished mental capacity.

*   *   *

Dr. David Goodrich Crane was the first to give his views and his answers to those questions. Assured and self-confident, Crane said, "I do not think Lieutenant Calley had the capacity on 16 March 1968 to plan or contrive the taking of lives." Most significant in helping him form this evaluation, he said, was the proverb test. Calley "gave a relatively concrete, simple interpretation," indicating that Calley saw things in either/or and black/white terms and so was unable to go into complexities.

Crane didn't think Calley could form a specific intent to kill on the basis of the conditions described in the hypothetical, his background, and his limitations. Neither did Calley have the mental capacity, Crane said, to give full consideration to the act of killing Vietnamese. "His thought processes were limited at that time so he could not give full consideration to the act." And, finally, "taking into full consideration his mental capabilities, his environment, the stress on that day, he would not be capable of making a complex decision at that time. He couldn't reason through a complex decision."

There was the insanity defense in the terms set forth in the *Manual for Courts-Martial.* If it went unchallenged, we could all go home and Calley would have his freedom, or at least a severely reduced penality, for there was mitigation.

But Daniel was not about to let it go. He took after Crane with an expertise in psychiatry that was surprising and he took after him with zest. For hours he cross-examined Crane, pulling apart his background and credentials—Crane was not board-certified, was not a member of the American Psychiatric Association, was not familiar with recent writings on stress or even with most recent psychiatric literature, had diagnosed Calley without ever having talked to him, though he'd had the opportunity to do that.

Slowly and with care, Daniel took Crane on a tour through all the schools of psychiatry and the ways of approaching a patient. He took him back over the answers to the four hypothetical questions. He took him through his reasons for coming up with his conclusions—there were sixteen of them, ranging from Calley's poor school performance to his feeling of fear in Viet-Nam to his fear of criticism from Medina to his literal interpretation of the proverb.

What Daniel was attempting, of course, was to force Crane to backtrack from his original diagnosis and admit Calley could premeditate the murders of the Vietnamese, that he knew what he was doing and intended to do just what he did.

And so, as he reached the end with Crane, he posed the questions for him precisely, pinning him down to legal definitions. Daniel defined premeditation as it is defined in the manual—"formulating an intent to kill and conceiving a plan to bring about the death prior to the killing." Using that definition, could Calley premeditate? For example, did he premeditate when he told Meadlo to take care of the people?

"No," Crane answered. "It would require the ability to think and comprehend in a psychiatric way."

Daniel: How about in a literal way, doctor?

Crane: In a literal interpretation, the answer is yes.

Daniel: When he ordered Meadlo to kill, did he mean for Meadlo to kill?

Crane: Literally, . yes.

Daniel: Did he form an intent to kill when he ordered Meadlo to kill before the actual act?

Crane: Literally, when he pulled the trigger it meant death, yes.

Daniel: He knew that would happen?

Crane: Yes.

But Crane kept trying to back away from saying that all this indicated that Calley could reason in complex terms. Daniel asked whether he knew when he fired into the people that they would die, that when someone ran away, he shouted to get them, that he gave orders to others to kill—all this indicated, didn't it, that he knew what he was doing and what the results would be. "Yes," Crane said wearily, "under the same literal interpretation. But I feel we're beating a dead horse. The fact is that he could know he was pulling the trigger and it would mean death, but that's not a complex decision to make."

Finally, with his last question, Daniel got what he wanted: "Isn't death the consequence of an event?" he asked. "Was he aware of that consequence when he gave orders for people to be killed and when he killed himself?"

"He was aware," Crane said slowly, "that pulling the trigger will kill individuals and bring about a loss of life."

"He knew the people would die? He meant for the people to die?" Daniel said, and waited.

"Yes."

There was no need to go any farther. The ground had vanished under the original contentions. His answers now indicated that legally Calley planned for the Vietnamese to die—premeditation—and he was aware of the results of that planning, of what those results would be.

So much for Crane.

Daniel was even better with LaVerne on his go-round with him in front of the jury.

After LaVerne's initial performance, there were many who wondered why Latimer stayed with him for a second time. When Latimer read the hypothetical to LaVerne, the psychiatrist looked as though he were falling asleep—but then so did everyone else, for it had been read to Crane and even before that had been gone over minutely in open court to clear the language to the satisfaction of both government and defense. When the reading was through, Kennedy asked LaVerne whether he had had all these facts before. "No, not all of them," LaVerne said. "Since the last time I was here, I have talked to him about March sixteenth, which Mr. Latimer had previously forbidden me to go into."

Then Latimer took him through the four questions, and LaVerne was in general agreement with Crane. Calley "suffered from a state of mind which prevented him from properly understanding his role as an officer in relation to an order." As a result, and because "of combat stress, psychological stress and his predisposition," Calley "couldn't contrive, plan or think out that day." And, he said, Calley's mental capacity was impaired. "He had an impairment of the faculty of cognition—to be able to analyze, understand the components of a complex decision and acts. And he had an impairment of volition—will, which was far greater. He was virtually paralyzed in this respect. He was acting in an automatic fashion, as a robot would, knowing what he was doing but not understanding it." In fact, LaVerne added, Calley was suffering from the same thing right at that moment: his denial mechanism was in progress, "he is suffering from the court-martial induced stress."

Calley, LaVerne concluded, "could not formulate, plan, contrive and carry out such a design" as the government charged. "His will was paralyzed. . . . He could not possibly, in my opinion, have premeditated on March sixteenth in that manner, based on his lack of mental capacity on that date."

He sounded so certain. It took Daniel less than a half-hour to destroy him, to leave LaVerne exhausted and send him from Fort Benning practically a broken man.

Daniel began immediately to question LaVerne on what Calley had supposedly told him about the events of March 16.

LaVerne: He proceeded to carry out his orders.
Daniel: How?
LaVerne: He was in charge of a platoon and he directed his men to carry out those orders.
Daniel: How?
LaVerne: One was to order Meadlo and another man to—
Daniel: What other man?
LaVerne: I'll have to check my notes.
Daniel: You do that.

LaVerne dug into his briefcase and pulled out several typewritten sheets. Kennedy, looking down from the bench, saw what he had and, the judge told me later, the first thought that went through his head was that here was trouble: "Oh, no, he's had it." Daniel came forward and took the notes from LaVerne and looked at them. They were not notes. They were copies of the hypothetical statement that had just been read to him.

Daniel: Are these your notes?

La Verne: Part of them. They're based on my notes, on facts given me by Lieutenant Calley that I gave to Mr. Latimer.

Daniel: Did Lieutenant Calley tell you all of these facts about March sixteenth?

La Verne: Well, I think I got more from the newspapers, radio, and television.

Daniel: You mean, you knew about what happened on March sixteenth before you talked to Lieutenant Calley?

La Verne: I'd have to be pretty stupid not to know.

Daniel: Well, can you remember what he told you that wasn't in the newspapers and wasn't in the hypothetical statement?

La Verne: No, all I can remember is what's in the hypothetical statement.

Daniel: Didn't you ask him a lot of questions?

La Verne: Yes.

Daniel: What were some of those questions?

La Verne: I don't remember.

Daniel: Why not? That's not so hard, is it? It doesn't take much energy to remember what you asked.

La Verne: I spent all my energy preparing for your cross-examination.

Daniel: Well, doctor, did you write down those questions so we can see them?

La Verne: The questions weren't in written form.

Daniel dug in hard, asking how Calley had acted while LaVerne was questioning him. "I couldn't get him to sit down," LaVerne said. "He was jumping up and down like a jumping bean. He was under stress." And then LaVerne looked with pleading at Kennedy and said, "Right now, I'm under stress and fatigued."

And Kennedy replied, "So am I. Let's recess and reconvene tomorrow."

But there would be no tomorrow for Dr. Albert LaVerne, at least not as witness in the Calley court-martial at Fort Benning. As soon as court was over, Daniel went immediately to Kennedy's chambers and was joined there by Latimer and Raby. LaVerne, Daniel said bluntly, was a liar who had been caught in a lie on the stand. He had, among other things, claimed that the hypothetical statement was his notes, and then that it was based on his notes when in fact it had been based on the report of the government psychiatrists at Walter Reed and was practically their verbatim language. As a result, Daniel said, he was going to cite LaVerne for perjury.

Latimer worked on Daniel and Kennedy, and then agreed to send LaVerne home and have his testimony stricken.

The next morning in court, with the jury absent, Kennedy had a statement to make: "Following yesterday's session, it was apparent to me that Dr. LaVerne was saved by the bell, so to speak, at four-thirty when we normally quit. At that point, he was hopelessly caught—well, it may not have been a complete falsehood at that point but if it had been developed it would have turned out to be. I know the defense was taken by surprise as well as the prosecution. The question is, what do we do at this point?"

Latimer moved that LaVerne's testimony be stricken, and said he would make that motion in front of the jury. And when the jury arrived, Latimer said. "Yesterday, during the afternoon, during the testimony of Dr. LaVerne, an incident happened that had created an adverse impression. Last night, I talked to Dr. LaVerne about strategy. I have the overall responsibility for what goes on in court. We had a disagreement. I now move that Dr. LaVerne be dismissed as a witness. I realize that this is denying the prosecution the right to further cross-examination of Dr. LaVerne. And so I move that all his testimony be stricken and expunged from the record and the jury be so advised. Let me say that Lieutenant Calley fully concurs in this decision."

Daniel said tersely, "The government concurs." (But later, he was to say privately that he intended to pursue the perjury charge before he left the Army. He was finally prevailed on to drop it.)

We had not, however, heard the last of Dr. LaVerne. He had flown back to New York and there declared that he was filled with indignation at Kennedy's characterization of his testimony. "You take half a statement and you formulate a conclusion and that isn't bringing out the facts. The impressions are completely false. The inferences are completely erroneous and to me that's a travesty of justice and character assassination. I am completely shocked that anyone in authority would make a conclusion without giving an opportunity to the person involved to defend his reputation. That's what I want and I insist upon that opportunity."

On Sunday night, I was at the airport seeing my wife on her way back to New York. Suddenly, there was LaVerne in the waiting room. He asked me what time the press got to court the next morning (between eight and nine, I told him) and whether he could just drive onto the base or did he need a pass? (He could just drive on, I said.) He would be at the base, he said, and he would be there to seek vindication.

And, indeed, LaVerne was there, with his three children. Standing outside the courthouse—from which he had been barred—he told reporters that he was demanding an apology. Some years earlier, LaVerne's wife had been murdered in the lobby of his apartment house by a former patient; their three children had witnessed the slaying, the youngest, only a baby then, held in her mother's arms as a shot hit the mother. Now, LaVerne declared, he wanted Judge Kennedy "to explain to my traumatized children, who have been more traumatized by this experience than by the murder of their mother, why he called me a liar."

Later, Kennedy and LaVerne had a meeting. LaVerne emerged smiling, and posed with his children for photographers. He was completely satisfied, vindicated, he declared. the judge was "a great man and my children think he's a great man. My children and I think he's tops."

What had Kennedy done? LaVerne would not say; we

should be in court at the afternoon session. Kennedy would make a statement, and "what he says will satisfy for me."

What Kennedy said in open court was: "During the noon recess, we had a discussion about your previous testimony," he told LaVerne, who stood in the middle of the courtroom listening. "You explained to me what you meant by parts of your testimony. I want to be perfectly fair. I don't want to hurt you or your career. So I'll strike all my remarks pertaining to you and your testimony from the record."

LaVerne beamed and walked around the courtroom shaking hands. Latimer gripped his hand tightly and thanked him "for his terrific help." But when LaVerne reached Daniel with an outstretched hand, Daniel just looked away, ignoring it.

Then LaVerne flew back to New York for good.

But we still had Wilbur Hamman to get through. Hamman seemed a compulsive talker and lover of publicity. All the time he was at Fort Benning, he was constantly cornering reporters in the corridors, on the sidewalk, even inside the pressroom to spout his theories, to ask how we thought he was doing. Hamman just sought us out, he was impossible to avoid.

At least one of his theories was intriguing. One afternoon, he told me that he felt nobody was to blame for My Lai and that he felt that perhaps the whole episode, though regrettable, was understandable. It was "better to kill a hundred Vietnamese," Hamman said, "if it saves ten Americans." When he was asked what he felt about the guilt of those killed at My Lai, beyond that truism, he came up with another: "Nobody holds bomber pilots guilty for the people they kill, do they?"

What do we do then, I asked him, just dismiss and forget about the dead, just write off the hundreds who had been killed at My Lai?

"Yes, I guess so," Hamman said.

"Isn't there someone who ought to take some blame for those deaths?"

"I guess," the psychiatrist said, "if you want to blame anyone, you can only blame God."

That was Hamman out in the corridors.

In the courtroom, he testified not from the hypothetical statement, but on the basis of his own interviews with Calley. But still he was asked the four questions, and replied that Calley "did not have the capacity to think out, plan or contrive" the killing at My Lai, was "not capable and did not have the capacity to form a specific intent," his mental capacity was "severely impaired," he "was not able to give consideration to the act intended," and his ability to analyze in detail a complex decision was greatly impaired as was his mental state." Calley, he concluded, "was not able to premeditate."

Daniel, of course, would not buy that. He kept Hamman on the witness stand for three days, pounding away at him, taking him over the same ground he had covered with Crane, and bringing out some similar answers—Hamman did not read the literature, for instance, and was not board-certified. He took Hamman through the various mental illnesses and then asked what his diagnosis of Calley was.

"Several, I guess," Hamman said. "He does not have mental illness. But he was in a tension state; his state of mind was that of a tension state most of the time he was in Viet-Nam."

Daniel: What do you mean by a tension state, doctor?

Hamman: It's a state of heightened anxiety and fear.

Daniel: Would you make such a diagnosis for any man who had ever been to Viet-Nam?

Hamman: In a general sense, yes. The same feelings and reactions are present in the men in Viet-Nam. In a general sense, Lieutenant Calley was just like anyone else in Viet-Nam. His thought processes were impaired by the state of stress he was under, by the things that caused him to be in that state.

But, Hamman added then, there was nothing unusual to that; it was common with just about everyone in the war. It was not a result of mental illness and Calley was "mentally healthy. I think he was reacting as a person who was reasonably well put together would react in that situation."

"Like everyone?" Daniel asked.

"Well, like a reasonably normal person. He had some problems. But he would be someone in the middle of the curve of normal level."

Daniel took Hamman carefully and in intricate detail through the story Calley had told him about March 16. It differed in several major respects from the hypothetical statement and even from the story Calley would tell on the stand (which put the surmises of the psychiatrists into a questionable category at best). To Hamman, Calley had denied killing any groups, claimed he had killed only couple of people in isolated incidents. He admitted, though, to the doctor that he had ordered Meadlo to "waste" some Vietnamese on orders he had gotten from Medina.

Daniel: Did you ask him what he said to Meadlo?

Hamman: Yes, and he said he shook Meadlo and said, "Get rid of them."

Daniel: Is that an exact quote?

Hamman: Yes, that's an exact quote.

Daniel: Well, doctor, what did he mean?

Hamman: He wanted them out of the way, he wanted them not to slow down the move through the village.

Daniel: Did you ask if he meant for Meadlo to kill them?

Hamman: Yes, I did.

Daniel: And what was his response?

Hamman: I think that when he said get rid of them, he didn't necessarily mean that he wanted them killed. He wanted them out of the way so they would go on and do what they were supposed to be doing.

That may have been the first time Calley talked to Meadlo, but how about later? "Did you ask him what he meant then?"

Hamman: No. It was clear what he meant.

Daniel: You never asked whether he intended to have them killed?

Hamman: I did not ask him that questions.

Daniel: Is there anything to indicate that Lieutenant Calley was hallucinating?

Hamman: No, of course he wasn't. He was aware of reality; he was aware of what he was doing and what was going on around him.

Daniel then read the definition of premeditation and asked whether, on the basis of that, Calley could premeditate.

Hamman: In my opinion, he did not have the mental capacity to form an intent to kill.

Kennedy intervened. "Just a minute. What does your answer refer to, a specific intent or a general one?"

But before Hamman could answer, Daniel rephrased the question: "Did he have the mental capacity to form an intent to kill someone?"

"In my opinion," Hamman persisted, "he did not have the mental capacity to form an intent to kill."

It seemed a standoff. But Daniel tried to circumvent it by asking about the incidents of killing Calley had discussed with Hamman.

"Yes," Hamman said, "he had an intent to waste."

"Isn't waste the same as kill?"

"Waste is not the same as kill to Lieutenant Calley."

"I don't understand, doctor," Daniel said. "What do you mean?"

"Lieutenant Calley's intent to kill is unique to Lieutenant Calley."

It was a bewildering dialogue—if it was even a dialogue, for Daniel and Hamman often seemed to be talking about different things, with Hamman sometimes the only one sure of just what he was talking about. On the faces of the jurors there were blank and lost looks. Hamman had gone way beyond them, and he had gone beyond most of those in the courtroom—except, that is, Daniel, who seemed to be enjoying the whole exercise, the only one who was.

"Tell me, doctor," Daniel posed, "if specific intent to kill means that he specifically meant for the man to die, could he form a specific intent?"

"Yes," Hamman replied slowly, "if it wasn't willful. He did

not have a free will then, he hadn't volition. He just knew that doing this act would have this result, but that's all."

Daniel: Was he deprived of choice by a diagnosable mental illness?

Hamman: He was deprived of choice by a state of mind, but it's not diagnosable.

Daniel: Doctor, in your opinion, was Lieutenant Calley suffering from any mental disease, or defect, or derangement?

Hamman: In my opinion, he was not.

Daniel: Did he know right from wrong?

Hamman: His ability to distinguish right from wrong was not affected by a mental disease.

Daniel: Could he adhere to the right?

Hamman: No—well, to some extent, yes.

It had taken three days, but finally Daniel had gotten the replies he wanted.

But before he let Hamman go, Daniel drove one more point home to the doctor, which left the jurors looking at the doctor quizzically. "Do you believe," he asked, citing the statements Hamman had made to me and which I had used in a piece in *The Times,* "that no individual should be held responsible for what happened at My Lai?"

"I do not believe that we should hold any one person responsible for My Lai," Hamman said. "I do not believe that we should hold any one person or the nation responsible. If you want to hold someone responsible, I think the only one you could point to would be God."

The cross-examination of the psychiatrists had been Daniel's high mark during the trial. He had taken what seemed clear indication on their testimony of Calley's lack of mental responsibility for his actions, and had demolished those statements. One psychiatrist had been sent from the court-room, his testimony stricken. The other two had been at least partially discredited. While Kennedy would have to instruct the jury at the end on the psychiatric testimony, it was already evident that Daniel had persuaded those six men that there was nothing to the evidence.

17

"That Was My Order"

"The defense will now call the accused."

We had come to the climax, at last. All the evidence for the defense was in, what there was of it, and now it was up to Calley to exculpate himself, if that were possible. He was the final witness for the defense.

It was two-fifteen on Monday afternoon, February 22, when Latimer spoke those words. Calley rose from the end of the defense table and walked quickly, a small, lonely figure, suddenly seeming even smaller than usual, to a place before Daniel, stood straight, and braced himself. "Do you swear the testimony you are about to give is the truth, the whole truth and nothing but the truth, so help you God?"

"I do."

"Will you state your name?"

"William L. Calley, Jr."

"And your present rank?"

"First Lieutenant."

"And your organization?"

"Headquarters, in Headquarters Company, TSB, here at Fort Benning, U.S. Army."

"Are you the accused in this case?"

"Yes."

Daniel turned to Latimer. "Your witness."

Calley walked to the stand and sat stiffly. Kennedy leaned toward him solicitously. "Let me say one other thing," the judge said. "I have a feeling that you are probably going to be on this witness stand for quite a while. If you reach a point where you want to stop regardless of what are the time limits, let me know."

"Yes, sir."

And so it had begun, the climactic moment in the testimony in this court-martial. Over nine hours during the next two and half days, Calley would be on the witness stand, most of the time nervous and tense. He answered "sir" to almost every question; he kept raising his eyes to the ceiling, and there were long pauses as he considered his answers, searched for words. He shifted in his seat constantly; he rubbed his mouth and chin with his fingers, with the same hand in which he held the small microphone into which he spoke.

It began slowly. Latimer, in a protective, almost fatherly way most of the time, with rambling questions which were often hard to follow, led Calley through his early years to his arrival in Hawaii and his assignment as Medina's platoon leader in Charlie Company.

Latimer: Now, I will ask you if during these periods of instruction and training, you were instructed by anybody in connection with the Geneva Conference?

Calley: Yes, sir, I was.

Latimer: And what was it—do you have a recollection, what was the extent and nature of that tutoring?

Calley: I know there were classes. I can't remember any of the classes. Nothing stands out in my mind what was covered in the classes, sir.

Latimer: Did you learn anything in those classes of what actually the Geneva Convention covered as far as rules and regulations of warfare are concerned?

Calley: No, sir. Laws and rules of warfare, sir.

Latimer: Did you receive any training in any of those places which had to do with the obedience to orders?

Calley: Yes, sir.

Latimer: What were the nature of the—what were you informed was the principles involved in that field?

Calley: That all orders were to be assumed legal, that the soldier's job was to carry out any order given him to the best of his ability.

Latimer: Did you tell your doctor or inform him anything about what might occur if you disobeyed an order by a senior officer?

Calley: You could be court-martialed for refusing an order and refusing an order in the face of the enemy, you could be sent to death, sir.

Latimer: Well, let me ask you this: what I am talking and asking is whether or not you were given any instructions on the necessity for—or whether you were required in any way, shape or form to make a determination of the legality or illegality of an order?

Calley: No, sir. I was never told that I had the choice, sir.

Latimer: If you had a doubt about the order, what were you supposed to do?

Calley: If I had—questioned an order, I was supposed to carry the order out and then come back and make my complaint.

At the beginning of December, 1967, Charlie Company shipped out for Viet-Nam as the advance party for the 11th Brigade, and there Calley found things "extremely confusing." Back in Hawaii and in the states, he said, "there was an answer for everything. We can go right down the book. We had no problems on almost everything. There was an answer to everything. When you got to Viet-Nam, nobody had the answers. You were expected to —everyone was expected to have the answers but it was quite obvious nobody really knew the tactic to be used or the basis of the operation over there or exactly what to do. There was no school solution, so it was just the disharmony right there. It is a frustrating point to get into, sir. I was extremely confused when I got there."

During those first weeks in Viet-Nam, the company prepared the way for the rest of the brigade, and began its first patrols, for "five to ten days to the west of Duc Pho in the mountain regions checking out the mountainous areas for enemy positions." But it was "very, very rare" that the enemy was ever encountered or a shot fired.

But in Calley's mind, he said, and in the minds of others, was fear, fear based on stories they had begun to hear and on the after-action reports he had read in Hawaii before ever reaching Viet-Nam. Those reports and those stories all told him to be afraid of the Vietnamese civilians. "It was essential," he recalled reading, "that troops in Viet-Nam put out of their mind World War Two and Korean concepts of giving candy and chewing gum and things to the children, because that was taking a heavy toll. This was not that type of war, and the Communists used that American philosophy on us. The women and children were used along with the men very, very effectively."

War began for Calley in January, 1968, when Charlie Company was moved from Duc Pho north, to northern Quang Ngai Province, to LZ-Dotti as part of the newly created Task Force Barker. Calley was told that the "area was heavily laced with mobile mine fields that could be moved within a matter of twenty-four hours. The Vietnamese could come in and pick up a whole mine field and move it on you. That was the main hazard."

Though there was danger, until the Tet offensive exploded, Charlie Company felt little of its reality. Then, at Tet, at least the company knew the war was real. "It was about two o'clock in the morning," Calley recalled, "and we could see Chu Lai, which was the Americal base. They were blowing some big ordnance in there. I believe a bomb depot went up and they cleared most of the Phantoms off the runway. It did extensive damage. I heard about that later in the day; but even from sixty miles away, you could see it and you could actually get a little bit of concussions off the tremendous explosions going on there. We were called up, about four o'clock that same morning and told we would drop our mission and proceed toward Quang Ngai city that was under seige at that time and be ready to move in and reinforce. But our basic mission at that time was to cut off the exits or retreating areas for the enemy forces that were attacking, or try to get in and cut them off so if they did try to pull out, to catch them. And we did catch them. They were trying to pull back into My Lai One. We didn't do a very effective job; about all we could do was get some gunships in on them, because we couldn't get close enough to them."

But from Tet, the company learned to be wary. "You take your stress of normal combat anyway," Calley explained, "and then realize that your division base camp, which is your home where you get all your supplies and, well, without division headquarters up above you, you don't have anyplace to really go home. And it's just like the enemy is closing in on you. And I would say any combat stress and everything that we had before came back on about twenty-fold. Because you realized the enemy was in such strength and had massed enough to take on your division elements, think what he could do to your company if he caught you alone."

If from Tet had come a wariness and fear of things at a distance, a new wariness and fear took over when the task force began moving out and south toward Son My, toward My Lai (1), the home base, it was thought, of the 48th Viet Cong Battalion. The first foray came at the end of February. Alpha Company made a direct assault on My Lai (1) and "was hurt very badly in there. They came in, were disorganized from fire from the rear, tangled in a mine field and could not effectively assault Pinkville." Charlie Company on that assault was given a blocking assignment to the north, mainly to cut some causeways across the river to prevent the enemy from fleeing. But the company was unsuccessful in its attempts to carry out its mission. "I lost my RTO," Calley said, "and by the time I could get him dusted off, I had a couple of other men go into shock on me. All I could do was try to get my men that were in shock back out. It was the first time we had ever had a volume of attack such as that."

Calley's RTO had "caught a round in his radio harness and, of course, the bullet flattened and smashed when it hit the radio harness. And when it came through, it just took his entire kidney out, so he died within a matter of minutes."

The impact of that fight, Calley said, was shattering. "Losing my RTO, of course, I was very hurt, and I think hurt was the main thing. I think basically I was of the opinion that the enemy had struck at me very personally, and I took it very personal. And I was very remorseful. And I had never been taught about troops going into shock. And I didn't know if you ever got used to going into shock, or would it be a recurring thing, and if we got hit much harder, would we all go into shock. So I would say it was terrifying, really. It's a terrifying experience."

A couple of days later, the task force went back into the area for a second assault, with Bravo Company making the main attack and Charlie Company again in a blocking position. "There was a lot of fire," Calley remembered. "They finally brought the Phantoms in and burned it and by noontime we were on our way home. But I know Bravo Company didn't get in there. They got shot out before they got near it."

But the worst day for Charlie Company in Viet-Nam came when Calley was not even there. He had been on R & R in-country, and as he got back to LZ-Dotti he heard that his company had been "caught in a mine field. . . and there was a chopper coming in bringing gear back, and I helped unload that chopper at that time and then I took the chopper back out to the field but Captain Medina told me not to come in and just to go to LZ-Uptight and he'd let me know when he wanted me to come in."

The chopper Calley helped unload "was filled with gear— rifles, rucksacks. I think the most—thing that really hit me hard were just the heavy boots. There must have been six boots there with the feet still in them, brains all over the place, and everything just saturated with blood, just rifles blown in half. I believe there was one arm on it and a piece of a man's face, half a man's face, on the chopper with the gear." What he saw, filled him with "anger, hate, fear, generally sick to your stomach, hurt." And he said he felt "remorse for losing my men in the mine field, remorse that those men ever had to go to Viet-Nam, remorse for being in that sort of a situation where you are completely helpless. I think I felt mainly remorse because I wasn't there."

The casualties mounted. When Calley arrived in Viet-Nam,

he had had forty-five men in his platoon; by the eve of the attack on My Lai(4), he was down to twenty-seven men, and of his casualties, "I would say ninety-five per cent with mines, booby traps."

Now we had come to Calley's story of the most momentous twenty-four hours of his life. He had been told early on March 15 by Captain Medina "to stay loose and stay in the area and keep my troops in the area." In mid-afternoon, "Medina told me to have my people assembled by the bunkers around his CP or near his CP, and he then went over to Colonel Barker's tactical operations center for a company commander's briefing. He returned about forty-five minutes to an hour later and the entire company, except for a few that were either on the bunker line or pulling KP. I believe just about everybody in the company was present, and then Captain Medina then briefed the company that we'd be going into Pinkville."

The men were spread out, sitting around on ammunition bunkers, and Captain Medina stood in front of them, Calley and Brooks to his right. First a chaplain Medina had run into held a short memorial service. Then Medina "started off and he listed the men we had lost which was—I think, surprised everybody. Not everybody in the company had known who exactly we had lost out of the other. I was quite surprised, some people in other platoons that had been lost and I had known. And then he went into that we were getting low in size, we had lost—we were down about fifty per cent in strength. And that the only way we would survive in South Viet-Nam would be to—we would have to unite, start getting together and fighting together and become extremely aggressive. And we couldn't afford to take any more casualties. And that it was people in the area that we had been operating in that had been taking the casualties on us, and that we would have to start treating them as enemy, we would have to start looking at them as enemy. The following day we would be going into Pinkville and Charlie Company was selected to be the main assault force, and Alpha and Bravo Company would be in blocking positions."

Medina took a shovel and drew a map in the sand of the Son

My area. "We were going to start at My Lai Four and we would have to neutralize My Lai Four completely and not let anyone get behind us. Then we would move into My Lai Five and neutralize it and make sure there was no one left alive in My Lai Five, and so on until we got into the Pinkville area. Then we would completely neutralize My Lai One, which is Pinkville. He said it was completely essential that at no time that we lose our momentum of attack, because the other two companies that had assaulted the time in there before, had let the enemy get behind him, or had passed through the enemy, allowing him to get behind him and set up behind him, which would disorganize when he made his final assault on Pinkville. It would disorganize him, they would lose their momentum of attack, take heavy casualties, and be more worried about their casualties than they would their mission, and that was their downfall. So it was our job this time to go through, neutralize these villages by destroying everything in them, not letting anyone or anything get in behind us, and move on into Pinkville."

Medina said that the "Forty-Eighth VC Battalion was in Pinkville itself, and he said they would be destroyed once and for all. the only remark he made as to civilians, about civilians, was that psych war had prepped the area and the area had been completely covered by psych war operations. That all civilians had left the area, there were no civilians in the area. And anyone there would be considered enemies."

According to Calley, someone at the briefing had asked "if that meant women and children." And Medina "said that meant everything." There were, then, to be no restrictions on the troops. "This area," Calley said, "was in the general classification of the word free-fire zone. On this operation, we had political clearance to destroy everything in the area."

Then there was a platoon leaders' briefing, at which Medina went over the same ground with more detailed instructions about movement and positions. And then it was the long night of waiting for the dawn and "the largest operation I had been on."

* * *

With Calley in the lead chopper, the twenty-seven men of the first platoon, all with triple loads of ammunition, left in nine helicopters from LZ-Dotti the next morning. (Calley thought they had left an hour late; nobody else has the same impression; all thought the seven-thirty time was met.) "The artillery prep was still going in when we came up on the village. I could see the artillery going in, and we circled down south and came back up. Originally, we were supposed to come in from north to south; being as the prep was still going on, we circled and came in from south to north [another element contradicted by others; that was the planned direction of attack everyone said]. We initially hit the ground—well, we came in on final and the guns opened up. The door gunner on our chopper didn't open up because the gunships were almost right off the side of him. But the only really significant thing I remember there, that on final, the AC [air controller] turned around and told me we had a hot one, we were coming in hot, and I believe he said, 'When I get low, un-ass.' And we definitely did. I think my first man went out the chopper when we were still at fifteen feet. I went off, it was about five feet off the ground. We laid down a suppressive base of fire and rushed up to the outer perimeter road of the village that gave us some protection and held there."

According to Calley, because they had come in the wrong way, the first and second platoons had gotten switched and Medina called and ordered them to change positions, which they did. And all the time the troops were putting "a heavy base of fire" into My Lai (4).

Then began the on-line movement into the hamlet. "We came up with an initial heavy burst of fire but, within three or four steps, most of the men were knocking back to semi-automatic fire, and assaulted straight on through the village. It was pretty rough going. It was hard to keep a line formation there because of the hedgerows and the buildings and the trees and everything would channelize men into files and they would have to break back out, and it was pretty raggedy-andy going through there as a line formation."

The troops swept through, attempting to quickly "neutralize" everything in the hamlet, dropping grenades down bunkers, firing into hootches to "neutralize any personnel inside any building." Calley said he had no idea how long the sweep took. "When I got to the eastern edge of the village, my men were—of my formation—had broken down. I immediately had to get my squad leaders to get my men reformed up to move out. At that time, I got a call from Captain Medina to put the contingency plan into effect, that the second platoon would be breaking off to the north [the plan called for the first platoon to spread out and sweep the entire hamlet if that happened]. I believe Sergeant Mitchell came up to me and asked me if I wanted to—if I wanted him to check out the small part of the hamlet to the southeast. And I told him to get his men gathered up and move over and check out this part of the hamlet. The second platoon leader called me and said that he had not—that there were some large bunkers on the northeast edge of the village that he had not had a chance to check out, and asked me if I could check them. Also, the whole eastern edge of the village. I would say there were five or six large bunkers there. I told my second squad leader, Sergeant Bacon, to get his people together and start checking those out real quick.

"And Six—Captain Medina—called me again and he asked me where I was going, or what I was doing. And I told him I had some bunkers up here yet to check out that I wanted to check, and I still had that small portion of the hamlet to the southeast. And also there was still a lot of enemy personnel I still had with me, sir, ahead of me."

We had come now to the point of death and Calley's part in it.

Latimer: Now, during the course of your movement through the village, had you seen any Vietnamese dead, or dead bodies?
Calley: Yes, sir.
Latimer: And how would you classify it as to whether it was a

few, many, how would you—what descriptive phrase would you use for your own impression?

Calley: Many.

Latimer: Now, did you see some live Vietnamese while you were going through the village?

Calley: I saw two, sir.

Latimer: All right. Now, tell us, was there an incident concerning those two?

Calley: Yes, sir. I shot and killed both of them.

Latimer: Under what circumstances?

Calley: There was a large concrete house and I kind of stepped up on the porch and looked in the window. There was about six to eight individuals laying on the floor, apparently dead. And one man was going for the window. I shot him. There was another man standing in a fireplace. He looked like he had just come out of the fireplace, or out of the chimney. And I shot him, sir. He was in a bright green uniform.

(Later, someone was to describe it as the time Calley shot Santa Claus; that he was color-blind and it was really Santa in a red suit. "But what about the reindeer?" someone else asked. "They were on the roof and he shot them, too." But Calley, in a different context, was later to say that he couldn't shoot a reindeer.)

Latimer: All right. Now that you gave that incident, did you see any other live individuals who were in the village itself as you made through the sweep?

Calley: Well, when I got to the eastern edge of the village, I saw a group of Vietnamese just standing right outside the eastern edge of the village, sir, the southeastern edge.

Latimer: All right. Was there anybody there with that group of individuals that you saw at that time?

Calley: I recollect that there were GI's there with them.

Calley didn't recognize any of the GI's at the time; he moved away, contacting Bacon and then Mitchell. Medina called and asked what was slowing Calley down. Calley told him some Vietnamese, and he said Medina "told me to hurry up and get my people moving and get rid of the people I had there that were detaining me." Calley "rogered."

He started over toward Mitchell and "ran into Paul Meadlo that was there with a large—well, a group of people." He asked Meadlo if the soldier "knew what he was supposed to be doing with those people. He said he did. I told him to get moving, get on the other side of the ditch."

Immediately thereafter, Calley came upon Conti "molesting a female. . . . I told him to get his pants back up and get over to where he was supposed to be." Conti made no reply, just started away. And Calley continued his own meanderings, he said, when he got another call from Medina, who "asked why I was disobeying his orders. Well, I explained to him why—what was slowing me down, and at that time, he told me to waste the Vietnamese and get my people out and on line—out in the position they were supposed to be." Calley yelled at Bacon to stop searching the hootches and move out. Then he started for Mitchell, found "Meadlo was still standing there with a group of Vietnamese, and I yelled at Meadlo and asked him—I told him, if he couldn't move all those people to get rid of them." Calley didn't stop to see what Meadlo would do, he said, continuing on toward Mitchell. Behind him, he said, "I could hear heavy volumes of fire starting back up." Finally reaching Mitchell, he said he told him to move out into the paddies and set up a defensive line linking with Bacon.

Calley turned away and started back north. "I heard a considerable volume of firing to my north, and I moved along the edge of the ditch and around a hootch and I broke into the clearing, and my men had a number of Vietnamese in the ditch and were firing upon them."

Latimer: When you say your men, can you identify any of the men?

Calley: I spoke to Dursi and I spoke to Meadlo, sir.

Latimer: Was there anybody else there that you can identify by name?

Calley: No, sir. There was a few other troops, but it was insignificant to me at the time and I didn't—

Latimer: What is your best impression of how many were there at the ditch?

Calley: Four to five, sir.

Latimer: Two of whom you can specifically identify, Meadlo and Dursi?

Calley: Yes, sir. I spoke to those two.

Latimer: What did you do after you saw them shooting in the ditch?

Calley: Well, I fired into the ditch also, sir. . . .

Latimer: Now, did you have a chance to look and observe what was in the ditch?

Calley: Yes, sir.

Latimer: And what did you see?

Calley: Dead people, sir.

Latimer: Let me ask you, at any time that you were alone and near the ditch, did you push or help push people into the ditch?

Calley: Yes and no, sir.

Latimer: Give us the yes part first.

Calley: Well, when I came out of this hedgerow, I came right up—came right up about the last man to go into the ditch. I didn't physically touch him, but if he would have stopped, I guess I would have.

Latimer: Well, did he—was somebody there with him to order him in or push him in?

Calley: They had been ordered in—to go to the ditch, sir.

Latimer: Do you know who gave them that information?

Calley: Well, indirectly, I did, sir.

Latimer: And indirectly, what do you mean by that, was it through somebody?

Calley: I had told Meadlo to get them on the other side of the ditch, sir.

Calley moved north again after the shooting at the ditch, had a brief discussion with the helicopter pilot, Thompson, who had landed, and then continued up the ditch. "The next time I fired, the helicopter had lifted off and I started walking over to this machine gun position and I fired on a head moving through the rice somewhere over in that area. I just saw a head moving through the rice and fired. One of my RTO's went over and checked it out. It was just a small boy."

"Did you do any more shooting there?" Latimer asked.

"The only other time I fired in the village was on coming in on the LZ. There was a man running out of the village on the trail. I believe I fired once and fired again, and he leaped off the trail and hit the rice paddy. I took it for granted I had hit him. I don't know, though."

How about the monk?

Calley said he did not participate in any incident with a "monk that I know of." However, there had been an incident with a man who "was brought up to me for interrogation and I interrogated him briefly.

Latimer: All right. Then what did you do?
Calley: I butt-stroked him in the mouth, sir.
Latimer: With what effect?
Calley: It knocked him down.
Latimer: Did you shoot him?
Calley: No, sir, I did not.

It had all taken place on the northern edge of the ditch. The man, Calley maintained, had not fallen into the ditch after the butt-stroking, though he eventually ended up there.

Latimer: What propelled him into the ditch?
Calley: I believe somebody's foot, sir.
Latimer: Somebody's what?
Calley: Foot.
Latimer: Do you know whose it was?
Calley: No, sir, I don't.
Latimer: Was it yours?
Calley: No, sir, it wasn't.

And then Latimer took Calley through each of the government's charges.

Latimer: Let me ask you another—your impressions of another incident. There has been some testimony in the record to the effect that there was a child running from the ditch, that you threw him back into the ditch and you shot him. Did you participate in any such event?

Calley: No, sir, I did not.

Latimer: Did you see a boy or a child running from the ditch?

Calley: Wait, let me backtrack. Now this child that I supposedly said I shot, now, was running away from the ditch, but it is not in the same location. It is east of the ditch, but he was running away from the ditch. Now, I don't—

Latimer: To the extent that you shot and it turned out ultimately to be a child, is that the only impression you have of any incident which involved a child?

Calley: Yes, sir, I do.

Latimer: There has been some information disclosed that you heard before the court that you stood there at the ditch for a considerable period of time; that you waited and had your troops organized, groups of Vietnamese thrown in the ditch and knocked them down in the ditch or pushed them in the ditch and that you fired there for approximately an hour and a half as those groups were marched up. Did you participate in any such shooting or any such event?

Calley: No, sir, I did not.

Latimer: Did you at any time direct anybody to push people in the ditch?

Calley: Like I said, I gave the order to take those people through the ditch and had also told Meadlo if he couldn't move them, to waste them, and I directly—other than that, there was only that one incident. I never stood up there for any period of time. The main mission was to get my men on the other side of the ditch and get in that defensive position, and that is what I did, sir.

Latimer: Now, why did you give Meadlo a message or the order that if he couldn't get rid of them to waste them?

Calley: Because that was my order, sir. That was the order of the day, sir.

Latimer: Who gave you that order?

Calley: My commanding officer, sir.

Latimer: He was?

Calley: Captain Medina, sir.

Latimer: And stated in that posture, in substantially those words, how many times did you receive such an order from Captain Medina?

Calley: The night before in the company briefing, platoon leaders' briefing, the following morning before we lifted off and twice there in the village. . . .

Latimer: Can you identify the east—what has been testified to as the east-west, north-south trails on a map?

Calley: You mean from being there or being in this courtroom?

Latimer: Well, from being there?

Calley: No, sir. I never had any idea where an east-west trail was, sir.

Latimer: Did you ever pass the area, in your maneuvering that day, which would bring you into a situation where you would see what was on the north-south trail south of the perimeter of the village itself? Did you go south far enough, or did you see along the north-south trail any group of bodies?

Calley: No, sir, I didn't, no. . . . I was never down in that area, sir. . . . I never went down there; I never saw anything down there.

Latimer: Did you ever, in your walking through this area, see any large group of Vietnamese of various sexes and ages dead in large piles or large groups?

Calley: Where I shot the two men, there was, I would say, a large group of people already dead in that building. It would have been five to six dead people there. Other than the ditch, no, sir. That was all, that was the only group of people I saw there, sir. Large, I mean.

Latimer: All right. Did you see some isolated groups of what you would call a small, or numerically might be around five or six, along that area?

Calley: Five or six sounds pretty large to me. I would say there would be groups of two and three here and there, sir, up to five and six in groups. But the only one that stands out in my mind is the one inside the building. And just people, dead people spread all over the village. . . .

Latimer: Tell the court, in your judgment, how many rounds of ammunition you expended?

Calley: I am not absolutely sure. I, during lunchtime, I know—that is the only time I changed magazines. I don't think I used—I still had rounds left in the original magazine, but moving out, I went on and made sure I had a full magazine. Just sort of precautionary.

Latimer: In your personal situation, what did you use as a full load for a magazine?

Calley: Eighteen, sir.

Totally, Calley had with him that day seven fully loaded magazines and a bandolier with 140 more rounds. According to him, he had fired only about a dozen rounds all morning.

So there had been another switch in the defense once Calley got on the stand. Until that point, especially with the testimony of the psychiatrists and the hypothetical question, it had seemed that the defense had conceded just about every one of the government's contentions of fact—that the murders had taken place as the government charged and that Calley had committed them. His defense, it had seemed then, would be based on extenuation and mitigation, not denial.

But as a witness in his own behalf, Calley had completely reversed the field. He had in substance denied all the government's charges. He had, he said, not picked up and thrown back into the ditch and killed a small child; he had never even *seen* that child. He had butt-stroked a man in white but he had not shot or killed him. He had fired only a few shots into the ditch, mainly into bodies that were already dead, and though he had given an order to Meadlo, it had been an either/or order—either get the people across the ditch or waste them. And he had never even been to the trail intersection and so could not have killed anyone there. (However, in the psychiatric report at Walter Reed, which was never made public, Calley admitted the killings at the trail intersection, and he admitted them, too, to Hamman.) Of the three specific killings he admitted—the two men in the house and the child in the paddies—and the one possible killing—the fleeing man at the landing zone—all were outside the government's specifications. He was not charged with them and so could admit them. And, too, all could in a battle, or an anticipated battle, be looked upon as justified.

And Latimer pushed this point of Calley's denial of the government's charges hard, driving the point that there had been no premeditation.

Latimer: I am going to ask you this: During this operation, My Lai Four, did you intend specifically to kill Vietnamese—man, woman, or child?

Calley: No, sir, I did not.

Latimer: Did you ever form any intent, specifically or generally, in connection with that My Lai operation to waste any Vietnamese—man, woman, or child?

Calley: No, sir, I did not.

Latimer: I will ask you whether during that operation you at any time consciously conceived or sat down and formed an opinion to waste any man, woman, or child Vietnamese?

Calley: No, sir, I did not.

Latimer: Now, did you on that occasion intend to waste something?

Calley: To waste or destroy the enemy, sir.

Latimer: All right. Now, what was your intention in connection with the carrying out of that operation as far as any premeditation or intent was concerned?

Calley: To go into the area and destroy the enemy that were designated there, and this is it. I went into the area to destroy the enemy, sir.

Latimer: Did you form any impression as to whether or not there were children, women, or men, or what did you see in front of you as you were going on?

Calley: I never sat down to analyze it, men, women and children. They were enemy and just people.

Latimer: Did you consciously discriminate as you were operating through there insofar as sex or age is concerned?

Calley: The only time I denoted sex was when I stopped Conti from molesting a girl. That was the only time sex ever entered the—my whole scope of thinking.

Latimer: In this instance, when you saw a group being supervised or guarded by Meadlo, how did you visualize that group? Did you go in the specifics in any way?

Calley: No, sir. It was a group of people that were the enemy, sir.

Latimer: And were you motivated by other things besides the fact that those were enemy? Did you have some other reason for treating them that way altogether? I am talking now about your briefings. Did you get any information out of that?

Calley: Well, I was ordered to go in there and destroy the enemy. That was my job on that day. That was the mission I was given. I did not sit down and think in terms of men, women and children. They were all classified the same, and that was the classification that we dealt with, just as enemy soldiers.

Latimer: Who gave you that classification the last time you got it?

Calley: Captain Medina, sir. . . .

Latimer: Now, I will ask you this, Lieutenant Calley: Whatever you did at My Lai on that occasion, I will ask you whether in your opinion you were acting rightly and according to your understanding of your directions and orders?

Calley: I felt then and I still do that I acted as I was directed, and I carried out the orders that I was given, and I do not feel wrong in doing so, sir.

And so we were back to the original defense once again. It was all Medina's fault; and besides the people may have all been enemies. But any way you looked at it, it was Captain Medina's fault and if anyone should have been on trial for what happened at My Lai (and there was obviously considerable doubt at the defense table that anyone should have been tried), it was not Calley but Medina.

As he neared the end of his direct examination, Latimer

drove harder at the theory that Medina was to blame. He began to talk about the body counts, and Calley explained that there was "a lot of stress on body counts. . . . every company was competing with body counts, everybody wanted their companies to have the highest body count. . . . During Tet, it was very important so we could tell the people back home we were killing more of the enemy than they were killing of us."

Latimer: In connection with this operation, were you asked by Captain Medina to give a body count?
Calley: Yes, sir.
Latimer: Were all the platoon commanders asked the same question, to your knowledge?
Calley: I know the second platoon was there with me, and he also gave a body count, sir.
Latimer: And did you hear the total results turned in to Captain Medina?
Calley: No, sir.
Latimer: You don't know what the other two platoons turned in?
Calley: Yes, sir, I think I know how the platoon thing ran, sir.
Latimer: All right, tell us how it ran?
Calley: My platoon, I believe, took fifty; second platoon took fifty; third platoon took fifty; and we gave fifty to the artillery and fifty to the gunships and just about roughly about that much. I don't have the exact figures but it was around in that area, sir.
Latimer: Well, it was now—when you say you took this and we took that, was that in the presence of Captain Medina?
Calley: Yes, sir.
Latimer: And did you sit down in his presence and figure out this body count and give it to him?
Calley: You just make an estimate off the top of your head. There is no way to really figure out exact body count. At that time, everything went into a body count—VC, buffalo, pigs, cows. Something we did, you put it on your body count, sir.
Latimer: Is that the procedure adopted in your task force?
Calley: It was about—I would say it was running that way,

yes, sir. I wouldn't say it was an adopted procedure, but that is about how it was being run and estimated.

Latimer: And in connection with that, at this luncheon, was there some discussion about the method to be employed or was that the method that was just employed by you and the other commanders?

Calley: I was—never heard of a method that was trained in employing to come up with a body count. As long as it was high, that was all they wanted.

Latimer: There wasn't any specifics, but this was desirable?

Calley: Right. I had been on it enough times where they told me, just come back with a body count.

Latimer: Were you ever criticized for a body count?

Calley: I was criticized for getting too many shot and not coming back with the enemy. . . .

Latimer: Did your commanders seek to get a high estimate from you?

Calley: I generally knew if I lost a troop, I'd better come back with a body count of ten, say I shot at least ten of the enemy, which was pretty hard when you are only fighting one sniper.

And there was one last point Latimer wanted. Did Calley ever hear of an investigation into the incident at My Lai—into, as Calley always called it, "the Battle of My Lai"?

"I wasn't told there was an investigation going on," Calley said. "I more or less concluded. It was about two days after the operation, we were still sweeping the area and we were moving back north and Colonel Henderson came in and talked to Captain Medina for a few minutes. And when Captain Medina came back over to us, he said something to the effect of, 'Well, looks like I am going to jail for twenty years.'"

Latimer was satisfied. He turned and sat down at the defense table.

Calley's ordeal had hardly begun.

18
No Big Deal

Daniel had not taken his eyes off Calley during that direct testimony, hardly even looking down at the pad in front of him when he jotted a note about something he would explore further when his turn came. He had watched, examined, with a coiled tension that could be felt just by looking at him, just by being in his presence. And when at last his turn came, he almost seemed to spring with joy and relief from his chair, a caged cat suddenly freed, with his prey right there before him.

Calley watched Daniel approach warily. They had hardly exchanged a word before this, Daniel, as prosecutor, being barred from talking with Calley in all those months and Calley avoiding even coming near Daniel, avoiding even a nod when they passed. This was now the moment both had awaited, Daniel with a barely contained eagerness, Calley with ill-disguised dread. And that dread must have mounted if he had sensed Daniel's watchfulness while he was testifying under the rambling and fatherly touch of Latimer. For there was little doubt in the minds of those who heard Calley that he had lied, and lied blatantly, on the stand. His denial of almost every charge against him, and his ingenuous admission of even the few shots he said he fired into the ditch, all in the face of the direct and damning testimony of so many members of his own platoon who had watched him and either obeyed or disobeyed his orders, seemed incredible. Did he really think the jury would buy his word, his denials, against the weight of the words of all those others? And if he was still pleading the defense of higher orders, of obedience to the orders of Medina, was it necessary to deny most of the charges against him as well? Did he think he could really have it both ways—that Daniel or the jury would let him say that he had done nothing and, besides, what he had done had all been in obedience to his captain's commands?

So he watched almost with fear as Daniel approached. The prosecutor's voice was hard, his whole manner unbending, his opinion of Calley clear from both his voice and his manner. The questions shot rapidly at the lieutenant, an edge to Daniel's Southern inflection, giving Calley little time to pause and ponder his answers; Daniel's tone demanded immediate, almost reflexive response. He asked for a minute breakdown of the platoon, who was in it, who was where on March 16, who was carrying what weapons, how the squads were divided, in what order they moved into My Lai, where Calley was. To most of the questions, Calley knew the answers—a point Daniel would remind him of later when his memory seemed dim and clouded.

And when Calley, as he had with Latimer, mentioned something about the "Battle of My Lai," Daniel sprang.

Daniel: Did you receive any fire getting off the helicopter?
Calley: I have no way to know, sir. I was not hit, no, sir.
Daniel: Were you consciously aware of receiving any fire?
Calley: No, sir, I wasn't. . . .
Daniel: Did you receive any fire during this period that you were waiting?
Calley: No, sir.

In no hurry, Daniel led Calley through every step of his passage through My Lai, from the moment he got off the chopper and fired at a man running away, to his entrance into the hamlet through "a tapioca patch, sir," and then in his "zig-zagging back and forth with no exact pattern, sir, just zig-zagging behind my men, trying to keep my men in line."

Daniel: Did you see any Vietnamese?

Calley: Yes, sir.

Daniel: Where was the first time you saw Vietnamese?

Calley: In the tapioca patch.

Daniel: Could you describe the Vietnamese you saw in the tapioca patch?

Calley: No, sir.

Daniel: What was he doing?

Calley: He was dead, sir.

Daniel: Was it a man or a woman?

Calley: I don't know, sir.

Daniel: When is the next time you saw a Vietnamese?

Calley: About three feet beyond him, sir.

Daniel: What was he doing?

Calley: He was also dead, sir.

Daniel: When was the next time you saw one?

Calley: I would say they were all throughout the village. I don't—I can't pick out every Vietnamese that I saw dead there. Just all the way through the village, there were dead Vietnamese.

Daniel: When is the first time you saw a live one?

Calley: On the eastern edge—well, the two that I shot while going through there, sir.

Daniel: Those were the only live Vietnamese you saw going through?

Calley: That I can remember, yes, sir.

Daniel: Did you give out any instructions to your men to gather up the people that were there?

Calley: Yes, sir.

Daniel: Who did you give those instructions to?

Calley: Sergeant Mitchell, sir.

Daniel: To have them gathered up?

Calley: Yes, sir.

Daniel: For what purpose?

Calley: Clearing the mine field, sir. I told him to hang onto some of the Vietnamese in case we encountered a mine field, sir.

But, Calley, said, he had not originated such orders to use

Vietnamese as human minesweepers. He had merely passed on to Mitchell as they boarded the choppers at LZ-Dotti an order he had just received from Captain Medina.

Though some were to be saved, more were killed. Calley's men swept through My Lai firing as they moved.

Daniel: What were they firing at?
Calley: At the enemy, sir.
Daniel: At people?
Calley: At the enemy, sir.
Daniel: They weren't human beings?
Calley: Yes, sir.
Daniel: They were human beings?
Calley: Yes, sir.
Daniel: Were they men?
Calley: I don't know, sir. I would imagine they were, sir.
Daniel: Didn't you see?
Calley: Pardon, sir?
Daniel: Did you see them?
Calley: I wasn't discriminating.
Daniel: Did you see women?
Calley: I don't know, sir.
Daniel: What do you mean you weren't discriminating?
Calley: I didn't discriminate between individuals in the village, sir. They were all the enemy, they were all to be destroyed, sir.

The soldiers were firing, there were dead all over, but what sex or age they might be Calley did not know; he was "not discriminating." But in this "Battle of My Lai," was there really a battle, were the people resisting, was there combat? Calley did not seem to know. He didn't know whether any of his men had received any fire, he was not informed whether his troops had suffered any casualties or encountered any booby traps, and he never made any attempt to find out, nor did he make any attempt to find out what his men were firing at.

What he was doing, he said, was moving back and forth, giving instructions to Mitchell, giving instructions to Bacon, putting the so-called contingency plan into effect, "checking hootches and destroying the enemy" along with his men, and mainly just acting as a go-between, passing on orders from Medina to his men. For instance, Calley said, there was that second call from Medina when he told the captain that the Vietnamese were slowing his troops down.

Daniel: How do you know they were slowing you down?

Calley: Well, I generally know how South Vietnamese people move, and if you are going to move South Vietnamese people, you are not going to move them very fast, sir.

Daniel: Why did you tell Captain Medina they were slowing you down?

Calley: Because I knew they were slowing me down. It was another element that I had to move. . . .

Daniel: Why were they being moved at all?

Calley: To clear a mine field, sir, if necessary.

Daniel: What did Captain Medina say when you had the group of people, when you told him—

Calley: He told me basically to get rid of the people, to get moving.

Daniel: He told you that basically?

Calley: To the best of my knowledge. I can't remember his exact words.

Daniel: You described the people to him?

Calley: No, sir, I didn't.

Daniel: How did you describe them to him?

Calley: Vietnamese. VC.

Daniel: Which?

Calley: Either one. I don't know, sir.

Daniel: You don't know how you described them?

Calley: In that area, I could have used either term.

Daniel: Do you know if there were women in that group?

Calley: No, sir.

Daniel: Do you know if there were children in that group?

Calley: No, sir.

Daniel: Do you know if there were men in that group?

Calley: No, sir.

Daniel: What did he say?

Calley: He told me to give—to get rid of the people and get moving.

Daniel: What did you do?

Calley: I rogered. . . .

Daniel: How did you interpret that?

Calley: As getting rid of them if I couldn't move them fast enough.

Daniel: Did you check with your men to see if they could move them fast enough?

Calley: Yes, sir.

Daniel: Was it fast enough?

Calley: So we could get into position in a relatively short period of time, sir. . . .

Daniel: What did you do to effect this order?

Calley: At that time, I ran into Meadlo there and I asked him if he knew what he was supposed to be doing with those people.

Daniel: When you saw him where?

Calley: With the group of people, sir. I was on my way to Sergeant Mitchell, sir. . . .[Then] I saw Conti trying to molest a female, sexually molest a female.

Daniel: What was that?

Calley: Same time, sir, that I talked to Meadlo.

Daniel: Were they together?

Calley: No, sir.

Daniel: How did you do that? Describe the situation.

Calley: I went up to him and told him to stop what he was doing and get over where he was supposed to be at, sir.

Daniel: Were you talking to Meadlo at the same time?

Calley: No, sir.

Daniel: How far was Conti from Meadlo?

Calley: I don't know, sir.

Daniel: You saw them both at the same time?

Calley: I talked to Meadlo as I continued to move by him. I saw Conti molesting a female.

Daniel: Where?

Calley: On the other side of the group, sir.

Daniel: How long did you talk to Meadlo?

Calley: Only for a matter of seconds, sir.

Daniel: What did you say to him?

Calley: I asked him if he knew what to do with those people.

Daniel: What did he say?

Calley: He said he did, sir. I told him to get moving, sir.

Daniel: What did you mean when you said to him, "Get moving"?

Calley: Get the people moving, get them on the other side of the ditch.

Daniel: You didn't mean for him to kill them?

Calley: Not if he could move them, no, sir. I am still worried about the mine field, sir.

Daniel: Did he move them?

Calley: No, sir. . . .

Daniel: How far did you get before you ran into Conti?

Calley: Two steps.

Daniel: Did he have one of the people out of this group?

Calley: Right, sir.

Daniel: What did you say to Conti?

Calley: Told him to stop doing what he was doing and get to where he was supposed to be.

Daniel: What did he say?

Calley: He said, roger, and moved out.

Daniel: That is all he said?

Calley: Well, I don't know what he said. To the best of my knowledge, he could have said nothing.

Daniel: You weren't—

Calley: No, sir. Unless he said something to the negative,which he didn't as far as I was concerned.

Daniel: Did he pull up his pants?

Calley: Yes, sir, I would imagine he would. He would look kind of funny if he hadn't.

Daniel: Did you see him pull up his pants?

Calley: I didn't notice, no, sir. I wasn't paying attention to whether he had his pants up or down. If he wanted to go around like that, that was his business.

Daniel: You weren't concerned with whether he was stopped or not?

Calley: Well, I stopped him, sir.

Daniel: Did he pull up his pants?

Calley: I don't know, sir. I didn't stand there to see if he pulled up his pants.

Daniel: How do you know if he stopped?

Calley: Because he released the girl's hair.

Daniel: And then what did you do?

Calley: She fell back.

Daniel: And you just left and walked away?

Calley: He started on his way.

Daniel: When is the last time you saw him?

Calley: That is the last time I recall seeing him that day, sir.

If Calley, in this exchange, had thought he was being humorous, that humor did not go over. Daniel did not pause long enough at any of Calley's one-liners to permit him to earn even a smile, and as Calley described his own response to Conti's actions, one could see several of the jurors look at him with souring expressions.

But there was little time to do much but just listen, for Daniel did not let up, he bore in on Calley, his questions drumming against the lieutenant. He took Calley from the encounter with Conti, after leaving Meadlo standing forlornly by the ditch with his group of Vietnamese, and followed him as he darted to the north to Bacon and back south toward Mitchell, and then we were back with Meadlo again, passed once again before Calley reached Mitchell.

And poor Meadlo was still standing where Calley had left him, Calley said, still guarding his group of Vietnamese. Calley told him, "If he couldn't move the people, to waste them."

Daniel: Were you angry when he hadn't moved the group?

Calley: I don't think a violent anger, no, sir. It was distressing. It was slowing me down. But it wasn't actually Meadlo's fault. I mean, I didn't take it personally out on him.

Daniel: You didn't feel like he disobeyed your order in not moving the people at all?

Calley: He had basically disobeyed my order. But I didn't know what his problem was. I didn't take out a resentment on him. As far as I know, he didn't move the people.

Daniel: He disobeyed your order?

Calley: Yes, sir.

Daniel: This didn't upset you in combat, that a subordinate had disobeyed your order?

Calley: Not that order, no, sir. I felt that the man was trying to do the job the best way he could.

Daniel: So it depends on the type of order?

Calley: Yes, sir.

Daniel: What did you say to him, then, on that occasion?

Calley: If he couldn't move the people, to waste them, sir.

Daniel: What did he say?

Calley: He said, roger.

What did Calley do next? Did he wait to see if that order was obeyed? No. He walked on toward Mitchell, not looking back even, sure, he said, that Meadlo would now obey because "Meadlo was a very good troop. I had no reason to doubt that he would." So Calley said that he continued down to Mitchell in the small area of the hamlet to the southeast, ordered him to move out into the paddies. While he was talking to Mitchell, though, he said, "I heard firing to the north of me," from the direction of the irrigation ditch. As soon as Mitchell was on his way, Calley started north, he said, to find out what was happening at the ditch.

Daniel: What did you find when you got there?

Calley: My men were shooting men in the ditch, sir.

Daniel: What men?

Calley: Vietnamese men, sir.

Daniel: They were all men?

Calley: I don't know, sir.

Daniel: Did you look?

Calley: I looked into the ditch, yes, sir.

Daniel: What did you do when you got there?

Calley: I fired into the ditch, told my men to hurry up and get on the other side and get into position.

Daniel: Who of your men were there?

Calley: I spoke—I recognized Meadlo being there and I recognized Dursi being there. There were other men there. I can't relate who they were, sir. . . .

Daniel: Did you say anything to Dursi?

Calley: Yes, sir . . . told him to get on the other side of the ditch.

Daniel: Did you say anything to Meadlo?

Calley: Yes, sir . . . told him to hurry up and get on the other side of the ditch.

Daniel: Did you shake him?

Calley: Yes, sir . . . Well, I didn't stand there and—I just grabbed him by the arm and pointed him in the direction.

Daniel: Was he crying?

Calley: I don't know, sir. . . .

Daniel: How long did you fire into the ditch?

Calley: I have no idea, sir.

Daniel: How many shots did you fire?

Calley: Six to eight, sir.

Daniel: One burst or semi-automatic?

Calley: Semi-automatic, sir. . . .

Daniel: Who did you fire at?

Calley: Into the ditch, sir.

Daniel: What at in the ditch?

Calley: At the people in the ditch, sir.

Daniel: How many people were in the ditch?

Calley: I don't know, sir.

Daniel: Over how large an area were they in the ditch?

Calley: I don't know, sir.

Daniel: Could you give us an estimate as to how many people there were in the ditch?

Calley: No, sir.

Daniel: Would you say it was a large group?

Calley: No, sir. . . .

Daniel: What were these people doing as they were being fired upon?

Calley: Nothing, sir.

Daniel: Were they being hit?

Calley: I would imagine so, sir.

Daniel: Do you know?

Calley: I don't know if they were being hit when I saw them, no, sir.

Daniel: Do you know if you hit any of them?

Calley: No, sir, I don't.

Daniel: How far away were you from them when you fired?

Calley: The muzzle would have been five feet, sir.

Daniel: You didn't see the bullets impact?

Calley: Not that I recall, no, sir. . . . My main thing was to go on, finish off these people as fast as possible and get my people out into position, sir.

Daniel: Why?

Calley: Because that is what I was instructed to do, sir, and I had been delayed long enough. I was trying to get out there before I got criticized again, sir.

That seemed about all Daniel was going to get out of Calley about the ditch, at least for the time being, so he took him north, to his encounter with a man in white who, he said, was brought to him for interrogation. Twice Calley asked the man whether "he was a VC or where are the VC," and the man replied twice to each question, "No Viet." It was a dialogue of two men who understood not a word of each other's language.

Calley: After he said "No Viet" again, I butt-stroked him in the mouth, sir.

Daniel: How hard did you butt-stroke him?

Calley: Quite hard, sir.

Daniel: What damge did it do?

Calley: It bloodied his face, sir.

Daniel: Did you hit him square in the mouth?

Calley: I hit his mouth, yes, sir.

Daniel: Did he go down to the ground?

Calley: Yes, sir.

Daniel: And then what did you do?

Calley: I had seen the helicopter by that time. I saw Sergeant Lagunoy come up toward me and I started moving toward Sergeant Lagunoy. . . .

Daniel: Where was the man when you left him?

Calley: When I started walking away from him, he was on the ground. By the time I got two more steps he was in the ditch, sir.

Daniel: How did he get in the ditch?

Calley: Someone drop-kicked him into it.

Daniel: Was he still alive?

Calley: I don't know, sir. I would imagine he was, sir.

Daniel: Did anybody shoot him?

Calley: I don't know, sir.

Daniel: You just left the man in the ditch?

Calley: Yes, sir.

Daniel: Did you search him for any weapons?

Calley: No, sir.

Daniel: Had you directed that any of those people be searched?

Calley: No, sir.

Daniel: How close were those people to you in the ditch?

Calley: Three feet, sir.

Daniel: Were you scared they might be booby-trapped?

Calley: Yes sir.

Daniel: Might have a grenade on them?

Calley: Yes, sir.

Daniel: Why didn't you direct that they be searched?

Calley: I feel much more secure in that situation not to search them, sir, or get that close to them. If a man made a move, you can defend yourself and get out of the way rather than bend down over to try to search him if he pulls a grenade.

Daniel: Did you ever direct that anybody be searched?

Calley: No, sir, not that day. No, sir.

Calley left the man in white—alive and kicked into the ditch, he said, dead and shot by Calley, the government charged—and went over to Thompson at his helicopter. "He said there was a lot of wounded people around the area and wondered if I could get any assistance in to them. . . . I called Six—Captain Medina—and told him that a helicopter had landed, said he didn't like the way things were being done down here and requested medical evacuation for the wounded in the area." Medina's only reply, Calley said, was "'roger.' I got the impression that the pilot had talked to Captain Medina. He said something to the effect that he knew and don't worry about it, and get up where I was supposed to be."

Thompson landed again a little later, again talked to Calley, and "said there were some people up in that area in front of us, and asked me to evacuate them. I told him there was no way I could evacuate them except to march them with me. That I had no means to. I told him that he had the helicopter and everything, if he could get some helicopters in there, I would be glad to help evacuate them."

Daniel: Did you tell him the only way you could get them out was with a hand grenade?

Calley: No, sir, I did not . . . let me retract that statement. I hadn't thought about it until now. I believe I might have, yes, sir. I said about the only means I have to evacuate them out of there would be a hand grenade.

Daniel: How do you evacuate someone with a hand grenade?

Calley: I don't have any idea, sir.

Daniel: Why did you make that statement?

Calley: It was a figure of speech, sir.

Daniel: What did you mean when you said it?

Calley: I meant just—I meant only that the only means I could evacuate the people would be a hand grenade. And that isn't exactly evacuating somebody.

Daniel: What did you mean when you said it?

Calley: A figure of speech, sir, basically meaning that I didn't have any means to evacuate these people with, sir.

Daniel: That you would kill them if he didn't evacuate them?

Calley: No, sir, I didn't mean that, sir.

Daniel: What would you have done with them if he hadn't evacuated them?

Calley: I don't know, sir.

Daniel: Would you have taken them prisoner?

Calley: I don't know, sir.

Daniel: The cease-fire order had been given, had it not?

Calley: Yes, sir, to the best of my knowledge, it had. My troops had stopped firing, yes, sir. . . .

Daniel: Did you remain in the area?

Calley: Until the people were evacuated, yes, sir. . . .

Daniel: How many people were there?

Calley: I believe . . . I don't remember the exact number, basically about—I really don't know, sir. . . . There were two gunship loads. I would say three or four on each gunship. Of course, they were Vietnamese, be much lighter, maybe they could have gotten six on the gunships, I don't know.

Daniel: Do you recall the sex of these people?

Calley: No, sir, I don't.

Daniel: Were there any children?

Calley: Yes, sir, I believe there were, sir.

Daniel: There were children in this group?

Calley: Yes, sir. Well, I am saying that they had to be definitely noncombatants, sir.

Daniel: You were discriminating at this point between sexes?

Calley: Yes, sir.

Daniel: Why were you discriminating then?

Calley: Well, I wasn't discriminating against sexes, let me put that up. But I had a means to discriminate, and we were no longer firing on—I had been given a no-fire.

(Several hours later, Daniel returned to this story, and this time Calley could not remember whether there were children or women in the group, had forgotten completely what he had said before, and claimed, "I didn't take the time to evaluate those people when they were evacuated, sir. I didn't know what they were.")

Daniel, as was his technique—and that of any good cross-examiner—drove along a line until he seemed, for the moment, to have used it up and then suddenly switched. He did this time and again with Calley, recalling suddenly Sergeant Cowan's testimony that he had seen Calley surrounded by troops interrogating a group of Vietnamese at the eastern edge of My Lai. Calley remembered, he said, that Cowan "came up and grabbed a couple of the troops and told them to spread out." But he was sure he was not then interrogating any Vietnamese, though there might have been some nearby; however, he wasn't even certain of that.

Again Daniel took another rapid turn, going after an area Latimer had made so much of on direct examination—body counts. Calley said he had joined Medina for lunch, had been told that "we had done a good job—but apparently we still weren't fast enough, still couldn't clear the area fast enough." Medina also said, Calley related, that word had been received that My Lai (1) was deserted, and so, too, were My Lai (5) and (6). Then they turned to body counts.

Calley: He asked me about how many—basically what my body count—how many people we had killed that day. And I told him I had no idea and for him to just go on and come up with an estimate, sir.

Daniel: Is that what you said to him?

Calley: Yes, sir. He had been to the area and seen the area, he could relate body count as well as I could, sir.

Daniel: Did he say what body count he would attribute to your platoon?

Calley: No, sir.

Daniel: How do you know he had been over the area?

Calley: I hadn't really known if he was over my area, sir.

Daniel: How did you know if he could arrive at a body count of your area?

Calley: Because he would have a better idea of what sort of body count he would want to put in than I would, sir.

Daniel: Just any body count? Just any body count, is that what you are saying?

Calley: Basically, yes, sir.

Daniel: Captain Medina could just put in any body count that he wanted to put?

Calley: Any body count that was reasonable. I would

imagine he would put in the highest acceptable body count that he could.

Daniel: Did you have any other conversation with him?

Calley: No, sir. We continued on that discussion for quite some time.

Daniel: Could you relate the remainder of that discussion?

Calley: After he had given the body count and called it in, we were getting ready to split up and start moving again, and higher called Captain Medina, called back and asked what percentage of that was civilians, that they had a report there was a high amount of civilians in the village, sir.

Daniel: What body count did he report?

Calley: I don't know, to be exact. I really don't.

Daniel: Did he give an actual count?

Calley: Yes and no. I don't remember exactly what it was. I remember that I took fifty, sir.

Daniel: You did not hear him make a report?

Calley: Not exactly. I don't know what he finally came up with, though I believe it would be between two hundred fifty and three hundred, sir.

Daniel: When did you take fifty?

Calley: When we were discussing body count. It was broken down fifty, fifty, fifty.

Daniel: When did this come up in discussion?

Calley: When we were sitting there discussing body counts, sir. . . .

Daniel: Did you tell Captain Medina that you had shot the people in the ditch?

Calley: Yes, sir. I did.

Daniel: Did he ask any facts about that?

Calley: No, sir.

Daniel: How did you tell him about it?

Calley: He asked—well, after the higher called back and asked—said it had been reported that a lot of civilians were killed in the area, he wanted to know what the percentage of civilians was.

Daniel: What did you tell him?

Calley: I told him he would have to make that decision, sir.

Daniel: Is that what you told him? Those were your exact words to the captain?

Calley: Yes, sir.

Daniel: Did he then ask you to describe the people you had shot?

Calley: No, sir.

Daniel: Did you offer any description of them?

Calley: No, sir.

Daniel: Did you give him any estimate?

Calley: No, sir.

Daniel: Did you tell him which of your men had been involved?

Calley: Involved with what, sir?

Daniel: Shooting into the ditch.

Calley: There wasn't any big deal, no sir.

Daniel: You told Captain Medina that you had rounded these people up, put them in the ditch and shot them?

Calley: No, sir. I didn't.

Daniel: What did you tell him?

Calley: I told him there was people shot over there in the ditch and people shot all through the village.

Daniel: Did you tell him the circumstances under which they had been shot?

Calley: No, sir. Why should I? He knew what—the circumstances they were shot under, sir.

Daniel: How did he know?

Calley: Because he had told me to shoot them, sir.

Daniel wove back and forth through that luncheon meeting with Medina, back and forth between the dead civilians and the body count, and Calley's statement that Medina had come up with the figure on his own, and then a change in the story, as Calley talked about splitting up the dead "fifty straight across the board."

Calley: I did give him an estimated figure.

Daniel: What was that estimated figure you gave him?

Calley: Between thirty and forty, sir.

Daniel: Lieutenant Calley, did you just not testify within the last twenty minutes that you did not give any estimated figure?

Calley: No, I don't believe I did. You asked me if—what Captain Medina said. I'd say he asked me for a body count. I told him to go on and make whatever he thought sufficient, that he'd been through the village.

Daniel: You didn't testify that you told Captain Medina that you—he would have to use whatever he thought was appropriate based on the circumstances and he could come up with a figure he wanted?

Calley: Yes, sir, he surely could, sir.

Daniel: Was it your testimony now that you told him thirty to forty?

Calley: Sometime during the conversation, yes, sir. . . .

Daniel: How did you come up with thirty or forty?

Calley: Off the top of my head, sir.

Daniel: Did he press you for a body count?

Calley: He said, just take something off the top of my head.

Daniel: So you said thirty or forty?

Calley: Right, sir.

Daniel: Did he ask for a weapons count?

Calley: Yes, sir.

Daniel: What did you tell him for that?

Calley: Zero that I had, sir.

Daniel: How did you know?

Calley: We didn't have any weapons, sir.

Daniel: You never questioned any of your men as to how many people they killed?

Calley: No, sir.

Daniel: And you didn't pick this thirty or forty based on the people you had seen?

Calley: No, sir, I didn't. . . . That was a relative high body count of what I figured I had seen dead in that village, sir.

Daniel: And you gave him thirty or forty, and why did he then give you fifty?

Calley: That is the body count that he wanted to submit, sir. I wasn't going to sit there and argue with him about body count. Mine was off the top of my head. That is what he felt—he thought

Daniel: I want this clear. Is it your testimony that you gave him an estimate of thirty or forty, or is it your testimony that you said, "I don't have any estimate; you pick whatever you want"?

Calley: I said both, sir.

He had also said something else when Latimer asked him about body counts.

The issue of body counts obviously fascinated Daniel—as it fascinated Latimer and as it has fascinated the whole American military in Viet-Nam—and Daniel worried the count for a considerable length of time, before he finally dropped the whole subject. He had made some points though; Calley had gotten confused and was steadily claiming a lack of remembrance.

Then he reversed the ground, demanding to know why Calley had not reported Meadlo for disobeying his orders or if not reported him, disciplined him in some way. "I think," Calley said, "I was perfectly right in not trying to court-martial him there. I was down to twenty-seven men as it was, and I couldn't afford to go down to twenty-six right in the middle of a firefight."

"Were you in the middle of a firefight?"

"I don't know, sir. I could have been the second after that, yes, sir."

Calley was beginning to fidget as Daniel hammered away at him. Latimer began to object frequently, claiming Daniel's questions were repetitious and argumentative, though those are accepted methods in cross-examination and Latimer had used them often in this court-martial. But Kennedy increasingly leaned to the defense in his rulings as he seemed to feel that the defense was outmatched by Daniel and was not up to the task of defending Calley. And thus the judge, in a sense at least, would have to act as counsel to Calley if the trial were to remain fair and just, so he sustained Latimer's objections.

But Daniel still had things he wanted to cover. He had not, for instance, asked about the human minesweepers yet, and so he aimed some darts there.

Daniel: Let me ask you this: Did you have any Vietnamese saved up for the mine field?
Calley: No, sir, I did not.
Daniel: Did you testify that you received an order before you left LZ-Dotti to save some of them for the mine field?
Calley: Yes, sir, I did.
Daniel: Why didn't you save some up for the mine field?
Calley: Captain Medina rescinded that order and told me to waste them, sir.
Daniel: When did he rescind that order?
Calley: When he called me on the radio, when he was in the eastern part of the village, sir.
Daniel: Did he specifically tell you to disregard the previous order?
Calley: No, sir. He said those people were slowing me down, waste them, sir.
Daniel: Save none for the mine field?
Calley: No, sir.
Daniel: So you interpreted it to mean save none for the mine field, is that right?
Calley: The second time he told me, yes, sir.
Daniel: Were you concerned about utilizing people for the mine field?
Calley: Yes, sir, I was.
Daniel: Did you ask him that you thought it might not be advisable to save people for the mine field?
Calley: Not after he told me the second time.
Daniel: How many people would you normally use to take to the mine field?
Calley: Never any larger than the front I was covering, sir. If I had five men on the front, I wouldn't use more than five, sir. If I had a twenty-man front, I would use no more than twenty, sir.
Daniel: One per man?

Calley: Yes, sir.

Though Daniel had been driving at Calley for more than four hours—spread over three court sessions—it seemed that he had hardly begun. There were still vast areas that he had hardly touched on and some he had not mentioned at all. He had not asked Calley anything about the shooting of the child, which Calley had denied under direct examination. And he had not asked a question about the killings at the trail intersection, where Calley told Latimer he had never been and so could not have killed anyone there.

But as the hours passed, Calley's answers became "I don't recall, sir," and "I don't remember, sir." Daniel was eliciting little at this point from the witness. And Daniel realized that to question Calley on incidents that Calley had denied ever occurring would be useless; all he would get would be more denials, flat and unequivocal.

He had, he realized—though no one else in the courtroom did—taken Calley as far as he could. Suddenly, one after another, he read off a string of names—Bob Maples, Ronald Grzesik, Thomas Kinch, Charles Hall, Lenny Lagunoy, Greg Olsen, Jim Dursi. All had incriminated Calley in one manner or another. Did Calley know, Daniel asked after each name was recited, any reason he would have to lie? Though Calley denied knowledge of the incidents each had described, he said he knew of no reason the former soldiers would have to lie.

And then, abruptly, Daniel spun around, turning his back to Calley, and walked to the prosecution's table. "No further questions," he said shortly.

There was a stunned silence in the courtroom. Had Daniel lost his cool? Why let Calley go now when, perhaps, he had him on the verge of breaking? But Daniel did not think he had him there, and he was certain it would be fruitless to go on any longer. He had drawn much from Calley, had revealed much about the man through these questions and answers. In those hours of cross-examination the jurors and the court had seen Calley as he had not been seen before, and any more would add little to that portrait.

On the witness stand, Calley was as stunned by this sudden halt as anyone. He was white, with surprise, shock, and relief. What was apparent was that he desperately needed a break at this point to gather his resources. One would think Latimer would have seen that and given it to him. But not Latimer; he began a redirect examination immediately, rambling and undisciplined as usual.

He had several things to cover. One was Calley's estimate of Medina, to show that there was no animus. "I felt," the still faltering and numb Calley said, "that Captain Medina was a very fine officer, and I respected him very much. He ran a good company, and I am now and always will be very proud to have served under his command." It was a nice sentiment, but it did not erase the sting of malice in what Calley had been saying for nine hours.

Latimer was still not through. He tossed Calley more questions about Medina, about Conti, about others in the platoon, about radio messages, about orders. "Now at any time," he asked, "did you stop and consider the legality or illegality of those orders?"

"No, sir," Calley whispered. Then he looked at Judge Kennedy, totally drained of all energy, and plead, "Sir, excuse me, can we take a recess at this time?"

Kennedy gave it to him.

Then it was the jury's turn to have a go at Calley. McIntosh had spent the entire half-hour recess writing questions he wanted asked, and so had some of the others. Mostly they covered ground Latimer and Daniel had gone over thoroughly already. One, though, asked Calley to define the term "civilians" he had used in describing the people to be collected to clear the mine field.

"Well," Calley said, "I used the term, when I say civilians, I mean non-regular troops, civilian VC forces, sir. The VC living in the area and the VC sympathizers, meaning non-regular forces."

And another finally elicited an estimate from Calley of his

guess as to the number of people killed at the ditch. "I wouldn't think there would be more than fifteen people."

Then it was over. With a sigh, Calley put down the microphone he had been holding and walked unsteadily back to his seat at the end of the defense table. For three days, the spectators had had a chance to see his face; now the only view of him was once again his back.

Judge Kennedy looked at Latimer. "Do you have any other evidence you are going to present?"

"Not tonight and not tomorrow, I don't believe, your honor," Latimer replied.

"Do you want to rest tonight?"

"Yes."

19
The Challenge Unmet

So the case for the defense of Lieutenant Calley was over after forty witnesses and more than two months. What had it all added up to, as a response to the case for the government, the case that tied Calley directly to the massacre of unarmed civilians at My Lai (4), that labeled him on direct and circumstantial evidence a mass murderer of unarmed women, children, and old men?

It had been confusing and confused, rambling and directionless, contradictory. There had been an effort to say that the killings were done by gunships and artillery. There had been an effort to say there had been no killings. There had been an effort to say that the people were all the enemy and so deserved to die. There had been an effort to say that the mines and booby traps and snipers of this war had so enraged the troops that a slaughter was inevitable and no one was to blame but God. There had been an effort to say that international law and the Army's own rules of warfare were meaningless and should be ignored and forgotten. There had been an effort to say that those rules had never been taught and so should not be enforced, and the men who had not learned them not punished for breaking them.

There had been a denial that Calley had done any, or most, of what he had been charged with doing. And there had been an effort to say that everything he had done had been done as a result of orders, or because of his diminished mental ability.

There had been an attempt to shift all the onus onto

someone higher in the chain of command—particularly Ernest Medina. And there had even been an attempt to shift the blame onto those lower—particularly Paul David Meadlo.

And there had been a portrait—which the government's case had drawn, too—of a meaningless war in which all were enemies, soldiers and civilians, and all were victims, soldiers and civilians; a war with no thought to homes and property and lives; a war in which allies were scorned, ignored, and even killed; a war in which no one knew why he fought or for what. A portrait of an obscene war.

But was it a defense which rose to the occasion? It did not seem so. Was it a defense that met the government's attack? It did not seem so.

Part Four:
Calley on Trial -
The Last Words

20
"A Nice Conservative Number"

The defense was done, but, as in all cases, because the burden of proof rested on it, the government had the last word. There seemed little more that Daniel could want to do. But he was not content. He wanted to seal this case in an unbreakable wrapper. For the next two weeks, he called a series of rebuttal witnesses, beginning with his own psychiatrists, three combat psychiatrists who had conducted the sanity board tests on Calley at Walter Reed. All agreed, as one of them said, that Calley was "free from any mental disease, defect or derangement," that there was "no evidence of any psychotic or neurotic condition, intoxication, disorganization, confusion, or disturbance in his behavior at all," that he was sane and suffered no more battle strain than any of his soldiers at My Lai that day. He was not even suffering from a "transient mental disorder."

Latimer could not shake them. But because psychiatric evidence had been introduced and Calley's balance brought into question, Kennedy said he would instruct the jury on the sanity issue at the end of all the evidence and it would be up to those six men to make a determination on Calley's sanity in their deliberations.

Psychiatric rebuttal was but part of Daniel's answer to the defense. He called and recalled witnesses to rebut the claim that Medina had given orders to kill everyone or that such orders had originated with Barker or Henderson or higher. And because the defense had opened up Calley's background,

Kennedy permitted Daniel to introduce testimony on other crimes Calley had committed in Viet-Nam to give the jury a larger base from which to decide whether Calley had the mental capacity to plan and design murder and the ability to form a specific intent to kill.

So Thomas Turner was back, and into the record at last went the story of how Calley killed a woman at the north end of the irrigation ditch. And three other former members of his platoon appeared to describe an incident some weeks before My Lai. James Bergthold, an obese young unemployed truck driver from Niagara Falls, his hair curling around his shoulders, his beefy face split by a mustache and goatee, his belly bulging through the buttons of the new shirt Daniel had made him buy, not even hidden by the new tie Daniel had bought for him, told how he had "seen a man in a rice paddy. I brought him in and turned him over to Lieutenant Calley. After a while somebody said, 'Let's see if he can swim,' and they threw him in the well. I heard a splash and I looked over and Lieutenant Calley was standing over him with his gun pointing down in the well. I heard a shot. Somebody said, 'He's blew his brains out,' and I went over and looked in the well and all I could see was blood."

Two others confirmed this story in its basic outlines.

And what orders did Medina give that March 15? Back came Turner, Dursi, and Paul to say that they had never heard the captain give an order to kill women and children, though, indeed, neither had most of the witnesses for the defense. And the three also disputed Calley about the use of human minesweepers, saying Medina made no mention of taking prisoners nor did he ever say that some civilians should be retained for the mine field.

Bridging the gap between Medina's briefing and Barker's was Captain Eugene Kotouc, the task force's intelligence officer and himself at the time still facing a court-martial for maiming a prisoner by cutting off his finger. Kotouc was granted testimonial immunity and agreed to talk when Kennedy gave him an order.

The operation at My Lai, he said, had been based on intelligence information he had picked up, and was planned the way Barker traditionally planned such operations. "Barker was like an artilleryman," Kotouc said, "taking on targets of opportunity. He planned operations that quick. I'm sure this operation wasn't planned anything like D-Day." All his information, Kotouc maintained, had indicated that "we would undoubtedly and most emphatically face a mainforce VC battalion that was well trained and well armed." Barker's orders, which he heard, and Medina's, which he also heard, were to "destroy the animals, poultry, trenches, bunkers, hootches—anything of use to the enemy was to be destroyed." There were no orders, he insisted, to kill women and children or not to take prisoners. "It was our final analysis and consideration that the civilian population—if you want to use that word, that's your word—would be in the market." As to what would happen to civilians not in the market, Kotouc grinned, "I'm not sure I gave it a whole lot of thought." However, on the basis of past experience, it was expected that once the attack began the civilians would leave. "That's what Colonel Barker said to me: 'Let's let 'em take off down the road to Quang Ngai and get on with the mission.'"

But it was hard to know whether Kotouc was really certain about anything he heard—for he was hard of hearing, something Latimer stressed repeatedly on cross-examination. And when Daniel tried to resurrect him by showing that Kotouc could read lips, the captain replied to a question on this, "Sorry, sir, would you repeat the question?"

Kotouc's contention that the killing of civilians was not ordered, at least not by Barker, was also the stress of testimony by higher officers who had been at that briefing, who had been under charges growing out of the cover-up and had been freed later. All testified exactly as Daniel hoped, though each managed as well to light up some of the dark corners of the later cover-up.

Lieutenant Colonel Frederic W. Watke had been a major commanding a helicopter squadron over My Lai. His pilots reported on returning from their missions that day that they had seen stacks of bodies at My Lai and had intervened to save some of those civilians from the advancing American troops. Watke said that he passed those reports on four times that day and the next, with no results. At noon on March 16, he said, he told Colonel Barker of the reports. That evening, he told Lieutenant Colonel John Holladay, commander of his helicopter unit. The next day he personally gave a report to General Koster's second-in-command, General George Young. And later the same day, he repeated those reports to Colonel Henderson.

Major Charles C. Calhoun, who had been Barker's operations officer, brought the link directly to Koster. According to Calhoun, he was on an overflight of My Lai during the assault when he "got a call from Colonel Barker, who called Captain Medina to make sure his troops weren't hurting any civilians or doing any unnecessary burning. I relayed this to Captain Medina. He rogered." But those reports kept coming in and growing during the day, and so later in the afternoon, after the troops had left My Lai and were in their night position some miles away, Calhoun said he got back on the radio and "issued some instructions to Captain Medina . . . to re-enter My Lai Four and see if any civilians had been killed and by what means they had been killed." But Medina did not return. "Captain Medina requested me not to have him go back to the village. He was getting near his night lager, or night position, and he was concerned about mines in the area. He said twenty to thirty civilians had been killed there. I told him the instructions were to go back. At that time, Sabre Six—the division commander, General Koster—interrupted and said there was no need to go back in there."

Daniel had one more point to make on rebuttal. Lieutenant Stephen Brooks, commander of Medina's second platoon, was dead. But Jeffrey LaCross, now a college student, had commanded the third platoon and he came to court to tell of his day at My Lai. He said Medina made no mention of killing everyone in the hamlet; he had just said that everything was to be destroyed and, further, he remembered Medina saying that if there were civilians in My Lai who had been helping the Viet Cong, "it wasn't all their fault since Americans had not been in the area and they were forced to help the VC."

As far as he was concerned, LaCross said, he assumed that during the attack the standard practice of gathering civilians in a central location, interrogating and then releasing them would be the order of the day. During the advance, he said, his platoon had come upon two soldiers guarding twenty-three Vietnamese civilians. "I called the old man and asked him what to do with them. He said leave them there and he'd try to come over and talk to them." LaCross heard later that Medina had talked to the people and then released them.

Later, as the company was leaving My Lai, LaCross's platoon picked up four military-age men. "I called the old man and he said bring them along."

And LaCross disputed Calley's tale of the body counts. He did not remember any such lunch near the ditch at which body count was discussed. It had come up that night and there Calley and Brooks had each decided to take sixty dead for their platoons.

"What body count did you give?" Daniel asked.

"Six." The number brought an audible murmur in the courtroom.

"Why?" Daniel asked.

"I thought it was a nice conservative number, and I figured somewhere along the way my men might have killed six enemy," though Brooks said he had not actually seen any of his men kill anyone. In fact, he said, he had seen "no more than twenty-eight and no less than twenty-two" dead bodies as he walked through My Lai.

About the only place LaCross agreed with Calley was on the use of Vietnamese as human minesweepers. He had even used some that way during the day, though they "were used as guides. They weren't put out there like cattle to explode the mines. The VC had symbols marking booby traps and mines and only the Vietnamese could read them. So we put the Vietnamese in front of us since they are not going to blow themselves up for the sake of their beliefs."

They may not have been blown up that day, but it didn't always work that way.

At the noon break, LaCross and Calley, smiling and friendly, had lunch together. During that lunch, LaCross leaned over to Calley and asked, "Hey, Rusty, what're are you doing these days?"

Calley stared at him in surprise. "I'm being court-martialed."

"No, I mean what do you do with your time otherwise?" LaCross persisted.

"That's what I do," Calley said. "I get up in the morning and go to court to get court-martialed and then I go home at night."

LaCross shook his head. "I know what your MOS is."

"What?" Calley asked with curiosity.

"Thirteen sixty-nine."

Calley looked at LaCross uncertainly. "What's that?"

LaCross laughed. "An unlucky cock-sucker."

21

"I Can Still Hear the Screaming"

The Lear jet swooped low over Columbus Municipal Airport, buzzed the field so that some of the people waiting ducked, roared back into the air, circled, and finally landed. Out stepped F. Lee Bailey, his own pilot, his famous mink coat draped casually across his arm, unneeded in the warmth of a March evening in Georgia. Bailey strode to the waiting crowd of reporters and microphones, said a few inconsequential words, and then strode off, followed by two other famous attorneys, Henry Rothblatt of New York, who would become Colonel Henderson's lawyer, and Melvin Belli of San Francisco, who was then considering taking on Henderson as a client—both looking slightly green and in no little distress after a couple of hours in a plane with Bailey.

Lee Bailey had come to Columbus to be with, to give whatever aid and advice was needed to, his famous—or notorious—military client, Captain Ernest Medina. It was Ernie Medina's turn, his chance to reply to Calley. He had come to Fort Benning from his assignment at Fort McPherson—he was now in charge of the post mortuary—ready to meet the man who had once been his subordinate and had now become his chief accuser.

Son of poor Mexican-American parents, his father a shepherd, Medina had been born in New Mexico and, when his mother died of cancer when he was less than a year old, had gone to live with his grandparents in Montrose, Colorado, thereafter seeing his father only on rare occasions. In Montrose, as in many small towns of America, the climate rings with patriotism, and Medina was imbued with its fervor. At fifteen he joined the Colorado National Guard, worked his way up to sergeant, but when he joined the regular Army refused to accept a similar rank on the ground that he didn't have enough training. Later he rejected several opportunities in the post-Korean period to go to OCS on the ground that he didn't have enough education to become an effective officer, and only after he had taken some after-hours college-level courses, had married a German girl, and was beginning a family was he prevailed upon to seek a commission through OCS at Fort Benning, where he graduated among the top five in his class. Both as a noncom and as an officer, Medina was considered tough and imaginative, a good officer of the kind the Army wanted and needed. The Army became his life and until the revelations about My Lai, it had seemed that Medina was destined for bigger things, to go about as high as an officer up from the ranks without much education, and a Chicano in addition, could go. When he returned from Viet-Nam in November, 1968, he had been sent to the Infantry Officer Career Course at Fort Benning to prepare for higher rank. His majority seemed in the offing. But then came the word of My Lai, and in November of 1969 his file was flagged and he was transferred to Fort McPherson while the Army tried to decide what to do with him.

A medium-sized, swarthy man who looked trim and erect and correct in his uniform—he had, since, the time his file was flagged, let himself go, gaining weight, becoming almost portly. But in the months since the Calley court-martial he had taken off almost all the excess and, while not as leather-hewn as when he was in Viet-Nam, nevertheless he looked hard and competent again—Medina had about him an aura of what could only be called command presence. It was there even through the wariness, caution, reserve, and tension—not unnatural or unexpected—he displayed as he arrived at Fort Benning on the eve of his appearance on the stand. He seemed a man who had come to know himself, who had discovered both his capabilities and his limitations and accepted both, who had come to discover a place for himself in life. He seemed a man, as some of his soldiers had said, whom it would not be difficult to follow with assurance and respect and loyality, if not love. (Indeed, when I mentioned to Medina that one of his former soldiers had been pretty bitter to me in private about him, he said, "I wasn't running a popularity contest; I was trying to run a company in a war"—an old cliché but one that fit Ernest Medina.)

Through the months of the Calley court-martial, Medina, from his duty-station at the Fort McPherson morgue while waiting himself to discover whether he would also face trial, had grown increasingly angry at the testimony about him that was going on the record at Fort Benning. That anger boiled over with Calley's testimony, the details of which were relayed constantly to him while Calley was on the stand by his two military lawyers—Captain Mark Kadish and Captain John Truman—who sat just inside the courtroom railing through those early days (as they had sat through much other testimony during the court-martial), making detailed notes.

Medina wanted almost desperately to appear as a witness, to tell his side, to rebut the stories. And Aubrey Daniel, as it happened, was just as anxious to have him appear for the government.

But on February 26, two days after Calley had left the stand, the Army seemed to doom the wishes of both Medina and Daniel. Colonel Robert M. Lothrop, staff judge advocate at Fort Benning, notified Daniel in writing that the Army would not permit him to call Medina as a government witness. That direction had come straight from Washington, from Secretary of the Army Stanley Resor and from the Judge Advocate General, Major General Kenneth J. Hodson. Their reasoning was that if Daniel called Medina, he would be vouching for his credibility; since Daniel personified the United States government and the Army, that would mean that the Army was saying that Medina was telling the truth on the witness stand, and how could it do that and still press charges against him?

Medina, Bailey, and the other lawyers didn't quite see it that way. What they saw was a blatant attempt by the Army to silence Medina, to prevent him from answering the very serious charges made against him by Calley, to let Medina be tried and convicted in the press and around the nation without having an opportunity to reply. They filed a petition with the Court of Military Appeals charging a "conspiracy" by the Army and its leaders to prevent Medina from testifying and asking that such action be stopped and that Daniel be given the right to call Medina. And, they said, the Army had "a special reason" to know that what Medina would say would be the truth. Though no one spelled it out at that time (nor was it ever officially spelled out), Bailey said privately—and others, including Judge Kennedy, confirmed—that Medina some months earlier had been given a lie-detector test by several of the nation's leading experts in the polygraph. He had been asked about his briefing and about the events of March 16. What the polygraph showed was that his answers were not false.

The Court of Military Appeals, however, never had to come to terms with the issues raised, for the jury at Fort Benning took the play itself. As Daniel's rebuttal witnesses were appearing in a seemingly endless parade, Judge Kennedy told the jurors that once Daniel was finished, they would have the right to call as their own, or court, witnesses anyone who had not appeared and whom they might want to hear as potentially vital—subject, however, to Kennedy's ultimate veto. The jury took the judge up on that and sent him a long list of names, ranging through General Koster, General Young, General Lipscomb, General Peers, Colonel Henderson, Captain Medina, Sergeant Mitchell, and more. Kennedy would not go the whole way. "You're not here to investigate the operations of Task Force Barker or whether the alleged events at My Lai were known to General Koster or anyone else after they occurred; the only question for your determination is whether Lieutenant Calley is guilty of the four specifications in the charge." Kennedy struck everyone off the list but Medina, Henderson, and Mitchell (who, when he appeared, took the

Fifth Amendment, refusing to testify, and was upheld by Kennedy in that refusal). The jury also demanded the right to go to Viet-Nam and examine My Lai on the spot; Kennedy put a stop to that too.

So Medina came to Fort Benning not as a government witness but as a witness for the court, for the jury itself.

And he and his attorneys were boiling as they arrived in Columbus, and not just at Calley. They all felt that at the last moment the Army had tried to put a major obstacle in Medina's path and force him to take the Fifth Amendment, not to testify. For the day before he arrived, he was formally ordered to stand court-martial on charges of murdering 102 Vietnamese at My Lai; there were three specifications, two of them relating to individual murders and the third to overall responsibility for the murders of no fewer than 100 Vietnamese. This, of course, was almost the same charge for which Calley was standing trial.

The night before Medina testified, I joined him and his lawyers for dinner in Columbus, at the hotel where we were all staying. It began as a tense meal, but gradually, over a couple of drinks, the talk lightened and even Medina began to relax (which was, of course, the whole purpose). Even Medina laughed loudly when Kadish, who is a very unsoldierly soldier, talked about how Medina, his client, was constantly criticizing him for walking around with his tie pulled down, his shirt collar open, and his uniform jacket unbuttoned. In the midst of the laughter, Medina leaned over to Kadish—who was sitting at the table in exactly the manner he had just described—and said in a stern voice, "Captain Kadish, pull up that tie and button that jacket! You're the sloppiest soldier I've ever seen." Kadish laughed and said, "Yes, sir, Captain Medina"—and left his jacket and tie as they were.

And Medina roared as Kadish told another of his seemingly endless stock of Medina stories: how one day soon after Kadish had come on the case, Medina had said to him, "Mark, why is it that all you Jews are lawyers and doctors and journalists? How

CAPTAIN ERNEST L. MEDINA, COLONEL REID W. KENNEDY
AND THE JURY.

come none of you are just plain ordinary soldiers? You know, if I'd have had two Jews in my company, none of this would ever have happened."

Bailey and Gerald Alsch, one of his associates, traded insults, attempting to see who could be more scabrous. Bailey told tales of other court cases; everyone talked about the bizarre episodes that had filled this court-martial.

By the time Medina went to bed, he had relaxed, even smiled often, which changed his face from one of stern foreboding—and so, perhaps, would be able to sleep. He would need all the rest he could get.

It was on Wednesday, March 10, at nine in the morning, that Ernest Medina, accompanied by his lawyers and by Rothblatt and Belli—presenting an array of the most expensive legal talent ever seen in one room at Fort Benning certainly, and perhaps at any court-martial—walked into the courtroom, nodded tersely to Calley, and said a short hello. Calley stared at Medina uncertainly but would not meet his eyes.

Once Medina informed the court that he was willing to testify fully and would request no immunity, Kennedy had a couple of things he wanted to say before summoning the jury. He warned Medina and all the lawyers that "I don't want to hear anything about a polygraph while those jurors are in here." Then he turned to Daniel and Latimer and said he had made a basic decision. "Being the court's witness, and also being under charge for similar offense, I know of no situation in the military court system where this has ever risen, so what I propose to do is: I will conduct what would be the direct examination and cover the areas posed by the individual jurors and provide each side with the right of cross-examination." Latimer didn't like that at all, giving Daniel the right to cross-examine someone he had wanted as his own witness, but Kennedy of course prevailed.

And then the day-long ordeal of Ernest Medina began; he would be on the stand for six hours of testimony, until eight that night.

Medina was an impressive witness. He answered each question at length, trying to cover all the details; he was fluent; his answers military, with a good memory for dates, unit numbers, and military terminology, stated in ways that could not but impress those officers on the jury, toward whom he almost invariably directed his answers (Bailey and Kadish obviously having done a good job in preparing him for this test).

Kennedy took Medina slowly through his military background, through his appointment as commanding officer of Charlie Company in Hawaii in December, 1966 (he finally left the company a month after My Lai, on April 24, 1968, going on to a position with the full brigade), through the training of the company, his problems in getting either enough or adequate personnel for both the ranks and for non-commissioned and commissioned officers. "Some of the replacements that were received were individuals that were referred to as McNamara's One Hundred Thousand," Medina said—men who could not normally have qualified for the Army on the basis of intelligence but had been inducted nevertheless under a plan by the then-Secretary of Defense Robert Mc-Namara to see if the Army could help them (and, perhaps, to provide needed fodder for the war in Viet-Nam). Medina described how even though the company, and the 11th Brigade, was promised two extra months of training, that was ignored—as was a later request for an additional month of training in Viet-Nam before combat duty—and on December 1, 1967, Charlie Company arrived at Da Nang, South Viet-Nam, as the advance party for the brigade.

Its initial job was to get things ready, to prepare a fire base for the brigade near Duc Pho, and to receive an orientation course to prepare for the war. "The training we received," Medina said, "lasted one day. . . . The course consisted of how to place batteries in a radio; proper radio-telephone communications; how to tell the South Vietnamese people, civilians that you encounter in your area of operations how to stop or if they were fleeing or trying to evade by using the words, 'dong la, dong la,' meaning stop, or 'di di moi,' move out of this area, or the words, 'la dai, la dai,' come out, come out. Words of this type. We were given an orientation on scout dogs, the use of scout dogs that were available to the Third Brigade, Fourth Infantry Division. We were also given instructions on how to open C ration cans and to eat our C ration meal, and how to use a C ration stove and use the C ration heating tablet to heat C rations. Our noon meal that day consisted of C rations. . . . We received instructions on the method of calling for gunship support, location of the enemy target, how to identify the location of the friendly positions. . . . We were given a demonstration by a gunship team on firing of the rockets on the gunships; the forty-millimeter grenade launcher, the miniguns, and how to prep an area with the gunships. . . .

"The only training that was given us as far as the treatment and handling of prisoners was basically the five S's—search, silence, safeguard, speed and segregate. The type of card that we were to use to tag the prisoners; how to fill it out; the location where he was captured, the capturing unit, whether the individual was evading with a weapon or without a weapon, whether we thought he was VCS or innocent civilian or indigenous personnel. . . .

"We did receive some training [on how to distinguish between noncombatants, Viet Cong regulars, suspects, and sympathizers] by the elements of the Second ARVN Division. The adviser was an Australian, also had some *cheiu hoi* [former Viet Cong] there. They told us it was very difficult to identify VC since they did not wear uniforms, unless they were carrying weapons or web gear. The Australian emphasized that you should be extremely leery of children; that he had lost one of his friends because a child had placed a hand grenade wrapped with masking tape in the gas tank and the gas had dissolved the masking tape and had blew up."

After a month in Viet-Nam, during which the company did little but patrol and secure its fire base, called LZ-Carrantan, near Duc Pho, Medina was not satisfied with the performance of his men. He did some switching around that he hoped "would give us a better combat operating structure." Among the switches: Calley was moved from commander of the second platoon to the first—which Medina considered more disciplined and, implicitly, less in need of a sterling leader— and to help him in that new assignment Medina transferred Mitchell, who was platoon sergeant in the third platoon, to squad leader in the first.

Late in January, Charlie Company was trucked north to join the newly created Task Force Barker at a new fire base, LZ-Dotti. In the process of the shift, some of Medina's better personnel were taken from him and assigned to the 11th Brigade. The same thing happened to the other companies, and the Task Force called itself Barker's Bastards. He complained to Colonel Barker and threatened to carry his complaints to the brigade commander, General Lipscomb, "that I did not have the proper support that I needed." Some of the men he requested were sent back to him.

But the area around LZ-Dotti was filled with mines and the casualties began to be taken. The first patrol Charlie Company went on "we had not moved from LZ-Dotti approximately fifteen hundred meters when the first individual detonated a home-made booby trap." More men fell to mines, wounded, and his first death came from an unseen sniper during Tet.

The worst day for Charlie Company, though, was February 25, 1968. The company stumbled into a mine field. It was on a long-distance patrol, moving through the northern part of its area of operations, feeling more and more illegitimate, more and more Barker's Bastards, for two of its better officers had been taken away, shifted to higher headquarters and replaced by two lieutenants who had never before been out from behind a desk, and the third officer, Calley, was away on in-country leave.

Throughout that patrol, Charlie Company had been under sniper fire and had taken four casualties. On the night of the twenty-fourth, at the bivouac, one soldier came up to Medina and "said, 'Sir, I have a problem. . . . I don't know how to go about. . . . I don't want you to think I am running out on you or that I am chicken or that I want to leave the people here, but I have a brother that is serving in Viet-Nam.' And I told him, I says, 'Why didn't you tell me before? I could have put you on the resupply ship that just brought in the resupplies, gotten you back to Chu Lai and we could have checked your story out.' He says, 'No, sir, that is not what I wanted. . . . I will wait until we get back in.'"

The next morning, the company started moving through an athletic field, three men with minesweepers out ahead. "We were moving rather slow trying to clear the area when the lead element detonated a mine. First I thought it was incoming artillery. Another one went off and another one. Immediately the cry started going up for, 'Medic! Medic!' In the mine field incident, I lost a number of people. My senior medic who had moved through the mine field very courageously also was—had given a lot of medical assistance, was trying to get to the third platoon leader when he detonated a mine and blew his foot off.

"We started sweeping the area as best we could with mine detectors, taking pieces of toilet paper and marking the mines that we found. We had one individual that we could not evacuate that was dead; it was the individual that had talked to me the night before about wanting to leave South Viet-Nam because he had a brother that was serving there. I took the medic that was with me, the platoon medic from the first platoon, and he and I moved through the mine field to where the individual was laying. He was split as if somebody had taken a cleaver and right up from his crotch all the way up to his chest cavity. I have never seen anything that looked so unreal in my entire life; the intestines, the liver, and the stomach and the blood looked just like plastic. We took a poncho and we spread it out and the medic started to pick him up by the legs. I reached underneath his arms to place him under the poncho and we set him on top of another mine. The concussion blew me back. I fell backwards, as I got up the medic was starting to go to pieces on me. He started to come out of the ditch and I looked at him as if he had stood behind the screen and somebody had taken a paint brush with red paint and splattered it through the screen. He was—had blood all over him. I grabbed him as he started to pass me and I shook him and I said, 'My God, don't go to pieces on me. You are the only medic I have got. I have got people that are hurt.' I hit him. I slapped him. I knocked him to the ground and I helped him get back up, and I seen on his religious medal a piece of liver and I tried to get it off the individual before he seen it. The individual was very shook up.

"We lost approximately sixteen wounded in the mine field and four—three—that were killed by mines and booby traps. As we were moving back, Lieutenant Brooks's platoon was—point man—was moving through a hedgerow, detonated a fifteen or a hundred-five artillery shell killing him and wounding a couple of others."

It was the company's worst day. But in some ways it showed many of the men they had a leader they could trust in Medina, for he led most of them to safety from that mine field, and for his actions that day he was awarded the Army's third highest decoration, the Silver Star.

A few weeks later, the company down to 105 men, having suffered 28 casualties since arriving in Viet-Nam, word came of the attack on My Lai, the first time, if the intelligence was right, that Charlie Company would be going into combat against a real live enemy; it would be an occasion to get revenge for all those mines and booby traps and snipers.

Medina heard about it at a briefing on the afternoon of March 15 given by Colonel Barker to him and the leader of Bravo Company, during a helicopter flight along the edges of Son My village. When the chopper was north of My Lai (4), Barker motioned to Medina to come to his side. "He pointed on his map and he says, 'LZ right here, your company. I want you to—we have permission to destroy the villages, to burn the hootches, to kill the livestock, to close the wells and to destroy the food crop.'"

When they landed, the three men went to Barker's headquarters and were joined by Calhoun and Henderson.

Barker expanded on the briefing, telling them that "the Forty-Eighth VC Battalion was located at the village of My Lai Four and that we could expect to be outnumbered two-to-one and that we could expect a heavy engagement. . . . Intelligence reports indicated that the women and children noncombatants in the village of My Lai would be going to the market at Son Thanh or Quang Ngai."

Henderson intervened at that point, Medina said, and declared that he wanted this, the first attack by elements of the 11th Brigade under his command—he had taken over from Lipscomb that day—to be a smashing success. "He mentioned that one of the failures with the other operations in that particular area had been that the failure of the American soldier to rapidly close with the enemy, that they had killed, and to capture the weapons—this is one reason why the weapon count in that area was low—and that he wanted them to move, wanted us to emphasize to move with aggressiveness, to ensure that the weapons were not picked up by the women, the children, or other VC and the individuals get away with weapons. He also stated that past operations were—it appeared that the people were not being thorough enough in checking the bunker complexes because once they had passed, the Viet Cong would appear behind the American forces and engage them from the rear, causing the people to become pinned down."

Then Medina moved to his own briefing of his troops and the operation against My Lai itself. And from this point on, his account diverged radically from Calley's—and from that of other soldiers. He contradicted Calley point by point on much of what Calley had said on the stand.

Medina's account of the briefing, in greater detail than reported by others, generally went along with much of what we had heard—and what he said Henderson and Barker had told him at the company commander's briefing—that they would meet the 48th Viet Cong Battalion, that there were between 250 and 280 enemy and so Charlie Company would be outnumbered two-to-one and could expect "a hell of a good fight and that we would probably be heavily engaged." The men were not to worry about being outnumbered because they would be supported by artillery and a double coverage of gunships, and so "we would finally get a chance to engage them in combat and we would be able to destroy the Forty-Eighth VC Battalion." And he told the men that all "innocent civilian or noncombatants," according to the intelligence reports "would be gone to market at seven hundred hours in the morning. . . . I did not make any reference to the handling of prisoners."

Kennedy: Let me ask you, were there any questions asked of you at that briefing?

Medina: Yes, sir.

Kennedy: Do you recall what they were?

Medina: Yes, sir. One of the questions that was asked of me at the briefing was, "Do we kill women and children?"

Kennedy: What was your reply?

Medina: My reply to that question was: "No, you do not kill women and children. You must use common sense. If they have a weapon and are trying to engage you, then you can shoot back, but you must use common sense. "

Kennedy: Were any provisions made by you for the treatment of any wounded Vietnamese?

Medina: No, sir.

Kennedy: Was there any provision made for the capture and collection of the Vietnamese in that village?

Medina: There were no instructions given as far as the capture or collection of any noncombatants in the village of My Lai Four. It was standard procedure in other operations that we had conducted that the sweep elements, when they moved through the village, they would move through as rapidly as possible, pushing any of the inhabitants to the far side of the village, segregating them in an open area.

Now it was on to the operation itself. Everything, Medina said, went as scheduled, the only delay being Calley. He was a little late getting to the pickup zone at LZ-Dotti and Medina went looking for him and told him "to get his butt moving, to get his people up to the pickup zone and get ready to go." Then it was on to My Lai. "For those of you that have been on a combat assault," Medina said directly to the jurors, "the adrenalin starts pumping, the pucker factor goes up."

The choppers moved in on My Lai as they were supposed to, from the south, after making a diversionary sweep westward over Quang Ngai city. As they set down on the western edge of the hamlet, "I did not hear the initial, or the familiar sound of incoming fire from somebody shooting at you, or a rifle shot cracking over your head. My first reaction was to notify the task force on the air-ground net that the LZ time was seven-thirty hours, LZ cold. At that time, the elements of the first platoon were moving to set up security toward the front of the landing zone. About that time, I received a call from a helicopter pilot that said, 'Negative! Negative!' He says, 'You are receiving fire! We are receiving fire! The LZ is hot!' at which time I relayed the information to my platoon leaders that the LZ was hot, we were receiving small arms fire, that the gunships had killed VC with weapons, VC evading from the village with weapons, to move with extreme caution and to get their people moving."

Medina remained at his command post outside the hamlet, waiting for the second lift to come in, then checked out a suspected booby trap—a box in which was found a Sony transistor radio, some documents, and medical supplies, he said. The lead elements swept through My Lai, overhead gunships were circling, reporting Viet Cong killed evading the hamlet with smoke dropped to mark their locations. Some men from the third platoon were sent out to check. More reports of dead Viet Cong came in and Medina sent the second platoon to the north to check those reports, informing Calley he was doing so and that Calley should spread out and sweep the entire hamlet until Brooks's platoon got back from the north.

More smoke was dropped, with reports of more dead Viet Cong with weapons and more requests that Medina send men to check the smoke. Now, however, Medina had nobody left to send. Over the radio came the voice of Calhoun: "Damnit, I want somebody to get over there and pick up that weapon." Medina went himself with some of his headquarters personnel. "The first location we came to that had been marked with smoke, there was a man, a woman, and a South Vietnamese girl, I would estimate her age, I guess, to be around fourteen or fifteen, that had been hit by shrapnel from artillery or from rockets from the gunships. I could tell that it was not done by small arms fire because they were ripped up very badly. I looked in the immediate area; there were no weapons."

Medina moved on, to where a helicopter was hovering over an area marked with smoke. "As I came up the incline, there was a small trail, the VC was laying off the trail in the rice. I see it was a woman. She was laying on her side, facing away from me. Her arm appeared to be under her. I did not see any weapon in the immediate area. I do not recall seeing any wounds on her whatever. I looked around the area. I didn't see a weapon. I started to turn away, my people were moving up behind me. And as I started to turn around, I caught movement from the corner of my eye. Her head started to move, her eyelid. She started—I could see her chest starting to move. And my immediate reaction was that the helicopter had marked a VC with weapon. 'She's got a weapon or hand grenade! My God, you have had it!' I just continued turning around and I fired twice, and I assumed that I killed her. I did not check her out. I did not turn her over. I assumed that I killed her."

Kennedy: Did you say your purpose in being in the area was to look for weapons?
Medina: Yes, sir.
Kennedy: And you thought this woman had a weapon?
Medina: Yes, sir.
Kennedy: Now, why didn't you look for one?
Medina: Well, I was a little concerned about having shot the woman. She was the first person I had ever killed. I was a little scared. I didn't see any weapon and I was upset about having shot her.

Almost immediately, Medina said, he received a report that Carter had been shot in the foot, and he led his group to that spot where he called for a medivac after being told that it had been an accident—Carter had been trying to clean a jammed .45 when it went off, was the story he was told.

Kennedy: Did you cross any major trails that intersected that village, that run from north-south, east-west?
Medina: Yes, sir.
Kennedy: Did you see any bodies anywhere near this trail intersection?
Medina: Yes, sir.

They were, Medina said, the bodies of twenty to twenty-eight civilians, the bodies that appeared in the picture taken by Haeberle, Prosecution Exhibit 12A. In addition, Medina said, there was "a small child that had been shot in the stomach; his intestines were protruding from the wound."

Kennedy: Now, had you received any radio communication from any part of your company concerning what the body count was up to that point?
Medina: Yes, sir.
Kennedy: Did you relay that to Task Force Barker?
Medina: Yes, sir.
Kennedy: Now, could you tell us who gave you these reports, or what the reports were?
Medina: The initial report that I had received was the first VC that the gunships had killed, the VC evading with weapons. The second report that I received was from the platoon leader of the first platoon, Lieutenant Calley, giving me a body count of approximately sixty-nine.
Kennedy: Did you transmit that body count to headquarters of Task Force Barker?
Medina: Yes, sir.

Once Carter had been dusted off—medivac-ed—Medina and his group entered My Lai and began wandering through the hamlet. They came on an old man who told his interpreter that forty or forty-five Viet Cong had left My Lai before six that morning. Continuing the tour of My Lai, Medina came on bunkers being blown, hootches being burned and, though he had given orders, he said, at the time of Carter's medivac, "to conserve ammunition . . . to ensure that no innocent civilians were being killed," there was sporadic fire all around.

As he passed the eastern edge of My Lai, Medina said he saw Calley for the first and only time that morning. Calley came toward him and said a helicopter had landed with a damaged rotor. "I asked him if this was the helicopter pilot that he had talked to earlier. He said no."

And what was that about an earlier helicopter pilot? It took Kennedy a little time to get it straightened out with Medina, who finally understood the questions and replied that even before he had moved his command group from their post outside My Lai, Calley had called and said "that a helicopter pilot had landed and had stated to him that he, the pilot, did not like the way the lieutenant was conducting this operation, and I asked him, I said, 'Well, what did you tell him?' And he says, 'I told him that I was the one in charge of this platoon.' And I said, 'Well, where is he at now?' He said, 'He's getting in his helicopter and taking off.' I said, 'Fine. That is good. You continue with your mission.'"

But that had all been much earlier.

This time Medina had the brief talk with Calley and then left him for a lunch break. He did not, he said, have lunch with Calley or any of his platoon leaders, actually had it by himself. There was no talk at that time, he said, with Calley or any officer of his command about body count. And when the lunch was over, he just gave orders to the troops to move out, head north and east. The Battle of My Lai was over.

Kennedy: Now, did you at any time on the fifteenth of March or at any time on the sixteenth of March order or direct Lieutenant Calley to kill or waste any Vietnamese people?
Medina: No, sir. . . .
Kennedy: After you left the village and you were some distance from the village, did you, at that time, ever receive a radio message to return to the village of My Lai Four?

Medina: Yes, sir. . . . between fifteen-thirty, sixteen-thirty hours on the sixteenth of March . . . I had received a radio communication from Major Calhoun and he instructed me to return back to the village of My Lai Four and to determine how many noncombatants had been killed. I told Major Calhoun that I felt because of the distance involved of my having to return back to the village from my night defensive position, we would have to clear the area that we had just crossed from My Lai Four to our night position. We would have to clear it again for mines and booby traps. I felt that it would be best not to return. Also at this time, I had an indication that the Forty-Eighth VC Battalion, which was supposed to have been in the village of My Lai Four, had not been there. That there had been a number of noncombatants killed. And this is the other reason I did not want to return back to the village.

At that time, Major Calhoun had instructed me to try to determine the number of innocent civilians that had been killed at the village of My Lai Four. I got my platoon leaders together and I asked them for a body count of innocent civilians that had been killed. The first platoon leader, Lieutenant Calley, told me in excess of fifty. Lieutenant Brooks, the second platoon leader, told me the like number. He said, "I believe the like number of fifty or more." Lieutenant LaCross, the third platoon leader, gave me a body count of six. At that time, I—"Oh, my God, what is—what happened?" I already had an indication that noncombatants had been killed. I did not know it was this large a magnitude, and at that time I made a remark to the platoon leaders that I had seen approximately twenty to twenty-eight, and that that was the body count that I was going to give to Major Calhoun. I got on the task force command net. I told Major Calhoun that I had a body count of twenty to twenty-eight noncombatants that had been killed. He said, "I want you to go back into the village of My Lai Four and make an exact count of how many men, women, and children had been killed," and about that time, an individual using the call sign of Sabre Six broke into the conversation and said, "Negative. What does Six," or

"What does Charlie Six say he has?" I said, "Twenty to twenty-eight." Sabre Six came back and says, "That sounds about right. Don't send him back in there."

Kennedy: Sabre Six is General Koster?

Medina: The call sign Sabre Six was the call sign of the division Commander of the Americal Division, General Koster.

Medina had finished his narrative of his part in and his experience in the Battle of My Lai and its immediate aftermath. But the jury was not through with him yet. It sent a bundle of questions to Kennedy to ask, and the judge posed them to the captain.

Kennedy: Did Lieutenant Calley ever radio to you, at any time in the morning hours of sixteen March, that any villagers were slowing his progress?

Medina: No, sir.

Kennedy: Did you ever issue an order to him to speed his progress toward a defensive position on the east side of My Lai Four?

Medina: Yes, sir.

Kennedy: Did you ever radio any of your platoon leaders, words in substance, "The party is over, the show is over, that is enough for today"?

Medina: No, sir. . . . I did place a cease-fire order to the platoon leaders to make sure that there were no innocent civilians or noncombatants being killed indiscriminately. This was done as I moved up to the area where the individual that had been wounded in the foot and after I had seen the twenty to twenty-eight people on the trail after we had evacuated the individual that had been wounded. I had received a transmission from Major Calhoun. I again relayed to the platoon leaders to cease fire, to make sure that no noncombatants were being indiscriminately killed, and there was another time that I called forward to the first platoon, and I said, "Damn it, what is going on up there? I want all this firing stopped."

. . *Kennedy:* With regard to body count, what was the total body count that you reported as being a result of this operation?

Medina: The total body count that was reported for the operation was one hundred twenty-eight. This was a combined body count for Bravo and C Company. Bravo Company had, I think, forty to forty-five.

Kennedy: What was your report as total body count?

Medina: The body count that I reported to the task force was between eighty and eighty-five.

Kennedy: Did you ever report to the task force headquarters anything about any prisoners that had been taken by C Company?

Medina: I reported to the task force that we had detained approximately twenty to thirty VC suspects.

Kennedy: Was that true?

Medina: Yes, sir.

Kennedy: And who detained those, where did you get that information?

Medina: The detainees that we picked up were in the second platoon, sir. It was on the northern portion of the village.

Kennedy: Do you know what happened to those persons who were detained, in your own knowledge?

Medina: Once we began moving toward the east from the village, we came upon a group of civilians that had been rounded up. I estimate the number somewhere between eighty to ninety, I guess, that had been gathered. There were men, women, and children. I had my interpreter talk to them. We selected the ones that appeared to be Viet Cong suspects of military age. The women and children and the old Vietnamese males, I instructed Sergeant Phu to tell them to proceed from this area and go directly to the refugee center either at Son Thanh or Quang Ngai and report in to the ARVN adviser there and they would be taken care of. . . .

Kennedy: Was it generally known to you after—immediately after—sixteen March or after you left the village of My Lai Four that many unarmed people had been killed in the village?

Medina: On the evening of the sixteenth of March, at the

night defensive position, I became aware of the magnitude of the number of people that—that there had been a large number of noncombatants that had been killed at the village of My Lai Four. I was not to learn until sometime later how many or, you know, the great number of civilians that had been killed. . . .

Kennedy: Did you ever give an order in My Lai Four, on sixteen March, over the radio or in person, to anyone that they should move the civilians out of the way, or get rid of them, or anything in substance like that?

Medina: No, sir.

Kennedy: Did you ever give an order in substance to save enough civilians so that they could be utilized to clear the mine fields for the rest of the Pinkville operation?

Medina: No, sir.

Kennedy: Now, immediately following the date sixteen March, did you ever make a statement to anyone, in substance, "I will go to jail for this"?

Medina: Yes, sir.

Kennedy: And when was that?

Medina: Could have been possibly the night defensive position when I found out what had happened, and also a couple of days later at LZ-Dotti.

Kennedy: All right. You testified that you made a radio transmission to the first platoon, in substance, "Damn it, what is going on up there?"

Medina: Yes, sir.

Kennedy: What prompted that?

Medina: I had received a—I had placed out a cease-fire order to the platoon leaders. By a cease fire, I mean that they were not—to make sure that there were no innocent civilians being killed. Then I received a call from the task force S-three stating that he had a helicopter report that there was indiscriminate killing of innocent civilians. I again put this out. After I had started moving from the evacuation, I again put— there was shooting over on the right-hand side. I then called the first platoon and told them, "Damn it, what is going on?" I wanted to make sure that there were no innocent civilians being killed. . . .

Kennedy: Did you ever see any Vietnamese being shot at in the vicinity of the dust-off area?

Medina: Yes, sir.

Kennedy: Would you relate that?

Medina: Yes, sir. Shortly after the dust-off, we started movinng in an easterly direction along the east-west trail. I was in the middle of the command group, there was a Vietnamese male, a small boy, that started moving from the edge of the wood line in front of the command group. I caught the movement. I turned and I started to raise my rifle. I seen that it was a child. I started to put it down. And I either uttered the words, "Get him! Get him! Stop him! Stop him!" or "Don't shoot! Don't shoot!" And somebody fired, the child fell.

The jury and Kennedy had reached the end of all they had for Medina. Now it was Daniel's turn. For the most part, Daniel was gentle, his questions designed to strengthen points Medina had made in direct testimony to tighten the chains around Calley. For Medina had been, after all, a sterling government witness; he had tried and, if the way the jury watched and listened to him was an indication, succeeded in reversing the defense tactic; he had taken the onus off himself and put it back on Calley, asserting that the slaughter of civilians had been Calley's doing and had been done in direct disobedience to Medina's direct orders.

Daniel took him first to the initial report of dead, the report by Calley, soon after landing, of sixty-nine dead Vietnamese. Calley had told him, Medina said, that they had all been killed by artillery and he was searching the area for weapons.

Daniel: Did he indicate he was having any difficulty in moving at that time?

Medina: No, sir.

Daniel: Did he indicate that he had gathered up any detainees at this time?

Medina: No, sir.

Daniel: Did you make any such inquiry?
Medina: No, sir.

Daniel directed Medina's attention to the call about the conversation with the helicopter pilot and asked whether Calley had told Medina that he had civilians with him then, men, women, and children. He had not, Medina said.

And what had prompted that first cease-fire order, that order to make sure no "innocent civilians" were being killed? Medina said, "I had seen the bodies on the north-south trail. I did not go over to inspect them. I was approximately twenty-five to fifty meters away, and I wanted to believe with all my heart that it had happened by artillery or gunship fire." But those bodies had been in the southern part of My Lai, and that was the area of Lieutenant Calley's responsibility.

Daniel went forward in time, to those days after the operation was all over, only a nightmare to be relived in the mind. Had there been any investigation and had Calley known about it from Medina?

Medina said that Barker had told him that an investigation was being conducted and asked him to find out from his platoon leaders "if there were any innocent civilians that had been killed." He called his lieutenants and put the question to them, telling them the reason—that there was an investigation and "I wanted to find out the number of noncombatants that had been killed and if they had any knowledge of any atrocities." A little later, he was talking to Calley and "I asked him if they were aware of any atrocities that had been committed. I did not read them any rights, under Article Thirty-One. Lieutenant Calley made comments as to, 'My God, I can still hear the screaming. . . .'"

Medina got no farther. Latimer leaped to his feet, objecting loudly, "If this is intended to be a confession of some kind extracted from this man, it would be inadmissible." And Kennedy agreed. But though the words were stricken from the record, they could not be stricken from the mind.

Then Latimer took out after Medina, sarcastically, angrily,

with venom. He had Medina draw his route on the aerial photograph of My Lai, and then when the captain commented that "this was probably not accurate," Latimer replied icily, "Captain, we all appreciate that everything you say is not accurate."

Latimer tried to get Medina to agree that the company was understrength, undertrained, underled, ill-equipped to face a hardened enemy. Medina wouldn't buy that; he still had pride in his company and in his ability to lead them, and "it was equipped as best the—probably any rifle company in conducting combat operations in South Viet-Nam. I felt that the people in Charlie Company were good soldiers and that with additional helicopter support and the artillery being placed on the village, that we could engage the Forty-Eighth VC Battalion and come out as victors. At the same time, sir, I also expected that we would take heavy casualties."

And Latimer turned time and again to his favorite subject—Medina's briefing of the troops, his claim that he had told his men not to kill women and children, to use common sense.

Latimer: I will ask you, Captain Medina, if one of the members of the platoon that was listening said—you were asked "if we were supposed to kill women and children and everything, and he replied, 'Kill everything that moved.'" Now, did you say that?

Medina: No, sir.

Latimer: And then the person who testified to that would be not telling the truth?

Medina: I did not state that, sir.

Latimer: Well, then, what he is telling is not the truth?

Medina: I guess so, sir.

Latimer: All right. If another asked concerning any men, women, and children that might be found, "He said they were also VCS or VC's." Did you make any such comment as that?

Medina: No, sir.

Latimer: So the member of the command that made that statement would not be telling the truth?

Medina: Yes, sir. . . .

Latimer: Did you tell them to burn all the buildings?
Medina: Yes, sir.
Latimer: Is that legal?
Medina: I had received—
Kennedy: Now, wait a minute, wait a minute.
Daniel: I object to that.
Kennedy: How would Captain Medina know whether it was legal or not?
Latimer: I supposed that is one of the things that might be barred by your treaties and Geneva Conventions and things that have been referred to here so generously because there is a provision against burning and destroying.
Kennedy: Well, I will put it this way: Do you know what the law is with regard to burning villages? That just requires a yes or no.
Medina: At that time, no, sir.
Kennedy: Well, that takes care of that.
Latimer: Well, Captain Medina, let me ask you this: It was your understanding that you were going to burn all the buildings, you were going to shoot all the animals and all living animals and chickens and fowls and things like that of a group of people that you knew were out of the village and were coming back. Now, was any thought given as to what might happen to those people under those circumstances?
Medina: No, sir.

Then Latimer turned to the issue of the civilian dead, the body count, and the fact that the body count he had given was nearly a hundred fewer than the body count he had been given by his platoon leaders—fifty for Calley, fifty for Brooks, six for LaCross against the twenty to twenty-eight reported by Medina. But then, Medina responded to Latimer's questions, this was the largest operation he had ever been on and the only one in his experience where there "was indiscriminate shooting of civilians," and he had already explained why he had given such a low body count.

By evening, Medina was clearly exhausted, his mind growing foggy and his answers less clear and direct than they had been early in the day. But Latimer had asked for only another hour, and so Kennedy let his cross-examination go on after a break for supper. In that final hour, Latimer tried hard to confuse Medina, make him contradict himself, and with Medina's fatigue it would not have been surprising if he had succeeded to a greater extent than he did. At first, though, Medina braced himself and held up under the onslaught.

He denied the conversations that had been reported in depositions by Phu and Minh, the interpreters. He denied having seen or talked to either Barker or Henderson on the ground at My Lai. He denied having given a body count of more than three hundred.

As Latimer drove at him, he said that he had not reported to higher headquarters about the group he had seen at the trail intersection or about having seen children shot in the hamlet.

Latimer: Did you indicate at any time that the information you had been given in a briefing was false and that there were men, women, and children in the village?

Medina: I did not expect to find noncombatants in the village of My Lai Four.

Latimer: Were you surprised when you did see them?

Medina: Yes, sir.

Latimer: Did you say anything to your lower command or your higher command about that?

Medina: No, sir.

Latimer: Why—when you first shot the woman, Captain Medina, you felt so horrified and sick about it, why, when you saw the small boy running by and you saw somebody kill him, and why, when you saw that body there, you didn't call somebody and notify them what you had seen and make it positive that you had seen it and reported it to higher headquarters?

Medina: There were four reasons, sir.

Latimer: Let's have them.

Medina: Number one, sir, I did not expect to find any noncombatants in that area; I expected to go in and do combat with the Forty-Eighth VC Battalion. The woman—I was shocked. It was the first human being that I had shot and I assumed that I did kill her. The four reasons that I did not report the shooting of any innocent or noncombatants at the village of My Lai Four and the reason that I suppressed the information from the brigade commander when I was questioned are as follows: Number one, I realized that instead of going in and doing combat with an armed enemy, the intelligence information was faulty and we found nothing but women and children in the village of My Lai Four, and, seeing what had happened, I realized exactly the disgrace that was being brought upon the Army uniform that I am very proud to wear. Number two, I also realized the repercussions that it would have against the United States of America. Three, my family, and number four, lastly, myself, sir.

Latimer: And those are the reasons you didn't report it?

Medina: Yes, sir.

Latimer: What has happened now because you didn't report it?

Medina: What has happened now, sir?

Latimer: Yes. Worse, isn't it?

Medina's answer sounded as though he had rehearsed it, almost too pat and too facile and it was, thus—if not by a military jury, at least by the nonmilitary—greeted with cynicism. He could admit to the crime of covering up because he had not been charged with that and the statute of limitations had run out, and he could admit to it with such an exclamation so that it would sound better. But later that night, over drinks, Mark Kadish was insistent that nobody had rehearsed Medina on that answer, that Medina had just spent three years of sleepless nights thinking about it and this was what he had come up with.

Latimer was not through with Medina quite yet, though the captain's face was drawn and haggard, and his shoulders were sagging. He got from Medina the admission that he was a disciplinarian with his troops, expected them to obey any legal order he gave—and as far as he knew, he didn't give illegal orders.

Latimer: All right. Then you would expect any order given by you they would comply with, wouldn't you?

Medina: I would expect them to obey an order, yes, sir.

Latimer: And you would give the same attention and devotion to orders given to you by Colonel Barker, would you not?

Medina: Yes, sir.

Latimer: So, when you were told to burn the hootches, you went out and burned the hootches, did you not?

Medina: Yes, sir.

It was just eight o'clock that night—Medina had been on the stand in one day for more than six hours, only three hours less than Calley had spent over three days—when his ordeal finally ended.

With his testimony, an issue had been clearly drawn. Medina's testimony and Calley's on the question of orders, that basic question that obsessed this trial and obsessed the nation, so precisely conflicted that it was apparent that one, or perhaps both, had lied. The jury would have to make the choice of which of them had told a story closer to the truth.

Among the spectators who had heard both of them, the consensus seemed to be that Medina's story in most of its essentials had the truer ring. Perhaps his remembrance of the question and answer at the briefing was self-serving, perhaps a lie, but what many seemed to feel was that Medina had little real recollection of that briefing, perhaps less than anyone else. He had been the leader of men who were frightened and demoralized and about to face a battle in which he expected them to be outnumbered. Did he, perhaps, like a football coach give them that stirring half-time speech to send them out to "win one for the Gipper" without ever really knowing what it was that he was saying?

When the utterly exhausted Medina left the stand, he turned in the middle of the courtroom and saluted Judge Kennedy. The colonel looked at him in surprise (Kennedy was later to say that he couldn't remember the last time anyone had saluted him) and gave a brief wave of his hand toward his forehead. Medina turned and left the courtroom.

He went back to the hotel, changed into civilian clothes, joined some friends in the dimly lit bar downstairs, and then proceeded to do what he rarely did—he got drunk.

22
A Little Joke on Henderson

Did anyone really want to hear Oran Henderson? After the long day and into the night with Medina, after the emotional strain of those hours, and after all the months and all the witnesses who had come and said their pieces and then gone, was still another one necessary? But then he was the highest ranking officer, a full colonel, to be called as a witness, he had been commander of the 11th Brigade, he was under charge himself for covering up the investigation of the massacre, and besides, he was a witness the jury had called. Maybe he would have something new to add.

But as Henderson walked into the courtroom the morning after Medina had departed, even the jury did not seem to be looking forward to more testimony with any anticipation. Everyone, jurors included, was drained, and besides, after Medina, just about everyone agreed with Mark Kadish's observation that now about 95 per cent of the story of My Lai was on the record and it was doubtful, with Barker dead and Brooks dead and a few others dead and some unwilling to talk, if that other 5 per cent would ever be known.

Henderson was a slight man who, despite six rows of campaign ribbons and decorations ranked on his breast, looked more like a schoolmarm than a professional soldier, with his thin-lipped waspish face, steel-rimmed glasses, and tightly brushed gray hair. And though under indictment himself, he told the court, in a surprisingly deep voice, "I have no reluctance to testify."

The 11th Brigade had been his. He had formed it, he declared, in Hawaii, only to be replaced as its commander by a one-star general; when that general left, he had, with only an eagle on his shoulders, been put in command once more, only to be passed over for permanent command when General Lipscomb arrived to take over and he once again became second man in *his* division. When General Lipscomb departed on March 15, 1968, command of the 11th Brigade was his again, but this time he held it only for a couple of months. He was obviously not one of the Army's favorites, not an officer thought of when command became vacant, not one destined for the stars.

And Henderson seemed utterly lacking in any levity, any ability to unbend. When Kennedy unwittingly called him "Colonel Barker" at one point, which brought a few chuckles, Henderson corrected him stiffly, "I'm Colonel Henderson."

The story he told was his view of My Lai, the story of the operation from on high. He had, the night before the attack, attended Barker's briefing, telling the company commanders that they should "aggressively pursue the enemy once contact was made, they should secure weapons and they should overrun the area." As for taking and handling prisoners, "The subject did not come up," although "I assume Colonel Barker had such a plan. It would have been normal. But I do not know if in fact he did have such a plan."

On March 16, Henderson "was present in both the My Lai Four complex and at LZ-Dotti." He had left his own headquarters at LZ-Bronco near Duc Pho, receiving a report as he departed that the LZ at My Lai (4) was cold, then that it was hot "and the gunships were firing at fleeing VC." When he received a report that two Viet Cong had been killed north of My Lai, he directed his helicopter pilot to fly over the area and "saw two dead bodies in a rice paddy." He knew they were Viet Cong, he said, because "they were dressed in green fatigues with web belts, similar to uniforms that the ARVN and American soldiers in the area wore."

Henderson remained over those bodies until a unit of ground

troops headed out from My Lai toward them, then went south over Highway 521, spotting three or four bodies at the edge of the road and, nearby, "a family group of three or four and a water buffalo, all dead." His chopper moved down over the highway, passing over a column of three to five hundred people evacuating the area in "an orderly movement." But running through that column were two men who seemed to be trying to avoid detection. Though it is almost unheard of to land a helicopter in an insecure area without protection, "we dropped down and picked them up and took them back to LZ-Dotti for observation."

Arriving back at the fire base, Henderson said that he found General Koster there waiting for him. They had a brief conversation, and Koster "expressed interest" in the two suspects that Henderson had brought back with him from My Lai. The two were brought out for interrogation in front of the general and the colonel and they "turned out to be PF's [members of the Popular Forces, one arm of the local militia loyal to the Saigon regime] from Quang Ngai who had been held prisoner for some time at My Lai Four. An old man had cut them loose that morning. General Koster had a little joke on me about that."

When the prisoners were led away, presumably to be sent back to Quang Ngai and freedom, Koster asked Henderson if he had heard anything about civilian casualties at My Lai. At some time earlier, Henderson said, he had heard—he's not sure how or from whom—that there had been "in the neighborhood of thirty VC KIA [killed in action]," and he himself had seen "between eight and ten" bodies at My Lai. In response to Koster, though, "I told him I had no report from Colonel Barker on that. And I told him about the family group I had seen. General Koster asked me to get a body count and I relayed that order to Colonel Barker."

Then, Henderson said, the general left and he left. "About ten-thirty, I left to pay a courtesy call on Colonel Duong of the Second ARVN in Quang Ngai city. I did not return to the area." The purpose of that call, as Henderson explained it, was

to try to calm the ARVN officer's ire at an American operation
and incursion into his area of operations without the support,
militarily, of his South Vietnamese troops and even without
advance knowledge that the attack was being made.

While he was at lunch, Henderson said, he got a call from
Barker that "ten or twelve, or twelve or fourteen had been
killed. I was concerned about the discrepancy of two in his
report, and I ordered him to send C Company back to search
and get a true count. And I must say I was disappointed in the
number of weapons captured; I felt they hadn't made a
thorough search." It was not until later that night, when he got
back to Duc Pho, that Henderson said he learned that
"General Koster had countermanded my order to send the
troops back to the village."

And at ten-thirty on the morning of March 11, 1971, Colonel
Henderson was excused as a witness. He was the one-hundred-
fourth witness to appear in the forty-four days of testimony
taken in the trial. He was the last witness.

All the evidence was now on the record. It remained only for
the jury to hear the last words of the government and the
defense and the judge, before it retired, to contemplate what it
had heard and to decide whether Calley was a murderer.

23
"We Didn't Make Those Facts"

"Please the court." Thus, five days later, did Aubrey Daniel begin his final arguments. For more than four hours Daniel went slowly over the evidence he had presented, summarizing his case for the jury. "I said in November," he told the six officers, "that this would be a long and difficult case, and it has been. We have come to the end of the presentation of evidence. My job is finished. You have a job to take all the evidence you have heard, resolve all the conflicts, judge the credibility of the witnesses, decide what the evidence shows. Has the Government proved beyond a reasonable doubt what happened in the village of My Lai Four on March 16, 1968? I think we have."

Then Daniel traced, with infinite care, what his witnesses had revealed about that morning at My Lai, his voice throughout often tinged with emotion, with anger, with disgust. In My Lai, he declared, the troops found "only unresisting females and males." They rounded them out into groups and marched them to various locations. At the trail, Calley came upon Conti and Meadlo with a group of thirty. "He ordered them to kill and he took part."

More people were gathered up, marched to the irrigation ditch, "over seventy people—men, women, children, babies—and they put them into the ditch and shot them and they died."

Calley left the ditch, moved north, came upon a man dressed in white, and "the accused butt-stroked him and shot him and blew half his head off." He came to a child, "picked him up, threw him in the ditch and shot him."

This, Daniel said, is what the government had charged and

what "the government did prove. It is not our function to judge the guilt or innocence of any other person at My Lai Four, just the guilt or innocence of the accused."

How much of what the government charged was in dispute? Daniel asked. There is no dispute, he said, on the time or place of the landing or that Calley was there; no dispute over the fact that the government's witnesses had been there; no dispute over the fact that the southern portion of My Lai, where these killings took place, was the responsibility of Calley's first platoon; no dispute over the fact that the platoon found only "unarmed old men, women, children, babies, and they were gathered up"; no dispute over Calley's encounter with people and his telling his men "to take care of, to waste the people. He testified about it himself"; no dispute that Calley was at the irrigation ditch and that "at least one group was put in that ditch and shot by members of the platoon"; no dispute about the encounter with the man in white, though there is dispute about whether Calley killed him, and there is dispute about the death of the child and whether Calley was at and killed the people at the trail intersection.

"The things you must resolve," Daniel said, "are all the conflicts. We are bound by the time sequence in our specifications, and we have proved that time sequence beyond a reasonable doubt. We are bound to prove that the victims are dead, and we have proved that beyond a reasonable doubt. It is not necessary for us to prove that thirty were killed at the trail intersection or that seventy were killed at the ditch. We are bound to prove only that at least one died, and that he died pursuant to the actions of the accused, that he shot them or ordered them shot. We must prove that that action was unlawful and that he had a specific intent and a premediated design, a formulated idea to take a human life before he killed."

The government's evidence, Daniel said, did not rest on a single witness. There were many witnesses, all corroborating each other. There were Conti and Dursi and Meadlo and Sledge and Turner and witnesses who didn't even know Calley and "even the defense's own witnesses corroborate the evidence," and he named Bacon and Haywood and others who had seen people, as many as sixty, being gathered up and marched toward Calley, had seen Calley with those Vietnamese. "That's a lot of people, gentlemen. Where did all those people go?" And Daniel pointed to Haeberle's picture of the dead bodies.

Calley had said he had never seen those bodies, but, Daniel asked, "Do you think that Lieutenant Calley would identify that photograph? Do you think Lieutenant Calley would tell you that was the enemy he shot? Do you think he could justify that to you?

"We didn't make those facts, gentlemen, and we didn't make a body count. You must make a judgment on how many were killed under his rifle and Paul Meadlo's. We have to show only that he killed only one. . . . How many people are shown in that photograph? If you count, you will see not less than twenty-five—nine clearly identifiable as children, three clearly identifiable as infants." And, Daniel added, twenty people had come to court and said they had seen the bodies on the trail, and among those twenty were six witnesses for the defense. "There is not much doubt that Lieutenant Calley shot those people and they are dead because of his actions on March 16, 1968."

But the trail was only one place where Calley had killed. There was also the ditch and there was direct evidence of his actions there, the evidence of Calley himself and of Meadlo, Dursi, Grzesik, Sledge, Conti, and Maples.

Certainly there were discrepancies and conflicts in all that testimony. But did those witnesses have "a way of fabricating this?" They had been out of the service, had not been in contact with each other, had come from all corners of the nation. Fabricate? "No way, gentlemen."

"And there is one man whose testimony permits you to sort out, to order the testimony. We give you Thomas Turner of Nebraska, student, husband. He blends the discrepancies. Why did people see different things? Because there was more than one group put in at different locations at different times. He sat up in the north on a paddy and saw Calley firing at the ditch. He recalls Calley and Meadlo when he arrived. He recalls Calley changed clips. He heard constant fire. Turner sat there and watched and looked south for an hour or an hour and a half."

Daniel turned and looked sarcastically at Calley. "Twelve members of his platoon place him at the ditch; that's half his platoon. Could he get up on the stand and deny he was there as he denied he was at the trail intersection? No way. So he admits he fired into the ditch. The evidence we have presented as to what transpired at that ditch is overwhelming."

The two individual killings were based mainly on Sledge's testimony, though LaCross said he saw the man in white dead in the ditch and Coburn had originally seen two children alive in the ditch and later one of them was dead. But "the issue is the credibility of Sledge and circumstantial evidence—which can be just as compelling as direct evidence—versus the credibility of Calley."

If, through all this testimony, the specifications had been proved "without the shadow of a doubt," there was, because of the psychiatric evidence, the question of Calley's mental balance. As he had done when they were on the stand, Daniel tore apart the testimony of Hamman and Crane. "What is the best evidence of a man's mental state? How about the accused himself? Doesn't his testimony show that he was thinking all sorts of things, that he was thinking all sorts of complex things beside just killing? There is no evidence that he was not aware of what was happening around him." After all, Calley knew the names of his men, the altitude of the helicopter when the first man went off, that he had talked with Thompson and Medina. "Do these facts demonstrate someone who was befuddled? They show he was thinking. They show when he gave orders to Meadlo, he knew what he was doing."

Did Calley have an intent to kill and was he premeditating? "When you stand up a group like this, you have intent. When you leave and come back, you must have intent. Don't the facts there clearly show what he intended?"

Like all soldiers, Daniel stressed, Calley was bound by the rules of law, rules explaining when human life may be taken in combat and when it may not be taken. "Summary execution is forbidden." Even if these people had been giving aid to the Viet Cong before March 16, that was not reason enough, and after "they held up their arms and surrendered, if any of them were killed and any order to kill them was given, it was an illegal order."

But, Daniel added, "we have shown that the people were unarmed and unresisting and were unjustifiably summarily executed nevertheless." No matter the order—if one were given—Calley was not expected to respond like a robot. He had "the obligation to make moral decisions. When he put on an American uniform, he still had an obligation to think and act like a reasonable person and have a proper respect for life."

And what about orders? "You think they thought they'd meet nothing but unarmed men, women, children, babies, and round them up and take them to the trail and execute them? You think that was the order? The testimony has consistently revealed that they expected to meet an armed enemy unit. There was nothing illegal in an order to fight that unit. Even the accused expected to meet an armed enemy unit. You think that indicates that the order was to kill unresisting men, women, children, and babies?"

Further, who heard such orders beside Calley that Medina had said "to waste civilians"? Not Sledge, his RTO. No one. Medina said he didn't give them. "You think the accused would have called Captain Medina and said I have fifty, seventy-five, one hundred unresisting civilians and his company commander would have told him to waste them? He never told his company commander. He was running the show, gentlemen, it was at his orders and at his direction."

But say, for some reason, you believe he made such a call and Medina ordered him to kill. It would have been an illegal order, and "if you follow an illegal order, all that's happened is that two are guilty—the issuer and the follower."

"If this was his great day, his big battle," Daniel declaimed, "where he met and closed with the enemy, wouldn't he want to give a big body count? If this was an armed enemy in a big battle, then couldn't he give an estimate of the body count? Were they the armed enemy met in honorable combat?"

Then Daniel came to his final point. In looking at Calley, in looking at his defense of orders, "you must still consider whether a reasonable man would have known it was illegal. A reasonable man should know without a reasonable doubt that any order if received to gather up thirty people, some children and babies, on the north-south trail and summarily execute them just can't be justified. To gather up more than seventy people and put them like cattle in an irrigation ditch and summarily execute them is illegal and the reasonable man knows it.

"Gentlemen, we have carried our burden and it now becomes your duty to return a finding of guilty on all charges."

It had been a long summation; the evidence had been analyzed minutely, often with eloquence that had rarely been heard at this trial. And the jury had listened closely, some even nodding at points Daniel made.

But Daniel had saved his real feelings, his real eloquence, his real emotion. He would have the final say after Latimer closed for the defense.

24
He Defended His Country

In a red shirt, blue and red striped tie, dark blue blazer, and light gray slacks, George Latimer stepped to the microphone on the small reading stand at the defense table. It was his final opportunity to recall from somewhere those talents he had once had but had so rarely revealed in this trial and, against the weight of all the evidence and of Daniel's logic, to sway the jury and pull it behind his client. A year and a half before, he had told a friend as he accepted this case that he felt he had one good case left in him; it had seemed to this point that he had overestimated. Perhaps in these final moments he could gather from his past all that had won him his reputation. Lord knows, Calley would need them.

But if any—and there were some in that courtroom that morning—had prayed and hoped that Latimer would find again his youth and his power, those hopes were doomed. As he began, and as he progressed through his arguments, he seemed no more up to this moment than he had been to any other moment in the months gone by. Where Daniel over six hours had been reasoned and logical and organized, Latimer's summation was diffuse, often divisive, aimed at a different generation and a different time, filled with issues and feelings of another age. It was not World War II and it was not a time to appeal to blind, unthinking patriotism, but Latimer did not seem to know it.

It was ten-fifteen in the morning when he faced the jury and began to speak in his droning, often muted and inaudible monotone, on the morning, fittingly enough, of March 16, 1971, the third anniversary of the attack on My Lai. (Though the date was the same, actually the anniversary of the attack, because of time and dateline differences, had been at seven-thirty the previous night, but few seemed to realize that; when someone told Calley as court adjourned the previous evening that a bunch of reporters were going to have a drink at seven-thirty to mark the exact moment of the landing at My Lai, he looked startled, for even he had forgotten about the twelve-hour time difference between Viet-Nam and Georgia.) And fittingly enough, before the day was through Calley's fate would be in the hands of the jury.

"What I say here," the aging lawyer began, with a paraphrase of Lincoln, "may not be long remembered, but what you do here will never be erased from the pages of history. If this prosecution was necessary to avoid tarnishing the image of the Army, then, in my humble judgment, the conviction of one Army lieutenant for the ills and vices which occurred at My Lai will sear the image of the Army beyond all recognition. Though many did many things there, the indications are that this tragedy will narrow to a death race between Captain Medina and Lieutenant Calley, and I am here to prevent that from happening."

With his rhetoric old-fashioned and outdated, his emotion maudlin, Latimer pulled out all the stops to win sympathy and tears and perhaps victory. But what he got, instead, was cynical laughter from the audience, stony looks from the jurors, and one of outright contempt from Daniel, especially when Latimer rose to defend himself. "Under cross-examination," he said with almost a whine, "Captain Daniel suggested that the defense experts were ambulance chasers. This was intended obliquely but it was clear to me. I want to tell you right now that I did not solicit this case and I do not practice criminal law and this case will not help my practice. Lieutenant Calley called me in my office in Salt Lake City and we agreed to meet in Washington. I saw a boy threatened by a nation that he had tried to defend. He needed help. There was a nation with hundreds of millions of dollars to spend on his prosecution and he had no one to help defend him. I saw this boy and I adopted a son. I was not adopting a murderer."

Latimer hit out wildly, at any available target. He talked about the trial of Charles Manson for the murder of Sharon Tate in California, which was then also coming to its end, and he talked about "draft evaders and that part of the citizenry that try to destroy our courts and turn our courtrooms into barrooms. They can always find someone to represent them all the way to the Supreme Court of the United States. Why deride someone who helps a man who tried to defend his country?"

Then Latimer took another avenue to try to win the jury. He tried to tell them that he was one of them, that he, too, had been a soldier and an officer and had served in battle. "I am proud of the Army," he declared, "and it grieves me to see it pulled apart from within. This case is a vehicle to hurry along that destruction."

There were three tragedies in the My Lai affair, he said, leading to this traumatic moment for the Army. "Each man at My Lai was part of a common effort; somebody called the wrong signals and something went wrong. The second tragedy was when the company commander hushed it up and was aided in that hush-up. I feel the facts will never come up and the real truth was forever buried and cannot be resurrected because memories are clouded and self-interest intervenes. The third tragedy, a year and a half later, is this prosecution."

And look at those who talked, who testified against Calley, who were responsible for this prosecution. "Many have been discharged and are shielded from prosecution. They pointed the finger at those who remained loyal, who wanted to make the Army their career. Look at the roster of outsiders," and he went down the list—Dursi, Olsen, Conti, Meadlo, Sledge, and the rest. "Trial counsel says they have no reason to lie. I dispute that. They seek to shed the cloak of guilt by accusing others. With few exceptions, they said others shot civilians but I did not. All, or most, seek to avoid the charge of accomplices to murder at My Lai. This may be all right in a criminal case, but it is not in a military case. Accusing your buddies damages military discipline."

Then Latimer drove at a point that, later, outside court, was to turn some military officers livid. He attempted to pit civilian against soldier, to show that the Army was a separate entity, not part of the nation. "Those unhappy with the service," he asserted, were the ones who had borne witness against Calley, "those who had a grudge, sort of, have an objective in degrading the service," and that was why they were so anxious to testify against the man who remained loyal, Calley, for it would help in destroying the Army. He would return to that theme.

He asked the question that many had asked—but that was not an issue at this trial. What about others? What about Medina and what about Meadlo? "Does the buckpassing stop with Lieutenant Calley or does it go down? There are many who should suffer the same consequences as those who are convicted."

Was there any excuse for My Lai? Could it be explained away? Latimer said yes. He talked about the philosophy of the soldier "when he goes into battle. He wants to get it over with and get home. Sometimes he goes a little farther than sitting in an office dictates. You are dealing with infantry troops here and that life is harder than any other service. Most men have a feeling that a fine distinction is drawn in the infantry. It's all right for the air corps to bomb cities; it's all right for the artillery to tear down houses and wreck the lives of the inhabitants. But it is wrong for the infantry."

Then take this group of men, inadequately trained in Hawaii and Viet-Nam, led by untrained officers, beset with insufficient equipment. "No wonder they were called Barker's Bastards. They were an orphan unit. There was no esprit. There were fears and stark horror present in the unit on its first assault, and when raw troops are used, disaster is courted. The lesson of My Lai is that it is no wonder civilians were killed. I'm amazed that they didn't kill their own troops. When you think of the small size of that place, when you think of hearing M-16 fire from all its corners, with all that fire, I just go back and wonder why there wasn't more disaster."

With all that, and with the conditioning of Viet-Nam before the attack, anything should have been expected, he asserted. He talked about how they had never seen the enemy on "the number of reconnaissance, sweep and destroy missions"—it was a term he could never get straight; he called it search and seizure, sweep and destroy, almost anything but search and destroy, but then he had had the same trouble with other terms, thinking, for example, that the North Vietnamese and the Viet Cong were interchangeable, one and the same, until a witness straightened him out. He cited "the loss of buddies to mines, never any security, darkness, and the inability to see. They all breed fear. The deaths of members of the platoon added to the fear. You never knew when your number was up, when the next step might cost you your life or your leg. There was always a visionary foe, you could not see him and did not know who he was. Women and children were operating with the enemy, being used to help destroy. They were lethal and could not be seen. This breeds hatred against the enemy and anyone who might be the enemy." This, then, Latimer was implying, excuses the killing of the unarmed who might be enemy another day.

What happened at My Lai, Latimer said, "is a one-time incident." The men who attacked the hamlet are "good men, these boys. You find they were boys trained to kill, sent overseas to kill, ordered to kill, sent in to level, destroy, and kill. Are they to be labeled murderers at My Lai or are they entitled to consideration from the fact that they were doing their job as they saw it? Perhaps they acted too aggressively, perhaps they were trying too hard, perhaps they were not using good judgment. But do the facts warrant hanging a young American lieutenant by the neck until dead because he was trying to do his job?"

It was to these emotions—emotions of blind patriotism, that Americans are somehow better than anyone else and so can be excused anything—that Latimer appealed and upon which he dwelt interminably. One wondered if he would ever try to deal with the evidence against Calley. Eventually he did come round to it, declaring that it was filled with "bias, prejudices, reason to falsify."

The testimony of the government's witnesses, he said, had been rehearsed and practiced until perfect, before Army and Congressional investigation committees, in public, everywhere. "If any group of witnesses ever had a better chance to prepare and rehearse, I never heard of it." And even with that opportunity, they couldn't agree on details. "My experience of human nature is not to cut down but to build up on war stories, the tendency is to move up. My own experience has been when I tell my war stories about Bougainville and other engagements in the Pacific, I tend to exaggerate more and more over the years."

He tried to deride all of Daniel's witnesses. Conti "was doing something other than fighting wars"; Meadlo, though "insulated by his discharge," was still worried about whether he could be tried and so "his emotional state made him an unreliable witness." And so it went through all the incrimination. Even for Turner, whom Latimer admitted he did not understand and about whom he wondered: Why did he want immunity, what did he have to hide? And everyone else had contradicted Turner, so forget about him.

If one wants to seek a culprit, one should look at the briefing the night before the attack, Latimer implied. That was where "parties start falling out, officer turns against officer, men against men, each becomes an accuser against his brother-in-arms." What did Medina mean "when he talked about innocent civilians? He led them to believe that no innocents would be in the village."

So we had come back to Ernest Medina, with, Latimer said, "sadness and reluctance. I, too, am forced to pit an officer against an officer, and somehow it just seems the wrong thing to do. They were brothers-in-war saving each other's lives. But the time has passed and we must measure Captain Medina against Lieutenant Calley."

Latimer went through the witnesses from all three platoons who had testified that Medina told them that everything should be killed and who had said, "I killed because Captain Medina said kill everything. . . . I obeyed that order. I killed everything that breathed." Even those who had not killed and couldn't remember Medina's precise language "got the impression they were supposed to kill everything." And there was supporting evidence that the orders were to kill everything, Latimer asserted—the depositions of Sergeant Minh and Sergeant Phu and the fact that "nothing was said about handling prisoners or wounded, the artillery was placed on or near an inhabited village and the LZ was extremely close to the village, within effective range of small arms fire. In spite of Captain Medina's denial that he used that language, every member of the company testified that he said men, women, and children or words to that effect, or didn't remember whether he used the words or not. And there is the contemporaneous construction by the people who heard him. They went in firing and some people were killed."

If one wants to examine Medina's testimony and Calley's testimony since they are such opposites, then one should examine "Captain Medina's motives and actions." Though he saw people killed, he said nothing about it to higher officers or his platoon leaders; at night he refused to go back to make a count of civilian dead. "Here was a question that might become a national tragedy, yet Captain Medina didn't want to go back. He knew what had happened. He hoped that someone would cover the evidence. If that were done, if he had gone back, there might have been an immediate investigation before anyone changed his story. He told someone he was likely to go to prison for twenty years. Why? What was his culpability? His four reasons ring very hollow to me. He was alarmed at the number of casualties that might have occurred. He knew what had happened. Captain Medina knew how his orders had been interpreted. . . . Gentlemen, if you can believe that story, you can believe that this man was not fit to be a commander. Yet the boys all thought he was a good commander."

It was apparent what happened, Latimer declared. "Self-preservation entered and he took steps to preserve himself. It has now all come down to an issue between Captain Medina and Lieutenant Calley, because they are both running the last yard to a life or death sentence. When the stakes are that high, someone has to try to escape responsibility. Of all the men in or out of the service, they are the only two who can face such a sentence. Everyone connected with the My Lai tragedy has a fair chance of getting an honorable discharge from the United States Army and these two men are fighting to see if they get a death certificate. There is tragedy all over and it's tough to have to choose."

It is almost unheard of to break into another lawyer's summation. But Daniel was on his feet in a rage—and there were others in the courtroom, the judge's aides among them, who were also incensed. There had been an agreement early in the trial that no mention would ever be made in front of the jury of the status of the charges brought against others involved in My Lai. Latimer had just broken that agreement, in violation of all court rules. And there had been a court rule, too, that neither during testimony nor during summations would the penalties for conviction be mentioned; that would be up to the jury when and if it convicted, and such consideration was not supposed to enter into the deliberations over guilt or innocence. Latimer had broken that rule, too. Kennedy mildly rebuked him, hardly soothing Daniel.

And Latimer almost ignored the rebuke. He continued to pursue Medina, noting that Medina could afford to admit the cover-up at this point because he could not be tried for that. Then, showing indignation, his voice rising for almost the first time, Latimer asserted, "I can for the life of me not understand how you take twenty or thirty men, all good men, and take them and put them over there and have an incident like this happen unless that has been ordered. Orders must have come from somebody upstairs, and I go no further in this case than Captain Medina. I leave it to you good men to figure out how a lieutenant, the lowest man on the totem pole, came to be issuing orders like that without a directive."

If the jury was buying none of this, if it was convinced of

Calley's own guilt, then there was still the question of how mentally responsible he was, and so Latimer brought back the psychiatrists. "We have never contended that he is insane," Latimer said, but there were factors present that could have had such an impact on Lieutenant Calley "where he could not tell Captain Medina to go to hell, where he did not appreciate that the orders were illegal, where he could not say this is illegal and I don't think I should obey it." Calley, he said, was beset with the fact of "combat, the stark terror, the fear, confusions, considerations of your buddies." And he had been trained "to obey and ask later. If not, your troops might be dead." With a tinge of disgust, he said, "You get tried for a death sentence if you don't carry out orders and you get tried for a death sentence if you do. What a wonderful choice."

Then Latimer began a close examination of the testimony against Calley, rambling on so inaudibly that no one could hear him. At one point he lost his notes and hunted for them haphazardly. And he lost the jurors. All looked bored and both Bierbaum and McIntosh smothered yawns on a number of occasions.

If it had seemed through all of this that Latimer was pleading for Calley's freedom, it became even more apparent that, as he neared his climax, he was actually pleading for mitigation, for a reduced finding of guilt on a lesser charge. For he began to talk about manslaughter, that a killing in the heat of passion is manslaughter and "there are certainly elements of that here."

After nearly two hours, Latimer was tired and hoarse. But he had reached the point where "I conclude my little presentation. I thank you for your courtesy. His fate is in your hands. You have to measure him by right and wrong, what's criminal in your conscience. But who cannot argue the morality of war. I say that killing may sometime make the difference, it may save millions of lives, it may make the difference between winning and losing. This is not another Nuremberg. A second lieutenant is bound to give credence to the orders of his company commander. The laws of war are tailored to meet these very circumstances. They give leeway and latitude to people far from home who are trying to save the United States of America.

"I cannot recall when the United States of America had a similar situation. Or when we have taken a similar group of people in combat and put them up for trial. You, gentlemen, must chart a course for what should be done. You are in a situation where if ever the presumption of innocence and the rights to protect members of the armed forces ought to be extended to protect the rights of the accused, it is now."

Those who have been discharged and cannot be prosecuted, Latimer stressed, have "come forward as witnesses. . . . But the man who stays in the service and tries to build the morale and efficiency of the service does not have that protection."

Then he made his final emotional plea in that flat, colorless voice of his. "Give weight to the man who wanted to make the Army a career. He was not told and a word was never said to Lieutenant Calley about any of his problems in the service until he extended in Viet-Nam. He thought he was coming back to the United States for a new assignment. All the time the finger was pointing to Captain Medina. All of a sudden it turned and the charges were made. Who became the pigeon? The lowest man on the totem pole.

"I ask you to give honest consideration to this. It ought to make a difference between errors in judgment and criminality. I ask you to let this boy go free."

The final words in defense of Lieutenant Calley had been said.

25
"Who Killed More?"

Daniel would have preferred to wait another day, but Kennedy wanted to get the case to the jury before this day was through. And so, after a short supper break, Aubrey Daniel began to speak the last words for the government.

"It's been a long day, gentlemen, a long trial, and my job is truly almost over. I have one final duty to my client, the United States government. Because it is my duty to prove beyond a reasonable doubt the guilt of the accused, I have the last word."

Briefly he went back through the witnesses Latimer had challenged, reprising their testimony and asking, "Did he have any reason to lie? How about the accused?"

But that took only moments. Then Daniel let his own feelings come to the surface—anger, scorn, sarcasm, horror, disgust. If Latimer had tried for emotion, it was an emotion of another era, an era that was dead. Daniel more than matched his emotion, and his was an emotion that was relevant to this era, to this time. The result was perhaps the most eloquent and moving moment in the whole four months of the court-martial. There was not a sound or a movement in the whole courtroom while he spoke. Even the jurors leaned forward and followed him with their eyes, listening raptly. When he was through, it was as though a long sigh had passed through the courtroom to break the tension.

Daniel said:

"Only the guilt or innocence of the accused is your

responsibility. The defense attacks everyone. It attacks the CID; it attacks Captain Medina; it attacks the bad training for what happened and then it attacks the training on orders for his following orders. It puts the blame everywhere except where it belongs.

"Calley was not an enlisted man. He was an officer. He had an obligation to think. He had an obligation to his fellow man. He had an obligation not to disregard human considerations. He had an obligation to obey lawful orders and to act as a reasonable man. He owed that duty to his country. And he failed in it.

"Nothing has been said for the victims. Who will speak for them, gentlemen, who will speak for them?

"Mr. Latimer says the boys were a little aggressive, that they used bad judgment a couple of times. But the people were put in the ditch like a bunch of cattle and slaughtered.

"They say others are to blame. But, I ask you, gentlemen, who killed more? Do you want to take a poll?

"Do you believe that Task Force Barker was given orders to go in and round up and summarily execute infants who couldn't even walk? Do you believe Captain Medina gave such an order?

"Did the accused show any remorse? Did he complain about such an order? He's as much to blame as the one who gave the order—if such an order was given.

"A reasonable man would not have followed that order. What can justify shooting in cold blood infants, children, or any human being who is unresisting?

"The choice is not Captain Medina or Calley, but the facts and the law those facts show. The accused is to blame and he should be held responsible. What happened in My Lai Four is the truth and you can't hide it and you can't cover it up.

"You took an oath to apply the law to the facts regardless of your personal feelings. We have carried our burden. We have proven that the accused gathered up and summarily executed unarmed and unresisting men, women, children, and infants in My Lai Four on 16 March 1968. There is no question about the fact that he killed these human beings without justification or excuse and with premeditation. Under the law of this country and the Uniform Code of Military Justice and the law regulating warfare, all human beings are entitled to be treated humanely. They are entitled to this under the law regardless of their race or nationality or their political affiliation. It is not just unlawful under our law to take the life of another American, and the fact that the accused's victims were Vietnamese cannot justify the taking of their lives by summary execution.

"What the defense asks makes us no better than our enemy. It makes us legalize murder.

"How could we call for humane treatment of our men who are held prisoners when we don't give their people humane treatment?

"These people may have been VC, they may have been sympathizers or supporters of the VC, they may have been Vietnamese people who just happened to have been at the wrong place at the wrong time in their lives. They may have been people who had been under the control of the Viet Cong because they had no choice because they were captives. But who stopped to ask? Did the accused attempt to make that determination?

"And what choice did the children whom the accused killed have about the fact that they were in the village that day? Or what about the infants whose only possible crime was the fact that they were born in My Lai Four?

"The accused has been accorded a trial before his guilt could be determined. The people of My Lai Four were also entitled under the law to a trial to determine if they were guilty of any offense against this nation. A trial which they never received. Would the evidence presented against these people have revealed them guilty of any offense beyond a reasonable doubt? Would any tribunal in this world have found one of those children guilty of any offense and ordered his execution? Would the evidence have proven any infant guilty of an offense which could justify his execution? Gentlemen, the children and infants would never have been tried and nothing under the law could justify their execution.

"The accused appointed himself judge, jury, and executioner on 16 March 1968. He appointed himself the Lord High Executioner of his victims but without trial. He assumed the responsibility for determining their guilt and for their deaths. This nation did not. He and he alone made 'that determination and now he must assume the responsibility for his unlawful acts.

"The laws of this country are only effective if they are enforced. Without enforcement, they have no meaning, for justice, like discipline, requires that the innocent be recognized and guilt be determined. Discipline, which this government recognizes as the backbone of the military, also requires that when the law is disobeyed that it be exposed and condemned.

"The accused was a commissioned officer in the armed forces of the United States when he slaughtered his innocent victims in My Lai Four. He has attempted to absolve himself of responsibility by stating that he did his duty there. That he acted in the name of this country and the law of this nation. He did not and upon that question there can be no doubt. To so rely is to prostitute the true mission of the United States soldier. It has been said [by General Douglas McArthur]: 'The soldier, be he friend or foe, is charged with the protection of the weak and unarmed. It is the very essence and reason for his being. When he violates this sacred trust, he not only profanes his entire cult, but threatens the very fabric of international society. The traditions of fighting men are long and honorable. They are based upon the noblest of human faiths—sacrifice.'

"There are rules that govern your profession, gentlemen. Rules of warfare and of humane treatment are the guidelines of the soldier. The United States government says to you that the accused failed in his duty. That he did not act in the name of and in accordance with the law of this nation. Within our society and under the law, the value of human life is sacred. When the accused put on the uniform of an American officer and took the oath of allegiance to this country, he was not relieved of his conscience, he was not relieved of his responsibility to make appropriate moral judgments. He was not relieved of his responsibility to know the difference between what is right and wrong and what is humane. The accused when he took the oath of an American soldier was not given a license to slaughter unarmed men, women, and children on his own personal supposition that they were the enemy. Such acts are not now nor have they ever been justified under the law of this country. The accused failed in his duty as a soldier. He failed in his duty to his troops, to his country, to mankind. He did not do his duty.

"And your duty in this case is clear. On the evidence we have presented to you, and under the law, you can arrive at only one decision and still fulfill your duty as a member of this court.

"You, gentlemen, are the conscience of the United States Army. You are the conscience of the nation in this case. Your duty is clear.

"We have carried out our burden and you are asked to fix the responsibility where it belongs under law, to find the accused guilty of the premeditated murders with which he is charged."

And Daniel, who had not looked at Calley all during this summation, who had looked only at the jury, turned and pointed a stiff arm at the lieutenant as he ended. Then he turned and sat wearily in his chair.

26
To the Jury

All that remained now was for Judge Kennedy to explain the law and the options open to the jury. Fifteen minutes after Daniel had taken his seat, the judge began. He read, in a flat, emotionless voice—so as, Kennedy explained, not to give color or weight to any particular point and thus unduly influence the jury—a charge that was so detailed and complicated that it took an hour and twenty-five minutes to get through and ran forty-one pages. By the time he finished, his voice was hoarse and cracked.

Calley, he explained, was not charged with a single act of mass murder but with four specific counts; each was separate and distinct and proof of one was not proof of another. In order to convict, the jury must be convinced that the government's time sequence was correct, that the locations were correct and, in the case of the mass murders, "two-thirds of you must be convinced beyond a reasonable doubt that the same identical Oriental human beings arr dead." And in order to convict Calley, there was no need to find that he had killed the exact numbers specified by the government; it was only necessary to find that he killed one person at the trail intersection or one person at the ditch in order to convict him of those offenses.

In each of the specifications, Kennedy said, there were four elements the jury must find before it could agree on a verdict of guilty of permeditated murder: that the person or persons charged, whose names and ages are unknown, are dead; that their deaths resulted from acts by Calley; that the killings were unlawful; and that Calley "had a premeditated design to kill." If it agreed on the first three points, then the fourth was crucial. If it found that rather than premeditation, Calley merely had "an intent to kill," it could convict him of unpremeditated murder. And if it found that he had killed "in the heat of sudden passion caused by adequate provocation," it could convict him of voluntary manslaughter. And in the case of the child at the ditch, it could also find him guilty of assault with intent to commit murder rather than any of the three types of murder.

In developing its case, Kennedy explained, the government had relied on both direct evidence and circumstantial evidence. "There is no general rule for contrasting the weight of circumstantial evidence and direct evidence. The assertions of an eye witness may be more convincing than contrary inferences that may be drawn from certain circumstances. Conversely, an inference drawn from one or more circumstances may be more convincing than the contrary assertion of an eyewitness."

Because of the psychiatric testimony, the jury would have to make up its mind about Calley's mental capacity. The jurors should carefully consider, Kennedy said, "all evidence tending to show that Lieutenant Calley may have been suffering from mental impairment or condition of such consequence and degree that it deprived him of the ability to entertain the premeditated design to kill required in the offense of premeditated murder." The burden of proving that Calley was in command of his faculties was on the government.

In assessing the various witnesses, the judge said, the jury might consider "intelligence, the acuteness of his memory, his apparent candor, his appearance and deportment, his demeanor on the witness stand, his friendships and prejudices and his character as to truth and veracity." On these criteria, some of Conti's testimony might possibly be discounted, so might Sledge's and Medina's, while the testimony of Meadlo, Kotouc, and others might be weighed because they had received immunity before testifying.

But the final determination was up to the jury. "When conflict appears in the testimony, it is your function to resolve it and to determine where the truth lies."

If the jurors were concerned as to whether the killings at My Lai were legal or illegal, Kennedy said, "you are instructed that the killing of a human being is unlawful when it is done without legal justification or excuse." The defense, of course, had claimed that the killings were done as a result of orders and were, thus, legal. So Kennedy went through the conflicting testimony on the briefing and the orders. The jurors, he said, would have to decide if Calley acted under orders to kill his victims, and if he did were those orders legal or illegal. In considering this, the jurors should bear in mind that "the conduct of warfare is not wholly unregulated by law. . . . I therefore instruct you, as a matter of law, that if unresisting human beings were killed at My Lai Four while within the effective custody and control of our military forces, their deaths cannot be considered justified, and any order to kill such people would be, as a matter of law, an illegal order. Thus if you find that Lieutenant Calley received an order directing him to kill unresisting Vietnamese within his control or within the control of his troops, that order would be an illegal order."

But the question did not end there. Soldiers, Kennedy said, are taught to obey orders, especially on the battlefield, and military effectiveness depends on obedience to orders. "On the other hand, the obedience of the soldier is not the obedience of an automaton. A soldier is a reasoning agent, obliged to respond, not as a machine, but as a person." Thus, if "a man of ordinary sense and understanding" would know that an order is unlawful, obedience to orders is no defense, just as it is no defense if the actual accused knew that the order was illegal.

It was up to the jury to decide, if it found that he was acting under orders, whether he actually knew those orders were illegal. To determine this, Kennedy said, there was a lot of circumstantial evidence and the jury should also consider Calley's "rank, educational background, OCS schooling, other training while in the Army, including basic training, and his training in Hawaii and Viet-Nam, his experience in prior operations involving contact with hostile and friendly Vietnamese, his age, and any other evidence tending to prove or disprove" that he knew the orders were illegal. If he knew they were illegal, "the fact that the order was given operates as no defense."

If the jury cannot decide whether Calley himself knew this, then it should use the "reasonable man" test. "Unless you are satisfied from the evidence, beyond reasonable doubt, that a man of ordinary sense and understanding would have known the order to be unlawful, you must acquit Lieutenant Calley."

The main element throughout every area of deliberation, Kennedy said, was the concept of "reasonable doubt—not a vague, speculative, imaginary doubt, but just such a doubt as would cause you, as reasonable men, to hesitate to act in matters of importance to you. The real question is whether after hearing the evidence, and from the evidence and the instructions on the law which I have given you, you have or have not an abiding belief, amounting to a moral certainty, that Lieutenant Calley is guilty. If you have such a belief so formed, it is your duty to convict. If you do not have such a belief so formed, it is your duty to acquit. . . . (But) Lieutenant Calley must be presumed to be innocent until his guilt is established by legal and competent evidence beyond reasonable doubt."

In the final moments of his lengthy charge, Kennedy went through the procedures under which the jury would operate, some of which were decidedly different from civilian juries.

There was no possibility of a hung jury. Each vote on each charge would be decisive. To convict would take a two-thirds vote, or four of the six jurors. Thus, if three voted guilty and three innocent, Calley would be acquitted on that charge.

And though the jurors had been permitted to return home every night during the trial, that would no longer be true. Henceforth, they would be locked into a bachelor officers' quarters suite, totally segregated from everyone and every outside influence, and watched and tended constantly by bailiffs. The standard hours for them to deliberate would be from eight in the morning to four-thirty in the afternoon in the deliberation room in the courthouse. If they wanted to deliberate at other times, they would have to return to the courthouse to do so.

At nine-twenty-five on the evening of March 16, 1971, the case of the United States of America v. First Lieutenant William L. Calley, Jr., was in the hands of the jury. All the words that could possibly influence them had been spoken. It was now all up to those six combat veterans.

27
Waiting

The long, excruciating wait began.

As the jury started deliberations the next morning, Aubrey Daniel and Brooks Doyle went out on the golf course. It was the first round Daniel had played since the trial began in November; he shot a 94, ten strokes higher than his last time out. Early in the afternoon, he was back prowling the courthouse, a sunburn flushing his pale indoor complexion, and he looked a little healthier, a little less drawn, a little more relaxed. His attention was obviously divided between the jury and his wife, who was expecting a baby and day.

Through the next days, Daniel played golf several times, wandered around abstractly sometimes in his rumpled captain's uniform, sometimes in civilian sports clothes, chatted, talked about having a party at his home with some of the reporters the night the jury came in with a verdict, a party no matter what the outcome, just to memorialize the end of the trial. He went to several small parties given for him, by the television networks and others, trying to relax. But mainly he did what everyone else was doing; he waited.

Latimer and Raby and Kay roamed the courthouse, from their offices to the pressroom and back. They would wander into the pressroom and talk fitfully to whatever reporters were there, growing less optimistic (if they had ever been at all) all the time. In the evenings, now, Latimer began to appear in public for the first time, joining reporters often for dinner and sipping a little wine through the meal (though a Mormon, he was not above some wine with food though his wife abstained), talking about himself and his career. He, too, waited.

Judge Kennedy played some golf, played some bridge, had reporters out to the house for a cook-out, relaxed in his office and talked with anyone who wandered by, presided over the sessions when the jury returned to court for rereading of testimony. At one point, the weather growing warmer, he installed an air-conditioner in the deliberation room, both for the jury's comfort and his. He wanted to open his windows but every time he did he could hear shouting from the deliberation room across a short expanse of lawn. The air-conditioner muffled the shouts and let spring into Kennedy's chambers. And he waited.

Reporters wandered back and forth between the pressroom in the courthouse, the press center a couple of blocks away, and their hotels and motels in Columbus and Phenix City. There was little else to do. Some kept a long, steady, and unfruitful watch on the area of the court leading to the deliberation room, clocking the jurors and trying to decide, whenever they emerged, what the signs meant—what did it indicate when McIntosh came out angry? When Salem, chain-smoking, stomped out with a grim expression? When Kinnard poked his head out and his face was flushed? It was possible to read anything or nothing into that.

Other reporters played bridge, joined sometimes by Kennedy; others played poker or read or pecked away at their typewriters, trying to piece together their wrap-up stories for when it would all be over; some just talked and stood out in the sun.

Out in front of the courthouse, the television cameramen and crews and the still photographers pitched pennies, as they had been doing for months during the days—sometimes threatened with arrest for gambling by the provost marshal—threw frisbies and footballs, dozed, and waited.

One afternoon there was a party in the pressroom for John LaFond, Kennedy's assistant, who was being discharged from the Army that day (he, after a while, had decided to stop waiting and get on with his life). The beer, brought in in kegs, flowed, much to the dismay of the provost marshal, who looked askance at the idea of beer or liquor in the courthouse but who seemed hesitant about doing anything while Judge Kennedy was there, enjoying himself. Everyone who had had anything to do with the court-martial, except Calley himself, was there to give LaFond a send-off; the judge's other assistant, Ed Hieronymous, seemed particularly jealous, but then he was supposed to be going to Heidelberg for the next two years and had already had to put off his scheduled departure three times because the trial had dragged on so long (he finally left a couple of days after the verdict came in). A poem celebrating LaFond was read, a dramatic recitation of his citations and discharge papers was enacted. Raby relaxed and even got a little high on the ice-cold beer; and so did the judge and Daniel and everyone else. It was a time for winding down and waiting.

And Calley waited, at one moment assured, optimistic, and at the next gloomy and pessimistic. Except when he was needed in court for the rereading of testimony, he waited, dressed in bell-bottom jeans and a crew-necked short-sleeved sports shirt, in his apartment a couple of blocks away. He was rarely alone. Anne Moore was almost always there; so were other friends and acquaintances and well-wishers and the curious and even reporters whom he began to ask to drop by for a drink. He invited just about everyone he knew for drinks and some talk, and just about everybody—with only a couple of exceptions—took him up.

It was a new world for Calley, a world into which he had suddenly found himself thrust a year and a half before, a world where the intellectual and the pseudo-intellectual abounded, where the talk was as much about ideas as anything else, where nobody put Calley down—at least not to his face—where, in fact, some people seemed to listen intently to what he had to say and even to agree with him or to argue with him as though he were an intellectual peer. It was a world he had discovered in New York on his visits there with John Sack, a world of people who dealt in words and ideas, a world many of whose denizens seemed to feel that Calley was a victim rather than a perpetrator, that it was a corrupt and venal system that had turned him into a killer and so it was the system and not Calley that was to blame for what happened. And that world, or much of it, surrounded him all during the trial at Fort Benning, and now that the trial was about to end, he did not want his involvement in that world to end along with it and so he seemed almost desperately to be clinging to it, to surrounding himself with those sophisticated men who dealt in words and ideas even if they saw him in a different light from Sack and his friends.

And it was apparent in those days that he could not bear to be alone (and who could blame him, who not sympathize?). He talked about a party being planned for him in Atlanta when he was acquitted and told those planning it not to forget to invite . . . Peter Range of *Time* (who had become a close friend) . . . or one of the young women reporters (to whom Calley seemed drawn; he didn't know that she had different feelings about him, that she had told other reporters that sometimes Calley would try to hug her and when he tried to put his arms around her, "all I can think of are dead babies") . . . or someone else from that world to whom he was drawn at that moment.

Jokingly, he told people that he had bought everything he needed for the trip to Kansas (the disciplinary barracks at Fort Leavenworth where, according to regulations, he would be confined if convicted) except a new toothbrush, and that everything was packed and ready.

Most of the time he stood behind the bar in his apartment, surrounded by visitors, pouring drinks for them and himself (bourbon mainly), keeping people late into the night, unwilling to let his visitors go and to face the rest of the night alone. Rarely did he talk about My Lai and what had happened there, usually turning the queries aside, repeating that he didn't think he had done anything wrong, but that the war was what was wrong. He gave interviews saying that maybe if My Lai had waked the nation up then maybe it was a good thing. If he were acquitted, he said, he was just going to relax for a while or go back to school or maybe make some speeches telling of the evils of war—more and more he expressed antiwar views—or help John Sack finish his autobiography.

"If you're acquitted, where are you going to go?" somebody asked Calley one day.

"Home for a while," he said.

"Where's home these days, Rusty?"

Calley looked startled and then a little forlorn and lost. He thought for a moment and said, in a muted voice, "Fort Benning, I guess. Here."

But despite those moments of optimism, Calley was not really convinced that he would go free. He maintained that he had always had confidence in his lawyers and that they had done the best job possible and he had no regrets, claiming this particularly when one day a reporter whom Calley had always considered an antagonist wished him luck. "From you, the enemy?" Calley said, startled.

"Yeah. Anyone with your lawyers needs all the luck he can get."

And Calley recognized that he would need luck. He had told some very close friends that he thought he would probably be convicted when it was all over—but of manslaughter, not murder. What he didn't know was that even on that charge he could have gotten up to twenty years.

On the walls of Calley's apartment were an American flag, a gift of a World War II veteran who said it had flown over Bastogne during the Battle of the Bulge, an abstract peace poster, and an animal hide. One night Dan Greene, a reporter from *The National Observer*, asked Calley what the hide was.

"A reindeer skin," Calley said.

"Where's it come from, Rusty?"

"From Norway."

"Did you shoot it, Rusty?" Greene asked. It was not meant in offense, just after a couple of drinks and in a sense of curiosity.

But Calley looked shocked and then pensive. "God, no," he said, "I couldn't shoot a reindeer."

(When the story made the rounds later, someone added sardonically, "Yeah, but what if he'd been ordered to?")

Almost wistfully, as though it didn't really have anything to do with him, he talked about Daniel. The prosecutor, he said, had done "a hell of a job." Calley saw it, though, as only a job; he didn't seem to understand that Daniel had really believed intensely in the morality and the rightness of what he was doing. And Calley would say that Daniel was the kind of officer he wished he had been, the kind of man he admired—smart, persevering, "the kind of guy you give an order to and you know he's going to carry it out."

But the days got to Calley, the waiting. He drank more, was edgier, detested those calls that brought him back to court to hear only that more testimony was going to be reread, and he would delay getting dressed as long as possible on those days, sometimes arriving long after everyone else.

In the deliberation room, the jurors went slowly and meticulously over all the evidence, poring over all the exhibits, using two blackboards. They asked for the testimony of the helicopter pilots to be reread and then the testimony of Conti, Sledge, Dursi, Meadlo, and others.

At one point, after they had been out only a couple of days, there seemed a danger of a mistrial. Brown was rushed to the hospital with severe stomach pains. It turned out to be minor and after a little treatment, a walk in the garden of Kennedy's home with the judge and a bailiff, he was back in shape.

As the days passed and the jurors demanded to hear more and more testimony, Latimer grew angrier and angrier. "They're getting way beyond anything that could be anticipated in this proceeding," he asserted one day. "They're not investigators, they're a jury." On another day, he declared that going over the testimony was "a second trial, that's what it is. I think that's cruel and unusual punishment, keeping this boy waiting, waiting, while we retry this case." Another morning, he was arguing against any more rereading. "I've got a kid over there sitting on dynamite. No one knows how it can affect a man. It's like a person waiting to be hanged the next morning. They'll give him anything he wants to eat, but he just wants to get it over with."

But Kennedy was not about to prod the jurors. "This case is much more complex factually and legally than any other I ever read about," he said. And he noted that, "If they acquit Lieutenant Calley, there will be accusations of whitewash. If they convict him, there will be allegations the other way." He would let the jury set its own pace.

Latimer kept complaining, though. The jurors were practicing "business as usual," not deliberating all the time; they were "watching the Glen Campbell and Ed Sullivan shows, and wining and dining themselves," taking time out for haircuts and on Sunday morning for a religious service. "It's a disgrace," he complained. "I worked eighteen hours a day almost seven days a week during the trial. This is not a siesta. This is a serious business. We've got a man's life at stake."

By that time, Kennedy's patience with Latimer had worn thin. "You have to eat, don't you?" he snapped. "You have to get your clothes cleaned, you have to get a haircut, don't you? From that standpoint, I totally disagree with you."

To the extent that a man's life was at stake, the jury agreed with Latimer—and that was why it was taking its time. Later Kinnard was to say, "We looked for anything that would prove Lieutenant Calley was innocent. We gave Lieutenant Calley every benefit of every doubt. Every piece of evidence given in that court and every witness that came before the court was closely scrutinized. It was related to the overall picture as we on the jury had it of what happened March sixteenth at My Lai. That operation that took place March sixteenth was relived every hour during the time we spent in the deliberation room by members of that jury trying to find some way, some evidence, or one flaw in the testimony of, I don't know how many witnesses, that would shed some light on some area not touched on so that we could find Lieutenant Calley innocent. The verdict did not come about as the result of our saying, 'The hell with it, he's guilty.' It was work."

And Brown added, "This is the most difficult job I ever had in my entire life. Because even to consider that an American soldier, any soldier, would do such a thing, it is almost beyond my comprehension. I wanted to believe it didn't happen. I was looking for this in all the testimony. That it was just a hoax, by any stretch of the imagination, that it didn't happen."

The question that was constantly raised in the minds of the jurors, when they came to discuss orders—and all felt that some orders had been given, though they weren't sure what kind—was put by Kinnard, and related to the principle of the reasonable man. "If you worked for me and I told you to go out and steal a car, would you do it? Well, would you?"

For nine days, the jurors did nothing but refight and relive and argue about the slaughter at My Lai. There were, one of them said, some "knock-down drag-outs" as they went through the mountain of evidence accumulated over four months.

On the tenth day of deliberation, Friday, March 26, they began to vote on the first specification, the killings at the trail. It took just that single vote: Calley was guilty on count number one.

But there was a dispute as to just how many he killed there. They studied the gruesome evidence in Prosecution Exhibit 12A. "I sat there and counted and counted and counted," Brown later said, "and I couldn't come up with thirty in that picture. There was no way you could come up with the exact number." Since it made no difference in the final analysis how many they did come up with, and since they couldn't agree on an exact number, they settled for "an unknown number, no less than one."

Two days later, on Sunday, they were ready to vote on the killings at the ditch. Again it took only a single ballot: Calley was guilty on count number two. Again they could not agree on numbers. "We tried," Brown said, "to give every benefit of every doubt to Calley's defense." Since the estimates by witnesses had ranged from a few to more than a hundred killed, they settled on "a conservative" estimate, reducing the number from seventy to "an unknown number, no less than twenty."

On Monday morning they reached the last two counts. Here

they chose to believe Charles Sledge over Calley. The vote was to convict Calley of the premeditated murder of the man in white, and to convict him of assault with intent to commit murder of the child because Sledge could not absolutely say that Calley had killed the child.

It had taken eighty-nine hours and fifty-eight minutes of deliberation during thirteen days in that small room in the courthouse for the jury to reach its verdict.

28
"The Court Finds You"

The phone rang in Calley's apartment just before three-thirty on Monday afternoon, March 29. It was time to go to court again, not this time to hear more testimony reread but now to hear the verdict. Calley took a long time getting out of his casual clothes and into his uniform. Brooks Doyle drove over to pick him up and drive him back to the courthouse.

It was not quite four-thirty when, accompanied by his lawyers, Calley walked into the crowded, hushed courtroom. When he had taken his seat, he rose again as Kennedy and the jurors came through the blue curtains behind the bench. "I have a communication that you have reached a verdict. Is that correct?" Kennedy asked. Colonel Ford said it was and passed the forms to the judge. Kennedy read them without expression and then passed them back.

So the moment toward which it had all been directed had arrived. At just four-thirty, Calley rose from the defense table and, according to military protocol, marched the few steps across the courtroom to stand before Colonel Ford. The only break in tradition was that instead of being alone, as the rules call for, he had Latimer on one side of him and Raby on the other (for Latimer had expressed fears that Calley, who had held up so well to that point, might break under the strain if the verdict went decisively against him). Calley saluted Colonel Ford stiffly and then waited.

Ford returned the salute. Then, in a soft, Tennessee drawl, he read: "Lieutenant Calley, it is my duty as president of this court to inform you that the court, in closed session, and upon the secret written ballot, two-thirds of the members present at the time vote was taken concurring in each finding of guilty, finds you:

"Of specification one of the charge: Guilty . . . of premeditated murder . . . of an unknown number, no less than one . . .

"Of specification two of the charge: Guilty . . . of premeditated murder . . . of an unknown number, no less than twenty . . .

"Of specification one of the additional charge: Guilty . . . of premeditated murder . . .

"Of specification two of the additional charge: Guilty of assault with intent to commit murder."

Calley's eyes, usually half-shut, widened as he heard the guilty verdicts read. At first he seemed to sag slightly, then braced himself stiffly, his face flushed, his eyes wide open, staring at Colonel Ford. When the reading was done, he tried to salute, but his hand seemed unable to reach all the way. Then he turned and walked stiffly back to the defense table.

There was not a sound in the courtroom. Judge Kennedy spoke briefly. "Gentlemen, we will go into the sentencing phase tomorrow."

If there had been no sound inside the courtroom when the verdict was read, there were plenty outside. Flushed and angry, Latimer emerged to face the television cameras, microphones, and reporters. The verdict, he declared, "was a horrendous decision for the United States, the United States Army, and for my client." It was, he added, "much tougher than I anticipated. Take my word for it, the boy is crushed." And then Latimer added, "This boy is a product of the system. He was taken out of his own home, given an automatic weapon, taught to kill. They ordered him to kill. And then the same government tries him for killing and selects the judge, the court, and the prosecutor."

As Latimer spoke, a crowd of more than a hundred people gathered across the street to wait for sight of Calley. A few minutes later, he came through the door, surrounded by military police (but not shackled, as had been, for instance, Dr. Howard Levy, who was convicted a couple of years earlier of refusing to train Green Berets in medical techniques for use in Viet-Nam), and marched down the sidewalk to a waiting car. Some in the crowd, one burly woman in particular with a German accent, screamed, "We're with you, Calley." He looked up, gave a brief wave, and then got into the car to drive to the post stockade and spend his first night behind bars.

29
"It Has Never Been Honor"

What remained was to decide Calley's punishment. With a verdict of premeditated murder, only two choices were open— death by hanging at Fort Leavenworth or life in the prison stockade there.

On Tuesday, March 30, the day after the verdict, the court heard pleas on what the choice should be. The defense could have called witnesses to show mitigation, in an attempt to sway the jury. Latimer decided against this and chose once more to make his pitch for emotion and patriotism. He flourished a handful of the thousands of telegrams that had poured into the defense office in support of Calley and declared that the verdict of guilty "has torn America apart. The flag may fly at full-mast over military installations, but it will always be drawn at half-mast over the homes of people whose sons may be going into military service. This case cuts very deep. When Lieutenant Calley went into the service of the United States Army, he was not an aggressive young man. Lieutenant Calley outside of an ordinary traffic violation was a good boy and he remained that way until he got into that Oriental area over there in Viet-Nam. Maybe, shall we say, he used bad judgment; maybe he became too aggressive. But who trained him to kill, kill, kill?

"You don't have to have eyes of glass and hearts of stone. Somewhere along the line, there is some place where a few humanities ought to be worked into this case, where a maximum sentence isn't given, where it should not be. I think some small consideration should be given to a boy who did not necessarily want to go to Viet-Nam but was sent there, a boy who did not want to kill anybody but who thought he had to. I think there is a place for Lieutenant Calley to go and make something of his life. But he can't do it in the graveyard. Thank you all so much. I go away with a heavy heart, for I see a life ruined."

Calley himself had decided that he would make a plea to the jury, too. He stood a lonely, dejected figure, smaller than usual, too small even to use the reading stand, often shaken with sobs, his voice quavering as he spoke for just over two minutes.

"I asked my attorney, George Latimer, and my other attorneys not to go into mitigation in this case. There's a lot of things that aren't appropriate, and I don't think it really matters what type of individual I am. And I'm not going to stand here and plead for my life or my freedom.

"But I would like you to consider a thousand more lives that are going to be lost in Southeast Asia, the thousands more to be imprisoned, not only here in the United States but in North Viet-Nam and in hospitals all over the world as amputees.

"I've never known a soldier, nor did I myself ever wantonly kill a human being in my entire life. If I have committed a crime, the only crime I've committed is in judgment of my values. Apparently I valued my troops' lives more than I did that of the enemy. When my troops were getting massacred and mauled by an enemy I couldn't see, I couldn't feel, and I couldn't touch—that nobody in the military system ever described them as anything other than communism. They didn't give it a race, they didn't give it a sex, they didn't give it an age. They never let me believe it was just a philosophy in man's mind. That was my enemy out there. And when it became between me and that enemy, I had to value the lives of my troops—and I feel that was the only crime I have committed.

"Yesterday, you stripped me of all my honor. Please, by your actions that you take here today, don't strip future soldiers of their honor. I beg you."

And the last word was left to Daniel. He did not ask for death, leaving the ultimate decision to the jury. The night before, he had held his party—and been criticized for ghoulishness in some papers—had several drinks, played the guitar, sang folk songs, gave some good imitations of Latimer and, early in the morning in discussion with some reporters, had decided that he would go with his natural detestation of the death penalty. So all he asked was, "You know the facts and I know you'll reach an appropriate sentence."

But Daniel wanted to take that sting from Calley's final plea. And so he reminded the jurors, "You did not strip him of his honor. What he did stripped him of his honor. It is not an honor—it has never been an honor—to kill unarmed men, women, and children."

The next afternoon, the jury had reached its decision. On that decision, it could have hung. For while it had taken only a two-thirds vote to convict, it would take a unanimous vote to reach a death sentence and five votes for life. But the jury—though Salem and Bierbaum would later express some hope that higher intervention would reduce Calley's punishment—did not balk.

At two-thirty in the afternoon, everyone was back in court and once again, flanked by his attorneys, the small lieutenant stood before Colonel Ford and saluted.

His face pale and tight, the colonel read the sentence: "First Lieutenant William L. Calley, it is my duty as president of this court to inform you that the court in closed session and upon secret written ballot . . . sentences you:

"To be confined at hard labor for the length of your natural life; to be dismissed from the service; to forfeit all pay and allowances."

Relief written all over him, Calley slumped, then straightened, saluted, and said in a barely audible voice, "I'll do my best, sir." He turned and strode back to the defense table.

"This court is closed," Reid W. Kennedy said sharply.

In the courtroom, two women wept. The crowd filed out slowly and, for the most part, silently.

Outside, another crowd waited for Calley, a woman screaming, "He's been crucified. Lieutenant Calley killed a hundred Communists single-handed. He should get a medal. He should be promoted to general."

About a half-hour later, Calley emerged, again surrounded by military police. He gave a brief acknowledgment to the crowd and was driven back to the stockade to wait for what the future—what the years of appeals through the courts—would bring.

The court-martial of Lieutenant Calley was over.

Part Five:
An End to Innocence

30
The Nation in Torment

So they marched Rusty Calley off to the stockade, which, if you believe that a man has to pay for his crimes, his sins, and even his mistakes, was what they should have done. The longest court-martial in military history was over, and now everybody could go home and try to forget the whole thing. Aubrey Daniel's new son could be born and he could get his discharge and go home to Virginia and then later announce that he was going to work for Edward Bennett Williams as a lawyer in that famous trial law firm. Al Raby could go back to JAG and continue with the courses he had instituted at Fort Benning, to explain the laws of war—and what was legal and illegal—to new officers. George Latimer could get on the next plane and fly back to Salt Lake City and begin to think about appeals. Richard Kay could go home to Cleveland and plan his right-wing political career. Reid Kennedy could go on to his next judicial assignment in the Army and preside over a less traumatic trial. All the reporters who had spent more than four months at Fort Benning could go back home too, and on to the next story. And Fort Benning could return to its old ways.

But no one would be quite the same again as he had been that day in early November when the trial had begun. No one would ever forget all that he had heard in that courtroom and outside it.

And there was the nation out there beyond Fort Benning, a nation torn by the torment over the trial and the verdict.

There was an evening early in the court-martial when my

wife and I were joined for dinner by John Sack. Early in the conversation, Sack said that we all had Calley wrong. "I see Rusty," he said, "as Christ on the cross being crucified."

In the days after the court-martial ended, it was apparent that a great many Americans agreed with Sack. A poll conducted soon after the verdict showed that nearly 80 per cent of Americans bitterly opposed the finding, that 20 per cent didn't think that what Calley did at My Lai was a crime at all, and that most of the rest thought he was a scapegoat (without, it seemed, understanding what the word meant, for a scapegoat is an innocent who takes the blame for others), a martyr, or a Christ crucified for his fellow Americans—and the trial was called by many the American Dreyfus affair.

Calley, the majority of Americans seemed to feel, was only a soldier doing his duty and obeying his orders, a soldier, an officer doing—as he himself maintained—his best to ensure the safety and welfare of his men. What happened at My Lai was only an act of war, an episode in combat, something that happens in any war (no one seemed to know or even care that there had been no combat at My Lai that morning). To condemn Calley was to condemn every American soldier who had tried to do his duty and would cause officers in combat to hesitate at critical moments which could cost the lives of their men. To condemn Calley was to condemn every American soldier who had fought not just in Viet-Nam but in every war. To condemn Calley would destroy the morale of all American soldiers henceforth and forever more. Instead of condemning Calley, he should have been hailed. Instead of sending him to prison for his crimes, he should have been freed and decorated.

Or he was the scapegoat taking the consequences for the massacre at My Lai while everyone else involved, as Latimer said, from generals to privates to discharged soldiers, went free. Others said he was the scapegoat for America's policy in Viet-Nam, a policy that by its very nature inevitably led to My Lai. They saw him bearing the burden of guilt not just for My Lai and those above him who gave him some kind of order, but for the entire nation and its leaders, military and civilian;

Calley would go to prison while those who had made the policy that led to the war crimes committed throughout that small nation in Southeast Asia went free.

And there were those who saw the whole nation filled with guilt for My Lai and for all those other crimes—and for the war itself, the biggest of crimes—that had led so inevitably to the destruction of Viet-Nam and its people. They felt that much of the nation, that both the Army and the government were using Calley as the sacrificial lamb to wash clean the conscience of the United States, of the Army, and of the government.

Practically no one was willing to look at Calley himself and at what he had done; almost everyone wanted to make him more than he was, wanted in a large sense to turn him into a symbol and as a symbol to reject or accept what they saw him standing for.

There was a national unity that has been rare in recent times. It was a unity about ends, if not about what had led up to them. From the left, from the right, from the center came a deluge of telegrams, phone calls, letters, petitions, demands. They flooded the courthouse at Fort Benning, the offices of Congressmen and other public officials, newspapers and radio and television stations, the White House. By a margin of more than a hundred to one, they challenged the conviction and the sentence on one ground or another. They demanded that Richard Milhous Nixon—the President sworn to uphold the law—take action. He should reduce Calley's sentence; he should commute Calley's sentence and set him free; he should personally overrule the jury and declare that Calley was innocent; he should decorate and honor the lieutenant. It was a unity that brought together behind Calley on one level or another those who could not conceivably have been allies before; there were George Wallace and Dr. Benjamin Spock, for instance, both crying out against the conviction and sentence.

If there was to be vilification, it was not for Calley and what he had done, it seemed, but for those who convicted him. The jurors, when they returned home, were met with letters and telephone calls so vile and obscene that they had to change their phone numbers and take steps to protect their families. Some had hoped that the occasion might be a beneficial one for Americans "because," as Harvey Brown put it, "maybe it will make them look within themselves to find out what's wrong."

But such hopes appeared to be in vain. Most Americans took the verdict not as an opportunity for a national self-examination but rather as an attack on the nation and themselves and everything they believed, an attack that had to be repulsed.

There were some—a very few—who agreed with the jury that on the basis of the evidence in this one particular case, the verdict was the only possible one (though they, like many others, believed it could not and should not stop with Calley). "If a man kills unarmed citizens that do not pose a threat to him, then he would be guilty of murder," said former Attorney General Ramsey Clark. "I could see no grounds for clemency under those circumstances."

And there were those who noted that to acquit Calley would have been an open admission that the slaughter of unresisting civilians, that war crimes are American national policy in Viet-Nam and so are beyond condemnation. It could not be expected that a jury of Army officers, all but one of whom had fought in Viet-Nam, would acquit and make such an admission.

There were, too, some in the Army itself—mainly professional officers, and particularly West Pointers—who saw the guilty verdict as a personal vindication. A captain, a West Pointer, who had served in Viet-Nam stopped me one afternoon outside the press center at Fort Benning and in angry tones demanded that I spread the word that the regular Army was not only for Calley's conviction but wanted him hung. "Goddammit," he said, "I didn't go around massacring civilians when I was in Viet-Nam like that little son of a bitch. But now, whenever I wear the uniform off the base, it's damn obvious that people think I did, that they think everyone over there is butchering babies. I don't know whether it's ever going to be possible now to persuade people that I didn't fight a war like that and neither did a lot of other guys, but if they don't convict Calley and hang him or throw away the keys, nobody's ever going to believe we didn't."

But such voices—judicious, narrow, self-serving, whatever— were drowned out by those coming to Calley's defense. Those who had long supported the war were particularly outraged. They saw themselves in the dock with him, and everything they had done to support the war condemned. "I am saddened," cried Senator Herman Talmadge of Georgia, for one, "to think that one could fight for his flag and then be court-martialed and convicted for apparently carrying out his orders."

There were those Viet-Nam veterans, torn with their own guilt for, perhaps, having participated in smaller My Lais and other atrocities, who sprang to Calley's defense. "We feel," said one, "like if this man is guilty, then he is guilty for the same things we did." There were those veterans who opposed the war now that they were home. At a Senatorial hearing during antiwar rallies, they bared their breasts about their own atrocities, as they had done earlier at the Winter Soldier hearings, but almost unanimously they did not want to see Calley convicted or jailed, for they saw him as only a tool of American policy, a tool just as they said they had been. They seemed not to want to admit Calley's own personal responsibility for what he had done, for in so doing they would have to admit their own.

There were other soldiers who supported the war and now took off their medals in protest at the verdict. Veterans groups—the American Legion posts, Veterans of Foreign Wars, and others—organized rallies and demonstrations, circulated petitions demanding Presidential clemency, and sought funds to help Calley with his appeals. Governors in some states flew the flag at half-mast and some legislatures debated the bills demanding clemency. One Florida Congressman even asked that Calley be invited to address a joint session of the Congress. Draft boards in Arkansas, Florida, Kansas, Michigan, Montana, and Wyoming resigned and other boards said they would draft no more men to go into battle and face possible court-martial if they obeyed orders.

American soldiers in Viet-Nam seemed, too, to rally behind Calley. "That's a bummer," one soldier said when he was told of the verdict, and an officer declared, "That's bad—it's bound to affect the troops in the field." Calley's name became a rally-ing cry for some hawkish soldiers, and one artillery battalion painted across one of its big guns the legend "Calley's Avenger."

With his penchant for always siding with the forces of law and against those of the lawless, with his sense of right and wrong, of morality and immorality, with his deep belief in the sanctity of the legal system and his scorn for those who seek to destroy or ignore it, Vice President Spiro Theodore Agnew roared like a diesel to Calley's side. He railed against those armchair soldiers who didn't know and didn't understand the pressures of battle and who were judging Calley. And he noted that Muhammad Ali was being "eulogized and captured for immortality on the pages of the sports magazines and newspaper sections in this country and now live the rest of his life in ease and affluence while a man who answered his country's call to service in the military now finds himself in a position, in what may have been a error . . . facing a life or death sentence."

On the other side, there were the doves, those who had long opposed the war in Viet-Nam and now found a new cause in Calley. While they did not necessarily defend what he did, they felt, as Senator Abraham A. Ribicoff of Connecticut put it, that he should not be made "to bear sole responsibility for all wrongdoing." There were more than a hundred soldiers on the ground at My Lai and higher officers in the air overhead, yet nothing was happening to them, only to Calley.

And there were those, of course, who took the argument farther, to encompass the entire war. Calley was being made to take the blame for everything while what he and his men did was only the inevitable end of the war policies developed by General Westmoreland and by the Johnson and Nixon administrations. "We as a nation cannot wipe away this blemish from the national conscience by finding one man guilty." anguished Senator Frank E. Moss of Utah, and Representative Richard Fulton of Tennessee declared, "We all share the guilt."

And then there was the President. He had run in 1968, it seemed, as much for sheriff of Dodge City as for President. Law-and-order was his cry, he would make the streets safe, he would make sure that the guilty were severely punished (indeed, his Attorney General, John N. Mitchell, was later to say that the courts were too "preoccupied with fairness for the accused"), he would uphold the law to the letter. When the first news of My Lai had broken, Richard Nixon had called it a "massacre" and said it was "abhorrent to the conscience of the American people." He had demanded that the guilty be brought to trial and, if convicted, punished to show the world that this was an aberration and that Americans knew how to deal with such things.

This was, too, the Richard Nixon who had declared over and over again that he was determined that justice and the law should be the rule in the United States and that he would never deviate from the course of law and justice no matter how loud the cries and demonstrations in the streets. But of course, when he said that, the demonstrators were from the left and were protesting the war in Viet-Nam. Nixon would not be intimidated by them.

Calley was convicted on a Monday; on Wednesday he was sentenced to life in prison. Under normal circumstances, he would have been transferred within the day to the disciplinary barracks at Fort Leavenworth, there to remain while his appeals ran their course through the appeals courts. But, on Thursday Nixon revealed that sometimes mass outcries could, indeed, affect him—if they seemed to be coming from those he considered his natural constituency, middle America, the proclaimed "silent majority." In an attempt to assuage the public clamor and growing outrage—and, we may be sure, in full awareness that he could count on some political gravy in the process—he bowed. In an almost unprecedented move, he not only refused to allow Calley, a convicted mass murderer, to be sent to Leavenworth, but he also ordered him released from the stockade at Fort Benning, where he had spent only three nights, and returned to his apartment on the base, where he would remain under house arrest (better, Calley was to say later to a friend, than being in the stockade, far better despite the restrictions that kept him almost always in his apartment) until all his appeals, through the military and civilian courts, had been exhausted—a process that could take years.

But this was not Nixon's final intervention. Two days later, after, he was to say, waking in the middle of the night in turmoil over the Calley case and his responsibilities to the nation about it (responsibilities, if he had thought at all and was concerned about the law, that were to leave hands off), he went farther. He announced that he would be, personally, the court of final decision in the case, deciding ultimately not merely on legal grounds but on all other factors involved, what Calley's fate would be. Legally, he would have been required to make a decision on Calley only if Calley had been sentenced to death. Without such a sentence, the case would never have reached his desk. But Nixon decided to intervene anway, because the public concern was so great and such intervention, he maintained, would have the effect of reassuring the public (what it would do to the system of military justice and the public's already well-known lack of confidence in the merits of that system, Nixon seemed neither to care about nor even to be aware of). Before any sentence took effect, the President declared, he would personally review the whole matter and decide whether the judges had come to the right sentence or whether he would reduce it. The implication was all too apparent, and one could only specualte on the effect of that implication on those in the military judicial review system who would pass on Calley's conviction and sentence in the years to come, knowing that their commander-in-chief, the man who had their careers and their futures at his command, was going to second-guess them later and was going to do that not just on the basis of law but, if his performance on other issues and on this one so far was any indication, on the basis of the political capital to be made. And as if to give credence to those who felt that Nixon was looking for every opportunity to appease Calley's supporters, the President in his press conferences, during which he would reiterate that he was convinced he was doing the right thing, constantly referred to the lieutenant as "Captain Calley."

If part of the nation was soothed and other parts outraged by Nixon's actions, it remained for Aubrey Daniel to point out to the President, in a long letter, that Nixon had failed in his duty to justice, to morality, to his office, and to the nation by his intervention. Daniel was highly distressed by Nixon's antics, but at first he thought it would be senseless and valueless for him to do anything. Finally, however, he became convinced that he could not remain silent and live with himself. So one night early in April, he sat down and wrote a lecture to the President—a lecture one would have hoped that a President would not have needed, but one that this President obviously did need.

"Sir:

"It is very difficult for me to know where to begin this letter as I am not accustomed to writing letters of protest. I can only hope that I can find the words to convey to you my feelings as a United States citizen, and as an attorney, who believes that respect for law is one of the fundamental bases upon which this nation is founded.

"On November 26, 1969, you issued the following statement through your press secretary, Mr. Ronald Ziegler, in referring to the My Lai incident:

"'An incident such as that alleged in this case is in direct violation not only of United States military policy, but is also abhorrent to the conscience of all the American people.

"'The Secretary of the Army is continuing his investigation. Appropriate action is and will be taken to assure that illegal and immoral conduct as alleged be dealt with in accordance with the strict rules of military justice.

"'This incident should not be allowed to reflect on the some million and a quarter young Americans who have now returned to the United States after having served in Viet-Nam with great courage and distinction.'

"At the time you issued this statement, a general court-martial had been directed for a resolution of the charges which have been brought against Lieutenant William L. Calley, Jr., for his involvement at My Lai.

"On December 8, 1969, you were personally asked to comment on the My Lai incident at a press conference. At that time, you made the following statement:

"'What appears was certainly a massacre, and under no circumstances was it justified. One of the goals we are fighting for in Viet-Nam is to keep the people of South Viet-Nam from having imposed upon them a government which has atrocity against civilians as one of its policies. We cannot ever condone or use atrocities against civilians to accomplish that goal.'

"These expressions of what I believed to be your sentiment were truly reflective of my own feelings when I was given the assignment cf prosecuting the charges which had been preferred against Lieutenant Calley. My feelings were generated not by emotionalism or self-indignation but by my knowledge of the evidence in the case, the laws of this nation in which I strongly believe, and my own conscience. I knew that I had been given a great responsibility and I only hoped that I would be able to discharge my duties and represent the United States in a manner which would be a credit to the legal profession and our system of justice.

"I undertook the prosecution of the case without any ulterior motives for personal gain, either financial or political. My only desire was to fulfill my duty as a prosecutor and see that justice was done in accordance with the laws of this nation. I dedicated myself to this end from November of 1969 until the trial was concluded.

"Throughout the proceedings there was criticism of the prosecution but I lived with the abiding conviction that once the facts and the law had been presented there would be no doubt in the mind of any reasonable person about the necessity for the prosecution of this case and the ultimate verdict. I was mistaken.

"The trial of Lieutenant Calley was conducted in the finest tradition of our legal system. It was in every respect a fair trial in which every legal right of Lieutenant Calley was fully protected. It clearly demonstrated that the military justice system which has previously been the subject of much criticism was a fair system.

"Throughout the trial, the entire system was under the constant scrutiny of the mass media and the public, and the trial of Lieutenant Calley was also in a very real sense the trial of the military judicial system. However, there was never an attack lodged by any member of the media concerning the fairness of the trial. There could be no such allegation justifiably made.

"I do not believe that there has ever been a trial in which the accused's rights were more fully protected, the conduct of the defense given greater latitude, the prosecution held to stricter standards. The burden of proof which the Government had to meet in this case was not beyond a reasonable doubt, but beyond possibility. The very fact that Lieutenant Calley was an American officer being tried for the deaths of Vietnamese during a combat operation by fellow officers compels this conclusion.

"The jury selection, in which customary procedure was altered by providing both the defense and the prosecution with three peremptory challenges instead of the usual one, was carefully conducted to insure the impartiality of those men who were selected. Six officers, all combat veterans, five having served in Viet-Nam, were selected. These six men who had served their country well, were called upon again to serve their nation as jurors and to sit in judgment of Lieutenant Calley as prescribed by law.

"From the time they took their oaths until they rendered their decision, they performed their duties in the very finest tradition of the American legal system. If ever a jury followed the letter of the law in applying it to the evidence presented, they did. They are indeed a credit to our system of justice and to the officer corps of the United States Army.

"When the verdict was rendered, I was totally shocked and dismayed at the reaction of many people across the nation. Much of the adverse public reaction I can attribute to people who have acted emotionally and without being aware of the evidence that was presented and perhaps even the laws of this nation regulating the conduct of war.

"These people have undoubtedly viewed Lieutenant Calley's conviction simply as the conviction of an American officer for killing the enemy. Others, no doubt out of a sense of frustration, have seized upon the conviction as a means of protesting the war in Viet-Nam. I would prefer to believe that most of the public criticism has come from people who are not aware of the evidence, either because they have not followed the evidence as it was presented, or having followed it they have chosen not to believe it.

"Certainly, no one wanted to believe what occurred at My Lai, including the officers who sat in judgment of Lieutenant Calley. To believe, however, that any large percentage of the population could believe the evidence which was presented and approve of the conduct of Lieutenant Calley would be as shocking to my conscience as the conduct itself, since I believe that we are still a civilized nation.

"If such be the case, then the war in Viet-Nam has brutalized us more than I care to believe, and it must cease. How shocking it is if so many people across the nation have failed to see the moral issue which was involved in the trial of Lieutenant Calley—that it is unlawful for an American soldier to summarily execute unarmed and unresisting men, women, children, and babies.

"But how much more appalling it is to see so many of the political leaders of the nation who have failed to see the moral issue, or, having seen it, to compromise it for political motive in the face of apparent public displeasure with the verdict.

"I would have hoped that all leaders of this nation, which is supposed to be the leader within the international community for the protection of the weak and the oppressed regardless of nationality, would have either accepted and supported the enforcement of the laws of this country as reflected by the verdict of the court or not made any statement concerning the verdict until they had had the same opportunity to evaluate the evidence that the members of the jury had.

"In view of your previous statements concerning this matter, I have been particularly shocked and dismayed at your decision to intervene in these proceedings in the midst of the public clamor. Your decision can only have been prompted by the response of a vocal segment of our population who while no doubt acting in good faith, cannot be aware of the evidence which resulted in Lieutenant Calley's conviction. Your intervention has, in my opinion, damaged the military judicial system and lessened any respect it may have gained as a result of the proceedings.

"You have subjected a judicial system of this country to the criticism that it is subject to political influence, when it is a fundamental precept of our judicial system that the legal processes of this country must be kept free from any outside influences. What will be the impact of your decision upon the future trials, particularly those within the military?

"Not only has respect for the legal process been weakened and the critics of the military judicial system been supported for their claims of command influence, the image of Lieutenant Calley, a man convicted of the premeditated murder of at least 22 unarmed and unresisting people, as a national hero has been enhanced, while at the same time support has been given to those people who have so unjustly criticized the six loyal and honorable officers who have done this country a great service by fulfilling their duties as jurors so admirably.

"Have you considered those men in making your decisions? The men who since rendering their verdict have found themselves and their families the subject of vicious attacks upon their honor, integrity and loyalty to this nation.

"It would seem to me to be more appropriate for you as the

President to have said something in their behalf and to remind the nation of the purpose of our legal system and the respect it should command.

"I would expect that the President of the United States, a man whom I believed should and would provide the moral leadership for this nation, would stand fully behind the law of this land on a moral issue which is so clear and about which there can be no compromise.

"For this nation to condone the acts of Lieutenant Calley is to make us no better than our enemies and make any pleas by this nation for the humane treatment of our own prisoners meaningless.

"I truly regret having to have written this letter and wish that no innocent person had died at My Lai on March 16, 1968. But innocent people were killed under circumstances that will always remain abhorrent to my conscience.

"While in some respects what took place at My Lai has to be considered a tragic day in the history of our nation, how much more tragic would it have been for this country to have taken no action against those who were responsible.

"That action was taken, but the greatest tragedy of all will be if political expediency dictates the compromise of such a fundamental moral principle as the inherent unlawfulness of the murder of innocent persons, making the action and the courage of six honorable men who served their country so well meaningless."

The White House acknowledged receipt of the letter, but the President never commented more than obliquely on the letter or on the issues Daniel had raised. Nixon went his own way, promising that he would make the final decision in the case of "Captain" Calley.

But Daniel's letter did serve one purpose, if no other. It seemed to shame many in the nation, and with its release much of the outward public debate and torment over Calley seemed to be checked.

31
An End to Innocence

It was the ironic twist, the nightmarish quality of our time in this nation beset by the guilt of Viet-Nam and My Lai. We had made murderers victims and victims murderers, responsible for their own deaths; we would punish those who had been killed and let loose those who killed the innocent, make them heroes. We had turned our world and our moral values inside out so that we could live with ourselves and with our ideas of this nation and what we had always believed it stood for.

If the nation looked, it knew that Daniel was right, as almost everyone who sat through the trial, who heard the evidence, knew he was right. There was no way, legally or morally, that Calley could have been acquitted, not if those jurors were to live with themselves as human beings in the years to come, not if this nation was to continue to consider itself civilized. He had murdered no one knows how many—not even Calley himself. Those he had murdered had done him no harm. They were unarmed; they offered no resistance. They marched to their deaths meekly, abjectly (much as the Jews marched to their deaths in the concentration camps of Hitler's Europe at the order of the SS). They were not soldiers, not men who had fought, though killing soldiers in such a way would have been equally a crime. They were women and old men, children and infants. Perhaps some time, somewhere, one or more had given aid to the Viet Cong, or may even have fought for that enemy. But on the day the Americans came to My Lai, these people were not hostile, they were docile.

Yet if we would believe Latimer, if we would believe the millions who came to Calley's defense saying he was not guilty, that he had committed no crime, then what can one say for his victims? That they are not dead, that they were not killed? Or that the victim has become his own executioner?

But Calley was not to blame, he was only obeying orders. We have heard that, too, often and resoundingly. But there were others at My Lai who did not kill, who did not obey those orders, orders given them by Calley (as there are men all over Viet-Nam who have not killed indiscriminately, who have not slaughtered the innocent). If we say that Calley was not guilty, that he was only following his orders as a soldier should, what do we say for those who did not follow those orders, who did not execute the unresisting? Are they, in this distorted morality that the Viet-Nam war has thrust upon us, the guilty? Are those who were killed and those who refused to kill, the guilty in this new world of this time?

But if Calley killed, it was because of his orders, and even if he is guilty, how can we pick on him, try and convict only him? There were others at My Lai, others who killed and there were those who gave Calley his orders. Why should only Calley be punished? We have heard that, too, since it all began. There are very few—perhaps only those who think no one should be blamed but God, and no one punished—who feel it should all stop with Calley. The sins and crimes of My Lai, and of all Viet-Nam, will not be washed clean through the sacrifice of one lieutenant named Calley (or even of a captain named Medina or a colonel named Henderson) while General Koster loses only a star and a medal, while General Young loses only a medal and retires with pensions and honors, while nothing happens to any of the other officers and men who were there that morning. And the sins and crimes of My Lai, and of all Viet-Nam, will not be expiated through the guilt of one lieutenant while General Westmoreland lives in honor and sanctimoniously proclaims his own noninvolvement and non-knowledge of war crimes under his command, while the politicians and planners who led the nation to Viet-Nam, who inflicted American troops upon the Vietnamese, write their memoirs telling how they were against it all the time.

But still there is the guilt of that one lieutenant, guilt undeniable. The fact that all those others have escaped—as they should not have—does that mean that Calley, too, should go free and My Lai just be written off? At the very basic level, there is Daniel's stinging rhetoric: "Who killed more?" Because Calley was guilty and was convicted of his guilt, he has to pay for his own crimes—who does not believe that a man must pay for his own crimes regardless of what happens to others? That others have gone free and will not suffer for their sins, is the nation's shame and the Army's shame. But it does not absolve Calley. Does anyone believe, because most of the crimes in this country are never solved and most of the criminals never sent to jail, that those who are caught, tried, and convicted should be set free?

What fills the mind with gloom and foreboding for the future is the twisted national reaction to Viet-Nam and to Calley, the celebration of Calley as hero and symbol, and the lack of a sense of outrage at Calley as murderer. Has this nation come so far in a decade that it now believes that My Lai is justified, that perhaps genocide is not only national policy with regard to the Vietnamese but a moral policy worthy of praise? Has this nation come so far that it feels the treatment of unresisting civilians—infants included—at My Lai is the correct and moral treatment of civilians in Indo-China? Has this nation come so far that it believes all its young men once they put on a uniform are Calleys, are murderers? If that is so, how different are we not just from our enemies in that war, the Viet Cong and the North Vietnamese, but how different are we from the barbarians of the past—the Nazis and the other despoilers of mankind?

Would this nation have reacted so strongly in favor of the murderers—and in blaming the victims for their own deaths—had the victims been Americans and those who slaughtered them the Vietnamese? Would anyone have said that it was just war, that it happens all the time, and let's just forget it? If one of the perpetrators had been brought to trial (and it may be the one saving grace of America that Calley was brought to trial), would anyone have accepted the plea that he was innocent because he thought his victims might be the enemy and besides he was just obeying orders? We did not accept that plea from those tried for war crimes after World War II. But then, they were losers.

If history affords us any insights, it is not likely that the slaughter of our men would be excused by our citizens as just an act of war. The nation screamed for blood when SS troopers massacred American soldiers—not children, not unarmed civilians, but soldiers who moments before had been engaged in combat—at Malmedy during the Battle of the Bulge, and when several of the SS involved were convicted and sentenced to death it was hailed as only fitting.

And consider how the nation and the world, the so-called civilized world, reacted when those slaughtered were civilians. This was a slaughter whose parallels are all too apparent. It was not one of the more famous, not Lidice; it was not the slaughter in the concentration camps. It was a slaughter where, *The New York Times* reported, the attackers entered a small village and "struck down old women with musket butts. They shot young boys and laughed at them as they died. They did unspeakable things to ten or twelve persons whose burned bodies were later found in a shed. There was no provocation. There was no trial. It was as though beasts had come out of the forest. It was worse than that."

It was not a slaughter in Viet-Nam. It was a slaughter at a small Belgian village called Pafenondroy in 1944, and the killers were SS. And what *The Times* and the nation demanded was that "we must make sure that these beasts are separated from the mass of humanity, including the less vicious mass of German humanity, and that they cease to exist upon this earth. When they are gone, we can talk of peace."

What would be the reaction in this country, in Mr. Nixon's White House, if Hanoi and the National Liberation Front were to demand the same for the murderers of My Lai?

But we have come a long way from those innocent and moralistic days of World War II, when we knew we were in the right and that the enemy was evil and had to be destroyed. In Viet-Nam, at My Lai, America lost its innocence. We had thought that somehow, some way we were better than other people. When we fought wars, it was never for national aggrandizement, never for gain, but for the weak and the oppressed, to free them from their bonds of tyranny. If war crimes were committed, if atrocities were perpetrated, it was always the other side that did them, not Americans. War crimes were the acts of the Nazis and the Japanese, of the Chinese and North Koreans, of the Viet Cong and the North Vietnamese, of all our enemies. We forgot, or ignored, the clearing of the Indians from the western plains, we forgot what we had done during the Philippine Insurrection. Americans believed fully that Americans were the good guys and the other side the bad guys.

Maybe we were better in those days with our naïveté, our sense of mission, the sense that we were devoted to principle. We were innocents at large in the world, stumbling and bumbling but thinking that we were trying to do good.

Viet-Nam and My Lai have ended America's innocence, ended it perhaps for good. In the hundreds of old men, women, and children and babies killed at My Lai, in the picture of those groups as they stood defenseless, 'at a trail intersection or alongside and then in a ditch, we have discovered that we were not as innocent as we thought we were and that American troops could massacre with as much will as any others. In the hootches burned and the livestock killed and the wells polluted in My Lai, with that whole hamlet so utterly destroyed it could no longer be inhabited, we discovered that Americans could commit war crimes with as little thought and with as much ease as anyone else.

We had not wanted to see the scarred children of Viet-Nam, the results of napalm. We had not wanted to see the crater-pocked landscape, the results of the massive bombings that have dropped more tons of bombs on the Indo-China peninsula in a single month of this war than were dropped over Germany in the whole of World War II. We had not wanted to see the devastated landscape, the result of defoliation, biological, and chemical warfare. We had not wanted to see the frightened and dead faces of the women and children crowded into miserable refugee camps all over Viet-Nam and Laos and Cambodia, driven from their homes, from the hamlets and villages, by the search and destroy missions of the American Army, missions that left nothing but havoc in their wake in an effort to deny shelter and food and support to the enemy.

We had not wanted to see all these things and more—the weapons we used that shattered and destroyed human flesh excessively and inhumanly; the indiscriminate shellings and bombings and strafings and killings in "free-fire zones" without thought that people lived there, had always lived there, and could be forced to move only by utterly destroying their homes and their means of living; the policy that led to what one American called the "forced urbanization" of Viet-Nam, the driving of a rural people into the squalor of overcrowded cities which could not shelter or care for them.

We had not wanted to see that in Viet-Nam we were not fighting, as our leaders constantly insisted, to guarantee democracy to a people who did not understand what we meant by the term and didn't care, and that we were not fighting to protect these people from being taken over by a Communist dictatorship, which would only replace another dictatorship under which they already lived.

We did not want to see that the war in Viet-Nam, and all over Southeast Asia, had brought to the front that arrogant racial superiority which seems a part of the American national character. We did not want to see, in the use of the words gook and slope and dink and all the rest, in our statements that "Vietnamese put a different value on life than we do," that our racial arrogance was blatantly expressing itself. We did not want to see that the rule in Viet-Nam was the MGR—the "mere gook rule": that it was no crime to kill or torture or rob or maim a Vietnamese because he was a mere gook.

We did not want to see that what we were fighting for in Viet-Nam and all over Southeast Asia was an old political principle which many Americans thought only corrupt Europeans ascribed to. We did not want to see that we were engaged in a game of power politics, that we were fighting for spheres of influence, and that we considered Indo-China within our sphere. We had not wanted to see that we were fighting not altruistically, for the Vietnamese, but for our own—or what our leaders thought was our own—political aggrandizement and selfish interests.

And we had not wanted to see that in that fight we were no better than those corrupt Europeans or anyone else. We did not want to see that we could develop the most devastating technology of war in the history of man and use it without thought of the human consequences, a technology that led to weapons and practices that violated every rule and law of humane warfare to which we and most other nations subscribe. We did not want to see that we could violate those rules with a self-righteous arrogance, that we could do that because we could blind ourself with the delusion that the rightness of our cause excused everything.

But My Lai ended our blindness and ended our innocence. Americans were forced to look at this nation, at what it had done and was doing. No one liked what he saw, for how could Americans brought up to believe in the altruism and romantic verities of the schoolbooks like it? But it was there, with My Lai, and it was there in all the testimony of all the months of trial. And it was there with the conviction of Calley. America's innocence was over; we had to recognize that we were no better than anyone else, and in some ways, because of our arrogance and our technology, we might even be a little worse than most.

Though Calley's deeds were his own—and he is accountable for them—there were others at My Lai helping him, and others at My Lai who did nothing to stop him. And My Lai did not stand alone. Too many other soldiers were arising to tell of their own personal My Lais, and too many officers were being charged with too many other atrocities in that devastated land—more than a hundred and fifty separate atrocities were being investigated by the CID at one point in 1970-1971.

Most of those who initiated and took part in those other slaughters, those mindless atrocities growing from this country's attitudes and weapons and policies in Viet-Nam, will go unpunished, just as most of the atrocities will go undiscovered.

And those who committed the greatest atrocity of them all—those, the Lyndon Johnsons and Richard Nixons, the Robert McNamaras and Melvin Lairds, the Dean Rusks and McGeorge Bundys and William Bundys and Henry Kissingers, the William Westmorelands and Creighton Abramses, who brought this country to this obscenity of a war, who developed the policies and the use of the weapons that have destroyed Viet-Nam, that led inevitably to My Lai, that gave Calley and the other Calleys the weapons and the opportunity to vent what was in them upon the innocent, and who then sanctimoniously proclaimed their devotion to peace and democracy and freedom—will face no trial as war criminals, will face no Nuremberg for their crimes against peace and against humanity. They will go unpunished, too, and will end their careers honored and celebrated.

And that, above all, is the outrage that lies at the heart of at least some of the deification of Rusty Calley.

We come back to him, as we must always return to him. While all those others go free, he was tried and convicted and will go to prison for as long as Nixon decides it expedient to keep him there. In this, perhaps, he is a symbol. Not a symbol, though, of all American soldiers or of all Americans, for that is blasphemy, that blasphemes those who did not kill the unarmed and the innocent at My Lai and everywhere else. And a symbol of America, for that blasphemes all those who fought against this war, all those who spoke against it and who did what little they could to halt it and call it by its right name.

It was Calley's misfortune to be caught, and once caught, to be convicted of the crimes he had committed. But he was caught and he was tried and he was convicted—and he committed those crimes. If now he were to be freed, if he were to go unpunished, if we make a hero of Calley for this time and this war, what do we say to those who did not kill, those who refused to obey the orders to kill the defenseless? Do we say that they were the ones who did wrong?

And what do we say to the Vietnamese whom we have slaughtered and destroyed and ruined if no punishment is assessed even against this one lieutenant whom so many Americans—and therefore so many Vietnamese as well—have turned into a symbol of everything that Americans have done to Vietnamese in the name of democracy and anti-Communism?

If we refuse to accept Calley's guilt for his own crimes, can we ever accept any man's guilt for any crime? Search out and find the others we must, if America is to emerge from the nightmare of Viet-Nam. Find and punish them we must. We cannot stop with Calley, but neither can we ignore Calley.

For if we do, what do we say to all those who were at My Lai, to Ngo Ngo Thininh, a young Vietnamese girl whom I found one day in a refugee camp in Quang Ngai, suckling a baby at her breast? Aubrey Daniel said the government could not give the names of the victims at My Lai. Ngo Ngo Thininh could have given him some of them if she had told him, as she told me, of that morning in March when Calley and his platoon swept into her hamlet.

"When my husband went to the city to join the ARVN, I stayed with my father-in-law. He was the richest man in our hamlet; some of the people said he was the richest man in all the hamlets of our village of Son My. I do not know about that. But he owned many rice paddies and he had the biggest brick house in our hamlet and he paid more taxes to the VC than anyone else.

"He did not like the VC. When they had first come to our hamlet, they had arrested him and taken him to the jungle prison. When he came back, he was very bitter against the VC. But he could do nothing against them if he wanted to stay in our hamlet as the head of his family name and take care of his family and the families of his relatives. He did not attend the meetings of VC unless they forced him to, and sometimes he spoke against them. When the VC began to recruit the young men in our hamlet for their army, my father-in-law said that his son, my husband, must go to Quang Ngai to join the ARVN and fight for the government.

"Three times before that day, the GI's came to our hamlet. My father-in-law said they were our friends and we should greet them with much friendliness, that we should share our rice with them and ask them into our house. But I did not stay in the hamlet when they came. I was only eighteen. I am only a woman and I was not pregnant at that time, so I knew that I must fear the GI's and that I must escape the house and the hamlet. My husband told me this and all the young girls knew that this was so. Each time the GI's came, when we saw them in the distance, I ran into the paddies and hid. Each time when I returned, my father-in-law was very angry with me. He said the Americans had been very friendly, they had given candy and gum and canned fruit to the children, they had shared the rice with the people and then they had left. They had been friendly to the people and the people had been friendly to them and there had been no trouble.

"Still, I was afraid to stay when the GI's came.

"That day it began very early in the morning when the first shells began to fall on our hamlet. We were just beginning breakfast. We were standing near the cooking pot in my father-in-law's house. My mother-in-law was serving the rice to the family. I remember that when the first shells fell my little brother, four years old, was standing near the rice pot. He had his rice bowl in one hand and his spoon in his other hand. The first shell fell right outside the door, and the bowl and the spoon fell from his hand to the floor.

"My father-in-law ordered everyone to go into the bunkers until the shelling stopped. We stayed in the bunkers for fifteen minutes or a half-hour while the shells and the rockets fell on our hamlet. Then the noise stopped and we could hear the sound of the choppers coming down from the sky and then we could hear the sound of the voices of the GI's.

"My father-in-law told us to come up from the bunkers and greet the GI's with friendliness as we had before. So the members of my family began to leave the bunkers and go toward the GI's. But I was frightened and I could hear the sound of shooting and the sound of screaming, so I stayed in the bunker for a little while after all the others had left. Then I left the bunker and did not turn to see what was happening, only ran the little distance to the rice paddies as fast as I could. I hid in the rice paddies and I heard shooting and screaming and I could see the smoke and the burning from my hamlet. Then I crept through the rice paddies to the next village to the west.

"I stayed there all that day. The sound of the shooting and of explosions came to us there and the people asked me what was happening in my hamlet, but I told them I did not know.

"Early in the evening, when everything was quiet and there was only smoke in the sky over my hamlet, I went back to my home. But my home was not there and my hamlet was not there. There were only ashes and cinders and the ruins of the houses and the bodies of many people.

"I came to my father-in-law's house, only I could not find it anymore. The house was not there, only cinders and ashes and some ruins. In the doorway of where the house had been, I could see three small bodies that had been burned. At first I did not know who they were, but then I realized that they were the bodies of my three brothers, eleven, seven, and four years old. When I saw them, I remembered the morning and my little brother standing in the kitchen with his rice bowl and his spoon when the first shells fell. Behind the house I saw two dead buffalo. Near them was the body of my mother-in-law. She had been shot many times. In the yard around the house there were many other bodies. As I walked near them, I saw that two of them were my sisters, fourteen and sixteen years old.

"While I was looking at them and wondering why the Americans had done this thing, my father and my father-in-law came into the yard. They were not harmed but they were covered with smoke and there was blood on them. My father told me that the GI's had shot at everything and killed everyone they saw. He and my father-in-law had hidden in a bunker when they saw the Americans shooting and they had hidden there all that day.

"My father-in-law said that the GI's had taken many people to the canal and we should go there because we could not find some members of our family. There were many bodies in the canal, lying on top of each other. There were many little children and mothers and old people. Among the bodies we found my husband's brother. He was still alive but he would die the next day of his wounds. Near him was the body of my sister-in-law, his wife, and her two sons, my nephews, aged twelve and four. They had been shot. A little way from them in the canal was the dead body of my mother.

"I do not know how we did it, but my father, my father-in-law, and I took the bodies from the canal and the bodies from the house and we took them to the graveyard outside our hamlet. My father and I dug a large grave and we buried my mother, my three brothers, and my two sisters there. My father-in-law dug shallow graves and he buried my mother-in-law, my sister-in-law, and her two sons in them.

"Then we made a stretcher from some bamboo poles and some cloth and we put my husband's brother on it. It was dark then and we left our hamlet to go to the city, to find my husband and to live in this refugee camp."